GOLF FOR THE CONNOISSEUR

By the same author

Sudan Today
A Day with the Aborigines
The Great Opens: the British and American Open Championships
Golf to Remember (with Peter Alliss)

GOLF FOR THE CONNOISSEUR

A Golfing Anthology

edited by Michael Hobbs

with a Foreword by Henry Longhurst

B T Batsford Ltd *London*

ISBN 0 7134 1397 2

Printed and Bound in Great Britain by
Redwood Burn Limited   Trowbridge & Esher
for the Publishers B T Batsford Ltd
4 Fitzhardinge Street London W1H 0AH

Dedication
For the members of Beamish Park Golf Club, whose company
both on and off the course has given me much
pleasure over the last several years

Contents

Foreword
by *Henry Longhurst*

Though cricketers might dispute such an allegation, I have no doubt in my own mind that the slow, pedestrian game of golf has brought forth better writing, and more of it, than any other game. This is not because those of us who perform in this line are such clever fellows, but simply because we have so much more to write about. Every cricket and football pitch and every tennis court are broadly speaking the same, apart from their playing qualities on any particular day, but not only are all the world's ten thousand-odd golf courses different from all the others but they each consist of 9 or 18 separate holes, each of which in turn are different from all the others. Furthermore, they are liable to be found in some of the most beautiful spots on the surface of the earth— hills, meadows, heaths, ancestral parks and the sea shore. No wonder they have attracted, or even created, some of the best writers upon any sporting scene.

Then, of course, there is the multiplicity of the instruments with which the game is played, all of them good for a chapter or two, together perhaps with, for the fiftieth time, the long-sought, ultimate and final discovery—the secret of golf. One very old friend of mine was found, when he died, to have more than sixty putters. Each one, for a while, had revealed to him the secret of putting.

An anthology, by very definition, cannot contain much that is new, but so vast is the mountain of material that has accumulated round the game of golf that much of any collection is certain to be new to a large proportion of its readers, while those who remember reading certain passages with enjoyment before will be grateful to the compiler for the chance of reading them again.

I suppose the earliest golf 'writer' was Sir Walter Simpson and I am happy to see a number of his words of wisdom included here. The younger generation, to whom he will probably be a stranger, may smile perhaps at his 'instructional' work, for he was only at the beginning of a long and complicated road, but they will find from his pungent observations on the game in general that the psychology of golf and golfers has not changed all that much in the past ninety years.

The second golfing essayist of real note was probably Horace Hutchinson, winner of the first two official amateur championships, who wrote as delightfully about fishing and shooting as he did about golf. He also produced the most marvellous bronze statuettes of golfers, mostly at the top of the swing and with what would now be called the 'flying right elbow'—due, it was always said, to their difficulty in holding the pose without the right elbow gradually rising. Hutchinson edited the first Badminton volume on Golf. He gave the first copy off the press to his wife, suitably inscribed, and she in turn, having survived him by thirty years, gave it to me. It remains the most prized possession in my golfing library.

No anthology would be thinkable without Bernard Darwin, whose light shone on a gentler golfing age but none the less brightly for that, and one is happy to see that he too is liberally represented. So also are the instructional writers and the 'personalities', and indeed the Editor could claim with his hand on his heart that there really is something for everybody. I think that as a matter of fact the best piece of instruction in the book was written by me! Let not the reader recoil in horror, however, for the instruction came not from me but from five-times-Open-Champion, Peter Thomson. We were playing in a practice round before a pro-am—it must have been in the late fifties—together with Ian Fleming, the creator of James Bond. I asked Thomson what I was doing wrong and the clarity and directness of his answers so impressed Fleming that he caused the *Sunday Times* to get me to do a couple of articles based on Thomson's ideas. We spent two half-hours together before the Open at St Andrews and the result was so simple and so intelligible that, believe it or not, the *Sunday Times* still receive requests for it and I still meet golfers who carry it in their pocket-book!

However, enough from me. Let me hand over to this really splendid bedside miscellany with its guarantee of so many hours of innocent pleasure and the comforting thought that there remains an unlimited store of 'plenty more where that one came from'.

Editor's Note

In collecting these writings about golf I had several aims in mind. But more than anything else I wanted to present those who have best written about the game from the far-off days of Sir Walter Simpson and Horace Hutchinson, through Grantland Rice, Bernard Darwin and Paul Gallico to their successors of the 1960s and 1970s. I began with an outline of the themes that I wanted to see them tackle and as time went on others forced their way in. For example, I had felt that above all else this must not be a book on how to play golf. As each new US or British open champion appears, soon after so does his book. It tells us how he does it and assures us that we too can do it very nearly as well if only we obey his commands and study the photographs and diagrams. So prejudiced have I become against this kind of book, dictated in haste, assembled from the tapes by a journalist who could do with the fee, and rushed into print before the glitter of a new champion is dimmed by later failures, that I set out determined to include no instructional material at all—but I came out with two or three chapters that contain a great deal.

The reader should not feel that he ought to read ploddingly through from page 1 to the end. There are, it is true, reasons for the order in which the pieces and chapters occur but he will probably do just as well if he starts with the subjects which interest him most. I hope he may find the one he puts last not without interest. I hope then that he will make this anthology a success by seeking out some of the books quoted from by half-forgotten writers of the past or present-day ones that he has not noted before. It is, incidentally, for this reason that I have reluctantly but usually omitted work that has appeared in newspapers and magazines only. You can always get hold of a book however long it has been out of print.

There has not yet appeared the complete golf writer, able equally to give us, drama, humour, emotion and make plain all the subtleties of technique. But if you lumped together all the talents that appear in this book I think you might have him.

MICHAEL HOBBS

Acknowledgment

The author and publishers wish to thank all the copyright holders who have given their permission for pieces to be reprinted in this anthology. In some cases, the original authors were concerned, in others, book, magazine or newspaper publishers or agents. In all cases their names are noted at the end of each piece, together with the original source.

A majority of golf books are published on both sides of the Atlantic and credit is therefore given to both US and UK publishers.

The author would also like to thank the staff of Gateshead Central Library for their very considerable help in obtaining long-out-of-print books from all parts of the British Isles—and occasionally further afield.

Photographs in this book are reproduced by courtesy of Peter Dazeley, H. W. Neale and the British Broadcasting Corporation to whom acknowledgment is given.

List of Illustrations

32. Alistair Cooke (*British Broadcasting Corporation*)
33. Laddie Lucas (*H. W. Neale*)
34. Bob Charles, Swiss Championship (*H. W. Neale*)
35. Peter Dawson (*H. W. Neale*)
36. Peter Alliss with H.R.H. The Duke of Edinburgh (*H. W. Neale*)
37. Ex-King Leopold of Belgium spectating, Canada Cup (*H. W. Neale*)
38. Spectator charge, Portmarnock (*H. W. Neale*)
39. Gary Player, Fulford (*H. W. Neale*)
40. Augusta during the U.S. Masters (*H. W. Neale*)
41. Frank Beard, Ryder Cup (*H. W. Neale*)
42. Henry Cotton (*Peter Dazeley*)
43. Bobby Jones, St Andrews (*H. W. Neale*)
44. Henry Longhurst commentating (*H. W. Neale*)

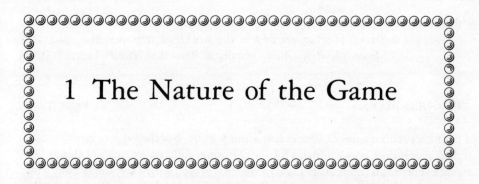

1 The Nature of the Game

WHAT golf is all about depends on the people who play it. For one player, a 5 at a long par 4 is something to savour briefly at the time and at some length in the bar afterwards; for another, it may be the hole where he hit a huge drive and failed to get his wedge shot as near as he should have for a birdie. But the score written down on a card for the hole or the round is just a part—not necessarily that important—of the whole experience that goes to make up a round of golf.

Just what that experience is, I shall leave to the contributors to this chapter to define.

THE ESSENCE   Sir Walter Simpson

Now golf is a game in which each player has a small hard ball of his own, which he strikes with a stick whilst it is quiescent, with the intention of putting it into a hole. Abstractly he wishes to do this with as few blows as possible, concretely in fewer than his opponent.

from *The Art of Golf*, David Douglas (UK) 1887

THE COMMON CAUSE   George Plimpton

. . .in a sense golf's special distinction is that it involves all those who play it in a *common* cause—whatever the level of their ability—namely the chance to achieve perfection, or even *better* it, as in the case of a birdie, or an eagle, or an albatross! Golf is one of the few professional sports—in fact I can't think of any other except perhaps such target sports as archery—which anyone can play and almost surely, sooner or later, hit a shot or sink a long putt or two during a round which would be the envy of the finest professional. High performance in the great spectator sports for the average man exists only in his daydreams; but the Olympian glory of a hole played in par, or a birdie, is always a possibility, even in the game of the direst duffer; all he must do (he keeps telling himself) is to put three or four shots together. That is the unique character of the game, and it binds us all as fellow players (or sufferers) in whatever area of the world we step onto the links.

from *The Bogey Man*, Harper & Row (US), André Deutsch (UK)

IN COLD BLOOD   Peter Alliss

Golf is a peculiar game. I almost said a funny game, but then it is not meant to be that. But it does pose problems for the performer different to those of almost any other sport I can think of. For one thing, it is played with a stationary ball. This simple fact in itself creates tensions, constrictions and inhibitions so peculiar that they make golf almost unique. A stationary ball means in essence a stationary performer. In games played with a moving ball, the movement of the performer is mandatory and instinctive, and this very physical movement creates its own relaxations. In such sports movement is incidental, incidental to the pattern of play or the final product of the game. In golf, movement is calculated, wilful, total. In golf, the achievement is concentrated into one fleeting, conscious action and is then over and done with beyond redemption. In other, moving-ball sports, the movement is continuous and intrinsic and for the performer acts as a stimulant and a tranquillizer combined. The golfer has to act in cold-blood. From a motionless posture he must generate a swift, sudden, powerful but rhythmic action which is complete in itself in perhaps three or four seconds. Golf is a solitary game. The golfer walks alone. In team play, in football, cricket, rugby and the others, the very existence of other team members gives the player a release, a safety-valve for his tensions, an excuse, a scapegoat readily to hand. The final responsibility is only partly his, whereas in golf, finally, it all gets down to the player, the club and the ball, and no other people. If you consider that the golf swing, the calculated shot at the ball, will take a generous four seconds, and if you further calculate that you will do it seventy-two times in a round, there is a total time *in action* of some four and a half minutes in a round which can take more than three hours to play. And in the intervals between the actions, the game is stopped absolutely. The ball has flown, rolled, come to rest. The golf course remains passive. Action is suspended. Thus, for the competitor as he walks forward for the next action, there is an intolerable amount of time for thinking, or rather for being subject to the mental process, regarding the shot he has just made, the one he is about to make, the bad shot he had made three holes back, the problems of the most difficult hole which will be coming up five holes ahead, the shifts of the wind, the people in the crowd, the face of a pretty girl in the crowd, a silly pop tune charging around in his mind, some reflections on a poor breakfast he had in the hotel and will dinner be any better, what his best route home through the traffic might be, how the children are at home, and so on. A round of golf lasts many hours. A tournament goes on for days. It is played at a low physical pressure, but always at a dangerously high mental pressure. Other sports make demands on the instincts and the reflexes. Golf makes its demands on the mind. Thus a golfer is terribly exposed, exposed in almost every way. The final responsibility is his, and there is no way to camouflage this, no hope of jettisoning it.

from *Alliss Through the Looking Glass*, Cassell and Co (UK)

BEREFT OF DRUGS   Tony Jacklin

Golf is *about* character. It's a very introspective game. You don't play golf against the other man. You play against yourself. You play against yourself in two senses. You are always trying to beat yourself, control yourself, *forget* yourself. And yet be terribly aware of yourself, trying to *change* yourself. Doing things which aren't natural.

Take the use of the left hand, for instance. In all games and sports, a right-handed man uses his right hand more or less as nature taught him—he hits or thrusts or fends with his right hand. But in golf a right-handed man gets his power with his left. His right guides. You wear a glove on your *left* hand, not on the right hand. And some people wear it there not to prevent the left hand getting calloused but to remind them that it is the *left*, not the instinctive right, which is the hand that really fights. Unnatural use of the left in golf *alone* makes the game psychologically exacting in a way no other game is.

It's a game of character partly because you're on your own. There's no team or partner to blame. There's no contact with him (unless he starts to sing as you commence to putt). You're out there on your own with a piece of wood and a ball, and the score you return tells your story. You are exposed. Everybody has time to observe you, not only read your score, but watch your shots. No game gives such a chance for highly focused post-mortems.

Unlike in the body-contact games, you can't bump and bruise some hot blood into yourself which suspends your self-criticism; or in the non body-contact sports, like running, generate some adrenalin which sends up your temperature and makes you forget, drugs you. No, the great intellectual fact about golf is that it is a cold-blooded activity in which your mind is completely bereft of the drugs and stimulants which nature provides in other competitive sporting activities. And you know all this as you play.

from *The Observer* (London), 14 July 1974 (interviewer: Kenneth Harris)

DOWN TO ESSENTIALS   Grantland Rice

With the possible exception of croquet 'for blood' and billiards, golf is like no other game. You are attacking an inert ball. Also, you are on your own. You are the referee. Nine times out of ten you must call the penalty on yourself—if a penalty is to be called. You can play the game by the rules or you can cheat. You are meant to play the ball as it lies, a fact that may help to toughen your own objective approach to life.

Golf gives you an insight into human nature, your own as well as your opponent's. Eighteen holes of match or medal play will teach you more about your foe than will eighteen years of dealing with him across a desk. A man's true colours will surface quicker in a five-dollar 'Nassau' than in any other form of peacetime diversion that I can name.

Golf lends itself nicely to the 19th hole, a period of refreshment, happy talk and commiseration. I've got a host of columns from the locker room . . .not only about and with name golfers but about and with headliners of every sport and business. Peeled down to his shorts, a highball in one hand, an attested score card in the other, it's hard for a man to be anything but himself.

from *The Tumult and the Shouting*, A. S. Barnes & Co (US)

AN X-RAY OF THE SOUL   Michael Murphy

'Gowf is a way o' making a man naked. I would say that nowhere does a man go so naked as he does before a discernin' eye dressed for gowf. Ye talk about yer body language Julian, yer style of projectin', yer rationalizashin', yer excuses, lies, cheatin' roonds, incredible stories, failures of character—why there's no other place to match it. Yer take ould Judge Hobbes, my God, the lies he told last week about that roond o' his in the tournament, 'tis enough to make ye wonder about our courts o' law. So I ask ye first, why does gowf bring out so much in a man, so many sides o' his personality? Why is the game such an X-ray of the soul?

from *Gold in the Kingdom*, The Viking Press (US) and
Latimer New Dimensions (UK)

MUCH BETTER THAN WALKING   Lord Brabazon of Tara

When I look on my life and try to decide out of what I have got most actual pleasure, I have no doubt at all in saying that I have got more out of golf than anything else. I am naturally lazy and would never in any circumstances go for a walk for a walk's sake. I share the view that Max Beerbohm takes in one of his essays: 'I always regret the time has gone when I had, and was not, a perambulator'. Consequently, the health I am able to enjoy now I maintain is very largely due to the quiet exercise of walking which goes with golf. But, apart from that, it is a game you enjoy both when you're bad and when you're good. It is a game which alone enables you to play, by a system of handicapping, with the best and the worst players in the world. Of few games can that be said. It takes you all over the world, you find new scenery on every course you play on, and you meet hundreds of new people under the pleasantest conditions.

I suppose I started golf too late—ideally one ought to be taught at about the age of twelve, then one would acquire the perfect swing. I never had a perfect swing, but was always what you call a 'puncher'—that is, rather a short swinger; but in my youth I hit an extremely long ball. A high ball with a slice, but very long. The best I have ever done in the championship is to play in the last eight games of the English Championship once—and then I was defeated by my dear friend, Harry Bentley, whom I often met in big competitions and who has always vanquished me; but on that particular occasion he had six threes in the first nine holes—which was a bit punishing.

But to get back to Calcot Grange and my mother- and brother-in-law at the time Charlie Rolls was killed.

Up to that time I had taken the view that golf spoilt a good walk. But Clarence Krabbé took a different view. He was a keen golfer and out of politeness I accompanied him to Huntercombe, near Henley, to play the game as a form of exercise. However, I had not played more than half-a-dozen times when I got the golf bug well and truly. Never have two young men concentrated on golf so closely as we did. He had a handicap of eight when I started. We played three rounds a day, four times a week. We putted on the lawn, we drove balls into nets, we had imitation bunkers, we had professionals down from every quarter to play with us and instruct us. Never was such zealous concentration known; and it is my belief that you only get such good golf by playing it, so to speak, in a row. Never do you improve by playing just an odd game then and now.

from *The Brabazon Story*, William Heinemann (UK)

IT CAN DO NO HARM   Patric Dickinson

When I began to play it, golf was not considered a suitable game for the young. It induced a spirit of selfishness, it was not vigorous enough, it was regarded as not quite 'healthy'. My mother I know was warned of the perilous influence it might be upon my malleable four-and-a-half-year-old character. But here we were opposite the Heath and the doctor had said I must be out in the air as much as possible. Why not, said Mr Padwick, give him a golf club? This solution had not occurred to Mama; she knew nothing about golf. She consulted friends: the general opinion was that I was too small to be affected morally and that it could do no harm, particularly since I was not taking to golf deliberately, as a game, but simply for the sake of my health. To keep this therapeutic approach pure, it was felt that I should not have lessons. Anyway I was too small. Nor was expensive equipment involved. Mr Padwick was going to give me a cut-down club and an old ball or so, and after that I could supply myself with the lost balls which I would find in the gorse-bushes. Going out ball-hunting became for me a delicious kind of adventure in itself. I spent hours tunnelling in the gorse worming about in the musty dry undergrowth or poking in the mud of the stream waiting for a bite. I could tell the feel of a ball from a stone in an instant. There was a shabby old man with a mongrel who spent every day, all day long, ball-hunting. 'Old Pocock' never gave me a ball once. He was a bit gone in the head, my mother said, but quite harmless. He hoarded golf balls like a demented squirrel; his rooms must have been piled with them. He had his 'rounds', which I soon learned, for it was no use following after him. His eyes and nose were always damp and when we met I'd say, 'had any luck?' He shook his head like an out-of-work mute. You could see the pockets of his old blue overcoat, which he wore summer and winter, knobby with spoil.

The club Mr Padwick gave me was old. He had cut down the hickory shaft to about two feet long. The head was iron and chocolate coloured, for the outer rust had almost a patina. He said it was a mashie. I loved it at once.

My mother's attitude towards golf was wary. I am sure that she never really wanted to play herself. When she found she had to, she played with a sort of resigned dissociation. But at first all was well. She came out with me once or twice and sat in the shelter of a gorse bush while I flailed away. She could not help me, and beyond telling me to watch other players and especially Mr Edmunds, the 'pro', left me alone. Soon, the cure was obviously working. Golf was making me sturdy.

I hated to be watched. Once through the gate I trotted or ran, bearing left round the slope until I was out of eyeshot. Then I'd drop a ball wherever I was and hit at it. Mr Padwick had told me a mashie was a club for getting 'out of the rough'. Even on the golf-course itself there was little difference between rough and fairway and I did not begin to venture on the real course. I kept to edges and out-of-the-way stretches. If I managed a good shot—say ten yards—I ran as hard as I could after the ball for fear I should lose it. I often did, even so, and padded up and down round and round with my eyes on the ground till I pounced on it. Then I'd hit it again.

This must sound dull. But I was intensely happy. I loved the wiry shiny knots of coarse grass, all the green and yellow and dun colours and the way one's boots could almost slide over it. I felt the whole scene, right to the Downs, close round me as if it were something I wore hidden against my naked skin. It clothed me secretly.

from *The Good Minute*, Victor Gollancz (UK)

DRIVING   Horace G. Hutchinson

Golfers are very fond of insisting, and with great justice, that the game is not won by the driver. It is the short game—the approaching and putting—that wins the match. Nevertheless, despite the truth of this, it may be quite safely asserted that if there were no driving there would be very little golf.

from *Golf*, The Badminton Library (UK) 1893

NATURE AND GOLF   Sir Walter Simpson

Golf has some drawbacks. It is possible, by too much of it, to destroy the mind . . .

For the golfer, Nature loses her significance. Larks, the casts of worms, the buzzing of bees, and even children are hateful to him. I have seen a golfer very angry at getting into a bunker by killing a bird, and rewards of as much as ten shillings have been offered for boys maimed on the links. Rain comes to be regarded solely in its relation to the putting greens; the daisy is detested, botanical specimens are but 'hazards'; twigs 'break clubs.' Winds cease to be east, south, west, or north. They are ahead, behind, or sideways, and the sky is bright or dark, according to the state of the game.

from *The Art of Golf*, David Douglas (UK) 1887

THE DULL MIND   Sir Walter Simpson

. . . excessive golfing dwarfs the intellect. Nor is this to be wondered at when we consider that the more fatuously vacant the mind is, the better for play. It has been observed that absolute idiots . . . play steadiest. An uphill game does not make them press, nor victory within their grasp render them careless. Alas! we cannot all be idiots. Next to the idiotic, the dull unimaginative mind is the best for golf. In a professional competition I would prefer to back the sallow, dull-eyed fellow with a 'quid' in his cheek, rather than any more eager-looking champion. The poetic temperament is the worst for golf. It dreams of brilliant drives, iron shots laid dead, and long putts held, whilst in real golf success waits for him who takes care of the foozles and leaves the fine shots to take care of themselves.

from *The Art of Golf*, David Douglas (UK) 1887

YOGA OF THE SUPERMIND   Michael Murphy

'Golf recapitulates evolution,' he said in a melodious voice, 'it is a microcosm of the world, a projection of all our hopes and fears.' I cannot remember all the phrases, but his words were an ecstatic hymn to golf, not golf the game I knew, but golf as it might appear in the Platonic World of Ideas, the archetypal game of games. As he talked I wondered what his course in 'cosmic ecology' must be like. No professor of mine at Stanford had ever talked like this.

He told about the technological changes in the game and how they brought new powers and awareness into play for those who pursued it with a passion. With its improved clubs and balls and courses, golf reflected man's ever-increasing complexity. It was becoming a better vehicle for training the higher capacities. And so it was becoming the yoga of the supermind, the discipline for transcendence. . . .

'Golf is played at many levels,' he was almost chanting now as he swayed in the firelight. 'Take our love of the ball's flight, the thrill of seeing it hang in the sky.' He made a sweeping gesture with his arm, tracing an imaginary trajectory against the fire's glow. 'How many games depend upon that thrill—archery, football, golf—the thrill of a ball flying to a target, have you felt it? The ball flying *into* the target; it's a symbol, of course. And here, friends, my theory leads . . .', he stepped down from the couch and crossed the room to the fireplace, ' . . . my theory leads to the simultaneity of past and future. For everything has a past *and* future reason for being. Projectiles for example, our urge to see them fly is derived from our paleolithic past, from the hunt, we love to see the spear or stone in flight. 'But,' he stood on tiptoes and his voice rose, 'it is also an anticipation. The flight of the ball, the sight of it hanging there in space, anticipates our desire for transcendence. We love to see it curve in flight as if it is free—why else do we hit a fade or a draw? We love to see it hang there, that is why we love to hit our drives so far. The ball in flight brings dim memories of our ancestral past *and* premonitions of the next manifesting plane.'

He rocked slowly back and forth, occasionally making a wide, sweeping gesture with an arm. We were all staring at him now with amazement. 'The thrill of seeing a ball fly over the countryside, over obstacles—especially over a stretch of water—and then onto the green and into the hole has a mystic quality. Something in us *loves* that flight. What is it but the flight of the alone to the alone?'

from *Golf in the Kingdom*, Harper & Row (US), Latimer New Dimensions (UK)

PERSEVERE!   Sir Walter Simpson

Golf refuses to be preserved like dead meat in tins. It is living, human, and free, ready to fly away at the least sign of an attempt to catch and cage it. It will confute your logic if you, as it were, stand aside and try to produce it by causes. With patient attention to hitting, not relaxed even when we are in the full pride of good play, our relapses will be fewer and less severe; but there is no means by which we can secure uniform progress. In proportion as the wave of advance is great, so will be the back draught. Let not the learner be discouraged by it, and begin to doubt lest the tide has turned . . .   It will come again soon, unless, indeed, he begin to ask, 'What am I doing wrong?' 'How did I stand?' 'How did I swing then?'

It is impossible to say how good a player a man may become; but every beginner ought, as much as possible, to play with better golfers than himself. He will unconsciously by that means aim higher. It should be his ambition to beat somebody, and, having done so, to attack a still stronger adversary.

from *The Art of Golf*, David Douglas (UK) 1887

THE TOURNAMENT WORLD   Peter Alliss

The marquees swell and billow, the flags stream in the breeze. The grass is green beyond belief, immaculately groomed. The roofs of a regiment of cars sparkle like breastplates in the sun. People walk, run, gasp, cheer, eat, drink. The scene is all movement and delight. The prospect pleases.

This is the façade of big tournament golf, but it is a façade which hides a tight, harsh world of success and failure, of emotion and envy, of greed, jealousy and sometimes hate; a jungle of individuals, of characters and champions, proud and pathetic. This is the public image of golf; yet it hides a hundred private feuds and falsities. In its way it is a fascinating world, bristling with promoters and performers, traders, manufacturers, hucksters and commission men, critics amateur and professional, do-gooders, philanthropists, publicity seekers, near-alcoholics, preachers and fringe characters galore; the famous ones, the modest ones, the young ones coming, the old ones going, the mass in the middle who are neither and never will be any of these, the people who want to say they talked to the champ—all sizes, all shapes, all nationalities, all the hopes and fears and passions of all mankind.

from *Alliss Through the Looking Glass*, Cassell & Co (UK)

BURN AND BURN AND BURN   Frank Beard

I have some theories about my own field, about what makes golf champions. I ran into Jack Nicklaus today, the first time he's been out this year, and we said hello and small-talked for a minute or two. That's about the extent of the relationship I ever have with a Nicklaus or a Palmer or a Casper. For a while, when Jack and I were both on the board of directors of the player's tournament committee, we spent more time together, but now I've drifted back in the crowd.

Jack Nicklaus is a golf champion, no question about that, one of the greatest players ever. If you judge by the past few years, the four greatest golfers in the world are Nicklaus, Palmer, Casper, and Julie Boros. I have nothing against any of them personally, but they're all off by themselves. They're isolated.

Cas tries harder to be friendly than the others do, but he's still in his own world. Palmer and Nicklaus don't have much contact with anybody except each other, and even that's mostly because they get thrown together, in business deals and social arrangements. I don't think either of them really enjoys the other's company. And Boros has nothing to do with anybody . . . .

The number-one guys have to be almost totally self-centered. They have to possess an incredible burning for success. They've got to be willing to do anything within morally, civically, and socially acceptable bounds to win. I don't mean they have to cheat, and I don't mean they have to go out of their way to stomp on people. Not at all. But they do have to stomp on people who get in their way. They have to ignore their friends and their enemies and sometimes their families, and they have to concentrate entirely upon winning, upon being number one. There's no other way to get to the top.

I'm sure I sound harsh, but I'm not really condemning them. They've got what we all want. They've got financial independence. They've got prestige. They've got power. I don't know anybody who wouldn't like to have his own airplane and his own secretaries and his own companies. There are many days I wish I had their drive, their singleness of purpose, their complete devotion to victory. I'm often tempted to try it, to push everything and everybody else out of the way and to pursue nothing but success. But I just can't do it. I don't mean I'm too nice a guy. I mean it's not my way. If I tried it, I'd fail. I couldn't survive that constant intensity, that constant burning. I admire—hell, I envy—their ability to burn and burn and burn.

from *Pro: Frank Beard on the Golf Tour*, Thomas Y. Crowell Co (US)

THE TOURNAMENT GOLFER   George Plimpton

As I sat there, listening, perhaps taking a drink too many to dispel my gloom of the afternoon, the golfers seemed to take on heroic, if slightly tragic, proportions. . . . But the exercise of the game itself in top competition was an ugly combination of tension and frustration, broken only occasionally by a pleasant surprise, but more often by disaster. The game required a certain cold toughness of mind, and absorption of will.

There was not an athlete I had talked to from other sports—the roughest of them: football, hockey, basketball—who did not hold the professional golfer in complete awe, with thanksgiving that golf was not *their* profession. The idea of standing over a putt with thousands of dollars in the balance was enough to make them flap their fingers as if singed. They would have none of it. Golf was the only major sport in which the tension remained throughout—where each shot was far enough apart in time for doubt to seep in and undermine one's confidence, so that there was no way of establishing an equanimity of mood. Other sports were not similar: the tension would mount, but as soon as the first whistle blew, or the contact began, that was the end of it. It was the familiar business of jumping into cold water—it was all right once you got in.

For the professional golfer there was finally only one pleasure, which was to come in on the top of the field and win the big prize. The possibility consumed them. It often crept into their conversation. That evening they talked about the win which symbolized their own struggles perhaps more than any other—Ken Venturi's victory in the 1964 Open—the year he won in the great heat, overcoming years of vicissitude and personal difficulties, which included a circulation problem in his hand. The history of that win, and his difficult career, was dramatic stuff to hear—right up to the moment when Venturi, barely able to put one foot in front of the other, dropped his putter on the 18th, the realization flooding in on him, and he cried out, 'My God, I've won the Open!' Many of the pros standing around watching at the Congressional broke down—Raymond Floyd among them. People stared curiously at him, rather hoping someone would come along and lead him away. They thought perhaps the heat had fetched him.

There were other great comebacks, of course, but somehow they didn't mean as much to the pros. Ben Hogan's recovery from the serious accident for example. On the operating table he had called out, 'Back on the left! Back on the left!' referring to some crowd bothering him in a match he was playing in his delirium. *His* comeback was expected somehow, he was such a champion . . . it was part of the natural progression of things. But Venturi's was a rise from a background much more like their own—toiling away in the pack, agonizing, never quite able to come out on top, and finally, in Venturi's case, being overwhelmed by the pressure and the disappointments, getting into fist fights, domestic problems mounting, physical quirks assailing him—all the miseries magnified so that in him the other golfers could see their own tribulations and foibles on alarming display.

On the banquet circuit that year Venturi would tell the story of his Open win—always in the same words—and when he got to the part where he dropped his putter, his chin would tremble and he would break down, and down the length of the long table the other golfers would look at their plates and there was never one who was embarrassed for him.

from *The Bogey Man*, Harper & Row (US), André Deutsch (UK)

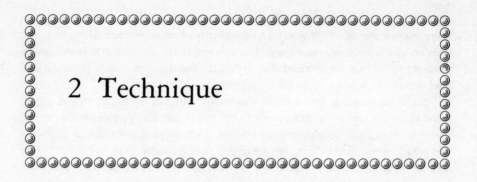

2 Technique

AFTER every new open champion there soon come glittering sets of clubs bearing his name. There are claims that they incorporate the latest thoughts on metallurgy, dynamics and the mechanics of the swing. Usually they do little actual harm. But there are new books too, and these may be less innocent. They are written—or rather 'talked' to a writer—by a supreme athlete at a peak of his career, and what they do is tell us how this maestro does it. His swing is a thing of smooth compact precision and power; his little finger stronger than the average golfer's thumb; his concentration all-excluding; his mental guts tempered by a hundred failures and successes.

Few except the young have the belief that, just perhaps, they might come to play their sport as well as the great names of the day, but this is not quite true of the golfer. Each one of us has hit a soaring drive, a long iron through wind dead at the flag, a biting wedge, a delicate flick off sand and holed an enormous putt or two. So the new champion's book is bought. There may be something in it that will make these things happen more often. For that is the secret of good golf: hitting it well most of the time.

The chapter that follows does not set out to teach how to play golf. Rather, it is a selection of pieces that covers some of the ground about how you ought to do it. But experts do not always agree ...

WORDS WITHOUT END   R. T. Jones

To me, golf is an inexhaustible subject. I cannot imagine that anyone might ever write every word that needs to be written about the golf swing.

    from *Bobby Jones on Golf*, Doubleday and Co (US), Cassell and Co (UK)

STYLE   Sir Walter Simpson

Do I maintain, then, the reader may ask, that every one ought to have the same style? By no means; on the contrary, for you or me to model ourselves on a champion is about as profitless as to copy out *Hamlet* in the hope of becoming Shakespeare. If we have a neat style, so be it; and if we have begun before our hair is grey or gone, it probably so is. But for a fat man to model himself on a swank youth is frivolous. We cannot ignore our deformities. Your shoulders are heavy, your fore-arm puny; it is useless to rebel. A very easy long swing is impossible with such a configuration: you may play well—beat the swank youth very likely,—but only if you are content with a stiff style. Are you lank and loose-limbed?—So will your driving be, if left to develop naturally.

On the other hand, there is no more fruitful source of bad golf than to suppose that there is some best style for each individual which must be searched out by him if he is to get the best results out of himself. In a broad and general way, each player ought to have, and has, a style which is the reflection of himself—his build, his mind, the age at which he began, and his previous habits. The ex-cricketer reflects cricket. The rowing man has a straight back, and there are characteristics in each golfer the history of which it is more or less difficult to trace. This is his style; and, however much he may feel he modifies it, to an onlooker, it will remain the same—because it is the same. It is not the general principles that a man has before him (of these he is seldom conscious) when trying to find out his absolutely best. It is some minor detail of which he exaggerates the importance—some particular twitch, which has arrested his attention after a very satisfactory drive. This will be stubbornly pursued till it is exaggerated into a mannerism, to which it is secretly believed everything good in driving is due. If golfers could only become convinced that no mannerism is of the slightest value, that there are fifty different styles (by style I mean here the petty variables of which alone we are conscious) in which a good shot can be made, that it is not indispensable to repeat in the next the same movements felt in one good shot, bad ones would be less frequent. There is, I repeat, a categorical imperative in golf—'Hit the ball;' but there are no minor absolutes. There is no best shape, or weight, or lie of clubs—no best stance, grip, or swing. From the nature of the case, one does not change his driver during the round; but the other things may vary every shot—nay, will, unless one makes a point of preventing them, sacrificing ease and accuracy to a consistency which, if stubbornly insisted on, may permanently cramp driving. There is no better proof of this argument than to watch a boy of about twelve, who hits every ball clean and (for his strength) far, of whom there are very many. At this age even the broad features of style are unsettled. At one moment he swings round his neck, at the next round his shoulder, his feet near together or wide apart, according to the unconscious fancy of the moment. And yet each ball flies away with unerring certainty. This should teach us that when we think we see what we are doing wrong, or what we are doing right, that when we cling to this bit of style or avoid that, we are merely distracting our attention from the main issue.

from *The Art of Golf*, David Douglas (UK) 1887

SWEEP IT AWAY   Sir Walter Simpson

From the very first some players, however, make the mistake of treating the ball as a heavy object, whilst in reality it has, for practical purposes, no weight, and ought to be swept away, not jerked. In a bunker or a hard hole it becomes heavy, and nothing will do but a jerk; but from the turf the problem is to shave it cleanly off. . . .   He must use his club like a scythe; must sweep, not strike the ball.

from *The Art of Golf*, David Douglas (UK) 1887

STRIKE EVERY SHOT FIRMLY   Sir Walter Simpson

One rule, without exception, is that no ball, however near the hole, should be played weakly. Even the shortest of all approaches . . . can only succeed if the ball is swept away, the grip tight, the muscles taut. A weak tap, however long or short the distance, will prove uncertain and disappointing. The length of swing, not the firmness of sweep, should regulate the carry.

from *The Art of Golf*, David Douglas (UK) 1887

WHY DID I MISS IT?   Sir Walter Simpson

A perfectly unconscious style in a grown man is very rare. It will oftenest be found among professionals whose education does not tempt them to think. There is one illustrious and venerable champion of whom it is proverbial that not even a whole round of bad shots can tempt him to consider his position. 'I've missed the ba',' is all he says. To hit it again, is all he tries. It is wonderful how soon he succeeds, too—much sooner than if he were to begin asking why.

from *The Art of Golf*, David Douglas (UK) 1887

THE VARDON GRIP   Harry Vardon

My contention is that this grip of mine is sounder in theory and easier in practice, tends to make a better stroke and to secure a straighter ball, and that players who adopt it from the beginning will stand a much better chance of driving well at an early stage than if they went in for the old-fashioned two-V. My grip is an overlapping, but not an interlocking one. Modifications of it are used by many fine players; and it is coming into more general practice as its merits are understood and appreciated. I use it for all my strokes.

I do not grasp the club across the palm of either hand. The club being taken in the left hand first, the shaft passes from the knuckle joint of the first finger across the ball of the second. The left thumb lies straight down the shaft—that is to say, it is just to the right of the centre of the shaft. But the following are the significant features of the grip. The right hand is brought up so high that the palm of it covers over the left thumb, leaving very little of the latter to be seen. The first and second fingers of the right hand just reach round to the thumb of the left, and the third finger completes the overlapping process, so that the club is held in the grip as if it were in a vice. The little finger of the right hand rides on the first finger of the left. The great advantage of this grip is that both hands feel and act like one, and if, even while sitting in his chair, a player who has never tried it before will take a stick in his hands in the manner I have described, he must at once be convinced that there is a great deal in what I say for it, although, of course, if he has been accustomed to the two V's, the success of my grip cannot be guaranteed at the first trial. It needs some time to become thoroughly happy with it.

We must now consider the degree of tightness of the grip by either hand, for this is an important matter. Some teachers of golf and various books of instruction inform us that we should grasp the club firmly with the left hand and only lightly with the right, leaving the former to do the bulk of the work and the other merely to guide the operations. It is astonishing with what persistency this error has been repeated, for error I truly believe it is. Ask any really first-class player with what comparative tightness he holds the club in his right and left hands, and I am confident that in nearly every case he will declare that he holds it nearly if not quite as tightly with the right hand as with the left. Personally I grip quite as firmly with the right hand as with the other one. When the other way is adopted, the left hand being tight and the right hand simply watching it, as it were, there is an irresistible tendency for the latter to tighten up suddenly at some part of the upward or downward swing, and, as surely as there is a ball on the tee, when it does so there will be mischief. Depend upon it the instinct of activity will prevent the right hand from going through with the swing in that indefinite state of looseness. Perhaps a yard from the ball in the upward swing, or a yard from it when coming down, there will be a convulsive grip of the right hand which, with an immediate acknowledgment of guilt, will relax again. Such a happening is usually fatal; it certainly deserves to be. Slicing, pulling, sclaffing, and the foundering of the innocent globe—all these tragedies may at times be traced to this determination of the right hand not to be ignored but to have its part to play in the making of the drive. Therefore in all respects my right hand is a joint partner with the left.

The grip with the first finger and thumb of my right hand is exceedingly firm, and the pressure of the little finger on the knuckle of the left hand is very decided. In the same way it is the thumb and first finger of the left hand that have most of the gripping work to do. Again, the palm of the right hand presses hard against the thumb of the left. In the upward swing this pressure is gradually decreased, until when the club reaches the turning-point there is no longer any such pressure; indeed, at this point the palm and the thumb are barely in contact. This release is a natural one, and will or should come naturally to the player for the purpose of allowing the head of the club to swing well and freely back. But the grip of the thumb and first finger of the right hand, as well as that of the little finger upon the knuckle of the first finger of the left hand, is still as firm as at the beginning. As the club head is swung back again towards the ball, the palm of the right hand and the thumb of the left gradually come together again. Both the relaxing and the re-tightening are done with the most perfect graduation, so that there shall be no jerk to take the club off the straight line. The easing begins when the hands are about shoulder high and the club shaft is perpendicular, because it is at this time that the club begins to pull, and if it were not let out in the manner explained, the result would certainly be a half shot or very little more than that, for a full and perfect swing would be an impossibility. This relaxation of the palm also serves to give more freedom to the wrist at the top of the swing just when that freedom is desirable.

from *The Complete Golfer*, Methuen (UK) 1905

HOW MANY KNUCKLES?   Henry Cotton

Good golf can be played with either two, three or four knuckles showing, and although I favour two knuckles myself I think that the muscle- and joint-construction of the left arm has much to do with the actual position adopted.

I am more than satisfied that with a four-knuckle grip there is a limit to the ways in which the left wrist can be used during the shot, and while this might seem to some golfers to be a good state of affairs, I consider that it makes the player get all the time on one side of the club . . . .

With the two V's up the shaft, the wrists have, in my opinion, the maximum scope, and the right hand can be employed to the full; with the four-knuckle grip, the effect of the right hand is to push the hands and the club-shaft through at the same time, and usually at the same speed.

I refer here to the case where the Vardon grip is used, the left thumb being inside the hands. Where the left thumb is outside, the left wrist gets an extra amount of freedom. The position of the right hand is, of course, affected by the position of the left hand on the shaft, and generally the more over the left the more under the right and vice versa, which is another reason why the left hand should not be too far over.

In the case of a short person of heavy build with short arms and a wide chest, it is not possible to play with the elbows together as is demanded by the two-knuckle grip, and so the attack on the ball must be made with a four-knuckle grip and an action inclined to the shut face. There is no way out of this. I have not mentioned three knuckles as this is the average position between the extremes and can be used in either method depending on the player's physique.

With the two-knuckle grip and the orthodox crook of the right-index-finger-control of the right hand, the hit, though accompanied by the maximum wrist-roll, can be used without danger of a smothered ball, because it takes place against the left hand. This cannot collapse under any more, as can happen when with a four-knuckle grip the left wrist is allowed to turn from open to shut.

I have experimented with all the various grips and, because I have big hands and long fingers, any grip other than the Vardon does not help me at all.

But it does pay to be original in approaching this part of the game, taking into consideration particularly the flexibility and strength of the wrists and the size of the hands.

from *This Game of Golf*, Country Life Publications (UK)

SHOW AS MANY KNUCKLES AS YOU LIKE   Max Faulkner

In my opinion, when playing golf both hands are equally important, but let us start with the left. When you take the club, the first thing to do is to ensure that the forefinger and thumb of the left hand are tight together, tight enough to show you that the muscle—I have no idea of the name of it—at the base of the thumb is large. This indicates that you *are* holding the club with your fingers, and that it is not away back in the palm of the left hand.

If you are holding the club correctly, you will notice that the top of the shaft is hidden behind the left wrist and that the left hand is very much on top of the shaft. Now, you hear a great many people talking about the knuckles of the left hand. But, if you are holding the club the way that I have said, you want to forget the left knuckles. I have seen people look down at their knuckles, and then I have heard them say, 'I am showing two knuckles,' or 'three knuckles,' or whatever it was. When I looked down at the head of their club I noticed that the face was away as wide open as it could get. There was no way they could get it into the ball if they lived to be a hundred. I have already talked about golfers going into all kinds of antics to get their grip right, but what half of them have forgotten is to see that the head of the club is correct. The face should be turned in, so much turned in that they cannot see the face at all. Then, when they have got the face that way, they hold the club in the manner I have directed.

Never mind about the knuckles. That is very difficult to do, this knuckle business, and just adds to the complications. Anyway, it is all so much nonsense. I should like them to show six left-hand knuckles if they had them. In other words the left hand should be as far over to the right as it is possible to get it, as long as the thumb remains in the correct position. I suppose you will be saying that you would have to be double jointed to do that. But that is not so. It is all a case of getting accustomed to it, and in time it will feel very comfortable. And, if you do hold the club the way that I have said, you will never slice a ball, and all of you know that slicing is the biggest bugbear that golfers have to contend with when playing . . . .

So much for the left hand, then. What about the right hand? Well, I am not concerned about that very much, as long as it is as far over the top of the club as it will go.

from *Play Championship Golf All Your Life*, Pelham Books (UK)

VARYING THE GRIP   Henry Cotton

I use the overlapping grip. I have large hands and use grips a little thicker than standard, as I find this allows the exact combination of flexibility and control in my wrists. A thinner grip accentuates the finger action during the swing and a thicker grip chokes the sensitivity of the fingers for me.

At times I have found it necessary to vary the thickness of the grip I use to work in with a particular action of the moment. Such need for a change of this sort, to produce as near perfect results as possible, would arise from a change in my general health and muscular condition, which vary considerably in my case.

I wear a special leather left-hand glove which is tight fitting. This is important, and when the leather stretches I take up the stretch so that it always fits snugly to my hand. Thus I have a constant surface between my hand and the grip which is independent of changes in temperature and the consequent difference in the tackiness of my skin and the grip, which affects directly the amount of 'squeeze' necessary to stop the club turning in the hands at impact.

The key points of the grip are the index finger and thumb of both hands—these must never move. It is not easy to hold tight with these points and slacken the rest of the hand, but I have trained my hand through deliberate exercising, squeezing rolled-up paper or a squash ball, to grip evenly all through.

I have many positions of the thumb at my disposal. My left thumb goes on the left side of the shaft, that is the hole side, to make my hand seem more solid and less liable to flap over at impact. This I use as an anti-hook trick. When it goes right into the palm of the right hand, that is to the right of the shaft, it loosens up the wrist and I can do a more lively turn over. This encourages the ball to fly to the left. An extended left thumb, where the ball of the thumb is pushed right into the palm of the right hand, stiffens all my action. I can play well in this way at times, but I always split the skin of my thumb as the extra pressure of the right hand is too much for the skin. A bunched-up left hand, that is to say, where the hands are not deliberately spread out to cover as much of the shaft as possible, helps me to hit later. This position helps me 'ring the bell', or, in other words, to get the maximum sag of the left wrist as the towing down of the club begins.

The right thumb plays an equally important role in my play. For example, if my thumb is put on the very top of the shaft and pressed there, it stiffens my entire wrist action, and so is used there for bad lies and for push shots. If I am to slice the ball, I put my right hand under the shaft—I repeat *under*—and press my thumb on the shaft. I can then guarantee not to close the club face at all during the stroke, but can bring the blade across the ball from outside to in.

If I force my right hand over the shaft to the maximum I am able, with my thumb on the side, pinching the shaft, to make my right wrist so free that it snaps through and over too easily. Consequently I hook best from this position. These are just the opposite positions to those ordinarily thought of as producing hooks and slices. I have no need to explain this further as I am talking of 'My Swing'. It is how it works in my own game, and how it might work with players using an elbows-together method like my own.

I find I hit earlier if I spread out my right hand down the shaft a great deal. Generally I do not need this feeling of extra control.

from *My Swing*, Country Life Publications (UK)

ARMS AND WRISTS   Henry Cotton

Using my hands and wrists in the way I do, and have done for a long time, does not put any abnormal strain on the spine, for the body plays a normal role: it does not have to do a kind of corkscrew movement in order to get the club face square to the ball.

Every golfer has to translate any golf action he sees into terms of his own physique. . . . I have a very loose neck, and unusually long arms, so that when gripping a club, I can make my elbows touch. Loose shoulders and collar bones enable this to be done.

Also I have very loose ankles; in fact, I can stand up on the outsides of the feet, my ankles almost on the ground. This makes it possible for my left foot to stay firm and not to spin round when I drive; my flexible ankle permits my left side to turn without the foot sliding at all when my left side braces. I have long fingers and my wrists are very supple in a hingeing way, but do not cock to the side as much as I would have liked.

This is responsible for my back swing being slightly less than the horizontal. I attach, however, little importance to the length of the back swing. I prefer to see a player hold on to the club and do a threequarter length swing rather than do a full swing at the expense of opening his left hand.

For the sake of effect, it might have impressed onlookers if my left wrist had had a little more cocking movement; I have worked on this point, but the bone structure prevented an increase in the freedom of this action.

I am round shouldered, which is a 'trade deformation' due to excessive practice when young. Later, no exercises I was willing to do could correct it. I do not think my posture was incorrigible, but when I made an effort, up to a point, to rectify it only my health benefited and not my game, so I stopped.

I strike the ball hard with my right hand, using my right index finger, which is very much bent back at the main knuckle joint, to guide the club face to the ball. I can made a real crook with this index finger.

My left thumb position varies slightly according to my form, for I have a sort of fine regulating adjustment at my disposal in this key position, inside my hands. I can place the thumb pulled up closely to the hand, extended down the shaft, or favouring the inside or outside of the shaft, all with minor efforts, which have a bearing on direction or trajectory.

My best positions vary from a bit more over to a bit more under; from being bunched up to being extended.

I have tried 'the club sliding in the hands' technique, but have found that this is worth while only to players with less wrist flexibility than mine. It is not a method I like, but I am quite prepared to encourage it in golfers who have very limited wrist movement, and if they have strong hands, they can even play first-class golf. However, I am satisfied that in the long run this method is less consistent than mine.

Many players do not persevere in making a change, I know. This is only natural, for golf is a sport, a pleasure, a pastime, not a drudgery or a sacrifice to make.

I am not setting out to tell you to play my way and to drop all your other methods. This is MY swing and all I will say at this stage is that I have taught it to many golfers—champions even. Yes! I have made a few as well! . . . It is sound; it merits the word orthodox, for there are no mannerisms which might complicate it, and I claim that it is simple, for it gives everyone, whatever his age or ability, a chance to build up his golfing muscles. The accent must always be on the fact that golf is 85 per cent. arms and wrists and 15 per cent. body.

My swing can be divided by time into these periods: going up, .90 seconds; from the top to impact, .36 seconds; impact to finish, .54 seconds, which totals 1.80 or just under 2 seconds.

I do at times swing quicker than I should, and at times I do not look at the ball as well as I can, but these failings, common to us all, I have usually been able to discipline myself to overcome by concentration.

You can play all your life if you play golf with your hands.

from *My swing*, Country Life Publications (UK)

THE STRAIGHT RIGHT   Henry Longhurst

I had not intended to go into golfing technicalities but in view of Hogan's eminence will risk one exception. After watching my puny efforts on the practice ground he asked why it was that British players brought the club up so abruptly after impact. When I demurred that, fat and forty, I was 'hardly representative . . . etc.', he said, 'No, no. All your team do it. I have often noticed. Why?' 'We reckon', he went on, 'to keep the left arm straight on the way back and the right arm straight on the way through, right to the end—like this.' It was here that he seized me and performed the armed combat demonstration.

To the original question I replied with some confidence that it was because we habitually wore more clothes for our all-the-year-round golf. Hogan and those who follow the tournament trail also 'follow the sun', as the title of his film confirmed. They play in shirtsleeves. For much of the year we play with a pullover, surmounted by a thick sweater or jacket, in which this right-arm elongation is impossible save to the ultra-lissom. Rees on the other hand thought it was because we were so often 'trying to get the ball up off hard ground'—but this, with due respect, is simply not true for at least half the year and I must prefer my own explanation.

At any rate, unimpeded by spectators, I watched Hogan closely in a practice round with Burke, Demaret and Claud Harmon. Each of these three was driving a colossal sort of ball which, when it should have been descending, would bore onwards towards the hole, and it seemed impossible that a man the size of Hogan, who happened to be driving last, could reach them. Time and again, however, he lashed the ball along thirty feet from the ground, or 'quail high' as they say in Texas. It ran perhaps thirty yards where theirs had stopped almost dead on the soft fairways, and finished five yards past the lot.

Since then I have been consulting his book, *Power Golf*, to see whether, unlike so many golfers who write books, he practises what he preaches. The answer is 'Yes, he does'. I never saw anything quite like it. By taking his club far away from him on the backswing, and then almost as far back round his neck as our own James Adams, and then thrusting it even farther away in front after impact (by which time he is already on the outside of his left foot, with the right heel high in the air) he attains, in fact, the swing of at least a six-footer. His right arm never bends after impact and it finishes in a position with which the middle-aged reader may care at his own risk to experiment, namely dead straight and pointing, almost horizontally, behind his head. 'The speed and momentum', says the caption, 'have carried me to a full finish.' They would carry most of us to the infirmary.

from *Round in 68*, T. Werner Laurie (UK)

PETER THOMSON TELLS ALL   Henry Longhurst

All this began in a practice round before the recent Bowmaker tournament at Sunningdale. Though I had watched him many dozens of times, this was the first time that I had had the pleasure actually of playing with Peter Thomson. I had always found it difficult to describe his style to other people because it seemed so straightforward. There was nothing peculiar about it. It turned out not only that his ideas about the golf swing were as 'simple' as his method but also, as I hope to prove, that he was equally good at communicating them.

I asked him, naturally, to cast an eye over my own manifestly unsatisfactory efforts and he said at once, 'Well, for a start you are set up all wrong.'

This expression, 'getting set up right', constitutes the absolute basis of Thomson's golf. 'If you get set up right and look like a competent golfer, you won't go nearly so far wrong.' Your set-up consists of how you stand, where you are aiming, your 'triangle' (i.e. the two arms and shoulders), and where you put the ball in relation to your feet.

The nearer you are, before you start, to the position in which you will be when you hit the ball, the fewer adjustments you will have to make in the course of the shot. 'Think how your body has to be when you strike the ball,' he says, 'and work back from there.' Lest this sounds too obvious, take a look on the 1st tee on a Sunday morning and see how many people's starting position bears any relation to any position in which they could conceivably be at impact!

There is no reason why any of us, tall or short, fat or thin, should not get set up right. The stance, about which volumes have been written, is a piece of typical Thomsonian simplicity. Lay a club down on the ground, pointing to the hole, and put your toes against it. That is the end of that.

Now put the ball opposite your left foot with your left arm and the club in a straight line, as they will be, or should be, as you actually hit the ball. Your arm and the club will now be at right-angles to the imaginary club on the ground against which you have lined up your toes. If they are not, you have got the ball—*as almost everyone has*—too far back. (We are talking at the moment of wooden club shots.)

We now come to the critical point, the make-or-mar of the entire set-up. Your right arm is not long enough. It won't reach. How are you going to get it on to the club?

You do it instinctively as nature tells you, the easiest way. You reach *over* with the right hand, bringing the right shoulder forward in the process, and at the same time, probably without realizing it, you bring the left hand back a bit to meet it. This is perfectly comfortable, but, to make it more so, you probably move forward a couple of inches at the last moment, thus, in effect, bringing the ball two inches back.

The whole set-up is now wrecked.

Let us retrace our steps. The right arm once again is not long enough. This time, keeping your right shoulder back and tilting your left shoulder up, you reach *under* with the right hand and attach it to the club.

I tried this experiment on many willing subjects and in every case, regardless of handicap, in this position they at once looked like a golfer. If it feels awkward at first, it only shows how wrong you were before. You can apply a simple test. When you have got 'set up', keep your body still, lay the club flat across your chest and see where it is pointing. In the 'easy' position you will find that it points yards to the left of the hole. If you are set up right, it will be pointing straight at the flag.

How far away from the ball should you be?
Thomson often uses the expression 'measuring off'. You will notice that he himself measures off quite deliberately before each shot. Stand relaxed, leaning slightly forward, with your knees slightly bent and the whole body *in balance*. Extend the left arm and the club in a straight line, not stiff as a ramrod, and you are now measured off. 'Picture in mind your position as you strike the ball and make final adjustments from that.' This applies to every club.

How do you grip the club?
Again, delightfully simple. *Get set up right and you won't notice!* Take it as you find it.

How hard do you hold on to the club?
'Often,' says Thomson, 'you can actually *see* the tension in a man's hand. You should start with a light touch, barely enough to lift it off the ground—so that it feels heavy. It is just like using an axe. You lift it with a light grip, just enough to raise it, and it feels heavy. As you bring it down, your grip tightens without your thinking about it and reaches its tightest at the moment of impact.

'There is another likeness with golf. Using an axe, you do not *hit* with it; you *accelerate* it. That is exactly what you should do with a golf club.'

How do you start the club back?
'Well, you just *draw it straight back*. Never mind about what the books din into you about turns and pivots. Just draw it straight back as far as is comfortable and let nature take its course. Don't turn away; just draw it back—*but*—keep your weight squarely on both feet and make sure you don't sway back with it yourself.'

Finally, what Thomson describes as the key axiom in the golf swing, namely, to be behind the ball when you strike it—not all of you, maybe, but certainly your head. '*A plumb line from your nose as you strike the ball should hit the ground several inches behind it*'—a sobering thought for us lurchers and swayers, to whom, as we heave forward, the ball so often appears to be moving rapidly backwards.

As a postscript I might add that, with the first shot in which Thomson was satisfied that he had got me satisfactorily 'set-up', I ricked my back—probably using muscles which had not come into play for thirty years—to such an extent that we almost had to terminate the game there and then. This in no way shook my faith in his principles and I wish you the best of luck. You have been warned!

from *The Sunday Times* (UK)

THE WRISTS   Max Faulkner

I hear a great deal and read a great deal about the cocking of the wrists. You will
not find anything about cocking the wrists in this book, except perhaps now,
when I say that it is unnecessary. All cocking the wrists does is to open the face of
the club. And when you open the face you have to pronate, or in other words roll,
your wrists. That is what pronate means, roll the wrists. And you have to do that
to correct having the clubface open. That, in my view, is out, and I will never tell
anybody to cock their wrists. This teaching, unfortunately, is all too common all
over the world, and it has held the game back for twenty-five years or more. That
is since World War II. It is the worst thing that can be taught to a club member of
over, say, ten handicap, because, when he tries to cock his wrists, he must make
his swing more upright. If you take the club back along the grass with the face of
the club pointing towards the hole, and then try to cock the wrists you will be
very upright and the face of the club will be open. You might as well lift up the
clubhead at the very start. No good at all!

When you have taken back the clubhead three feet the weakest part of the body
at that point is the wrists, and, as you take back the club, your wrists will give,
anyway. They are bound to do that. If they did not, they would hurt, so you do
not need to tell them what to do. They will do it on their own, and at the correct
time. So you have got it made. The face of the club is not open at the top. It is
square, so you can forget about the rolling of the wrists. It is all past and done
with without your knowing about it. They have given way of their own accord,
and the hands have gone back and up without your fiddling about with them. If
you do muck about with this pronating nonsense then you will not have a wide
arc, and that is essential. The arc going back must be as wide as you can make it,
then you bring the clubhead in towards the right shoulder. But you do not have to
try to do this. It will happen automatically if you have swung the club low
enough.

from *Play Championship Golf All Your Life*, Pelham Books (UK)

FULL BODY-TURN   R. T. Jones and O. B. Keeler

If there is any special merit in my style of play, it is the free body-turn. Of this I
am convinced.

Now, the hitting area in the down-stroke does not begin at the top of the
swing, and the first motion of the club should not be inspired by the wrists; that

is, the club-head should not start first, which would use up some valuable wrist action before hitting is possible. For me, as near as I can work it out, the correct way to start the down-stroke of any full shot is a slight sway to the left. The arms get under way with the wrists still 'cocked,' or wound up. It is a difficult sort of speculation, but it seems to me that the hitting area starts at that part of the stroke when the right hand begins to assert itself, the right arm begins to straighten out, and the wrists begin to unwind. In my stroke, this seems to be when the club is about parallel with the ground and the hands opposite the right leg. I suppose the speed of the club, from a gradual beginning, has been sharply accelerated to this juncture, and then the unwinding wrists and the straightening right arm provide the punch in the stroke.

It seems fearfully complicated, this trying to take a swing to pieces and see what makes it tick. I'd hate to try to learn to play golf synthetically. These attempts at analysis are quite puzzling enough. But it has been deeply interesting to me, in my feeble efforts at analysis, to encounter so many times, and in so many ways, the factor of body-turn in all shots.

One bit of earnest admonition. Stewart Maiden [the professional at East Lake where Jones 'grew up' as a golfer] maintains that he cannot think of any of these details, or of any other details, during the execution of a shot—that is, if the shot is to come off. He adds that he does not believe anybody else can think of these or other details and perform a successful shot. I find this to be the case with my own play. I have to do all my thinking as I prepare to play. Once the swing is under way, the only thing I can think of is hitting the ball. To attempt to think of anything else is the most certain method of courting absolute ruin.

from *Down the Fairway*, George Allen & Unwin (UK)

DON'T WAVE THE CLUB ABOVE YOUR HEAD   Max Faulkner

I have heard one member of a golf club saying to another, 'You know, George, you were swinging very flat this morning.'

'Was I really?' replies George. 'I had no idea I was.' And he looks utterly miserable.

What a pity, because that was the way that man should have been swinging. I am unable to understand it, but it seems that there is something built in golf that wants to make everybody try to wave a golf club way above their heads. It seems to be the same all over the world—this idea that, if you are not swinging a golf club above your head, you are not swinging it properly ... To my idea, when you have the clubhead at the top it should be two or three feet from the neck, and you can't do that with an upright swing. The shaft has to be right away from your neck, and if you can get the shaft of the club horizontal round your back, then you are in a perfect position, but the shaft must be laid off the right shoulder, a couple of feet or so away.

from *Play Championship Golf All Your Life*, Pelham Books (UK)

FOULED UP IN THE MECHANICS   Frank Beard

I was paired today with Lionel Herbert and Harold Henning. Lionel is one of the sweetest people I've ever met. He's been on the tour almost twenty years. He won the PGA championship more than ten years ago, and even now he's a fine golfer. Lionel and his brother, Jay, and Gardner Dickinson are very close—they travel together and stay together—and they're three brilliant golfers who've won a bunch of tournaments. All the rest of us on the tour respect these fellows for both their records and their ability; but once in a while we like to tease them, in a friendly way, about how hard they work trying to find exactly the proper swing and proper shot for every situation.

Lionel, Jay, and Gardner are fanatics on mechanics, on working on the swing, on experimenting. When they play a golf course, they feel they have to hit a perfect shot for each stroke on each hole. They've got to fit a little three-iron in, or hook a little six-iron, or fade a little wedge. And all three of them except maybe Lionel, are almost embarrassed when they have good putting rounds. They don't think putting's an art like hitting picture shots; they figure anybody can make a ten-footer, but only a real pro can deliberately hook one shot and then fade the next. They're artists all right, but over the years, if they'd just played their games and left all the mechanics alone, they might have run away from the rest of the tour.

from *Pro: Frank Beard on the Golf Tour*, Thomas Y. Crowell Co (US)

CORRECTING FAULTS   Patrick Campbell

The verbal hint or tip is the thing to go for. It, at least, contains a message of hope, and gives the player the feeling that he is doing something different, even if the resulting blind slash looks exactly the same as it has always done to his friends.

I should like to illustrate the application of the verbal hint or tip by Case History Number Three.

Case history number three

I used to play in a regular Sunday morning fourball with David F., a man who took golf books like cocaine in an effort to rid himself of a hook so virulent that the ball, on leaving the club-head, became almost visibly egg-shaped in its efforts to get round the corner, causing David to have to take a step back with his left foot in order to keep it in sight while it passed over the road.

When the toss of a coin condemned us to partnership I tried with everything I had ever heard about the game to bring about a cure, particularly at the second hole, a short one, where the tee was set back deeply in an avenue of trees, making it impossible for David's tee-shot to emerge into the open.

On one such Sunday morning I applied myself to his grip, it being the only physical feature of his game over which it looked as if he might have some control.

We had, frankly, become involved in a small game of cards—half a dollar ante and five bob jackpots—at his house the previous evening which had been interrupted—only, it seemed, a bare couple of hours later—by the arrival of his wife with breakfast, an intrusion for which she apologized. But then, she said, she couldn't have borne it if we'd been late for our morning round, particularly as there was so little to do about the house now that she'd got the children off to sleep again after the singing, or whatever it was, which had broken out round about dawn. Unless, she went on, we cared to stay to tidy up the sitting-room and in particular to shift the crates of stout which, even though empty, might prove too much for her strength, undermined as it had been by a somewhat sleepless night—

I could tell on the first tee that David, unfortunately my partner, had been more adversely affected than the rest of us, because he asked me if it was raining. It was, in fact, a hot still morning in July.

We lost the first hole to a 6. I was unable to take much part in it myself, suffering from the vertiginous feeling that my clubs had been shortened or the whole course lowered several inches by some outside agency during the night, so that even by striking sharply downwards I could reach only the top half of the ball.

David, of course, was in the car-park on the left with his tee-shot and picked up, after hitting the side of the pro's shop twice.

To stop the rot, before the opposition ran right away from us, I had a word with him on the second tee, the one buried in the trees.

'I can't help you much,' I said, 'until my clubs get longer or the course comes up a bit, so that if we're going to get anything like a six here and a possible win you'll have to hit yours straight, or at least straight until it gets out of these trees. Try gripping very tight with your left hand and forget about the right altogether. I'll watch it for you, if I can see it. It's only thirty yards out into the clear.'

He replied, as so many players do to helpful advice, by trying to defend his own method, one which, he said, he'd just picked up from a book by Henry Cotton. 'I'm piccolo-ing my hands,' he said. 'It helps me to snap the wrists through.'

'However the hell you piccolo,' I said, 'it snapped your opening blow into the car-park, from which you failed to emerge after two more.'

He made a conversational detour, then, to tell me that my back swing off the first tee had put him in mind of an elderly woman of dubious morals trying to struggle out of a dress too tight around the shoulders. He was interrupted by the other two players, who said that they were both on the green and did we feel it was worth playing on?

I took, I have to admit, rather a quick swish at mine, jarring myself badly with a punchy little 5-iron which buried itself, after a very short, low flight, in the back slope of the ladies' tee.

It was David's turn. 'Never mind the piccolo,' I told him. 'Just have a good bash with your left hand. If we're two down after this we can walk in.'

He shaped up to it quite well, very relaxed, but leaning a little too far over the ball to promise complete control. Whatever he meant by piccolo-ing, I guessed it hadn't started yet. I was, in fact, just about to remind him that golf clubs had no connection with musical instruments when he suddenly played a stroke with a long, flowing arm action reminiscent of one of the supernumeraries in *Les Sylphides*. The ball passed harmlessly between his legs, but it was the other development that the rest of us found hard to credit. We turned back to look at the striker.

He was standing there with his hands held high in a good finish. After a moment, however, the suspicion seemed to enter his mind that all was not well. He lowered his hands slowly and looked at them. He examined the ground in front, and then behind. 'Where,' he said, after a short interval, 'is my driver?'

from *How to Become a Scratch Golfer*, Blond & Briggs (UK)

SWING VELOCITY   R. T. Jones

The great fault in the average golfer's conception of his stroke is that he considers the shaft of the club a means of transmitting actual physical force to the ball, whereas it is in reality merely the means of imparting velocity to the club head. We would all do better could we only realize that the length of a drive depends not upon the brute force applied but upon the speed of the club head. It is a matter of velocity rather than of physical effort of the kind that bends crowbars and lifts heavy weights.

I like to think of a golf club as a weight attached to my hands by an imponderable medium, to which a string is a close approximation, and I like to feel that I am throwing it at the ball with much the same motion I should use in cracking a whip. By the simile, I mean to convey the idea of a supple and lightning-quick action of the wrists in striking—a sort of flailing action.

from *Bobby Jones on Golf*, Doubleday & Co (US), Cassell & Co (UK)

WHAT IS A SWING?   Horace G. Hutchinson

Now what, after all, is the meaning of the word 'swing' . . .? It has a meaning which it is useful to fully realise. The upward swing should be slow and even, downward swing even and swift. But though the upward swing should be slow, it should, we have said, be a swing, and not a lift. And the essential difference between a swing and a lift, and between a swing and a hit, is this:—that in a swing one is all the while conscious of—one can all the while feel in one's hand—the weighty thing, the head of the club, *swinging* upward or downward, at the end of the shaft. We are to feel that the weight of the head has its influence upon the movement of the club—we must rather try to follow and be guided by this influence than to interfere with it with our tautened muscle; for this it is that produces jerkiness, and unevenness, and misses, and disaster. Encouraging and accelerating the speed of this swinging thing at the end of the club means hard driving, in its true sense—above all, accelerating the pace to its utmost at the moment that the club-head meets the ball. But directly we begin to force the swing out of its harmony—to over-accelerate the pace—from that instant it loses the true character of a swing and becomes a hit, a jerk—and this is 'pressing.' *Festina lente*—'Don't press.' Let the club swing *itself* through. Help it on, on the path of its swing, all you can, but do not *you* begin to hit with it. Let it do its work itself, and it will do it well. Interfere with it, and it will be quite adequately avenged.

from *Golf*, The Badminton Library (UK) 1893

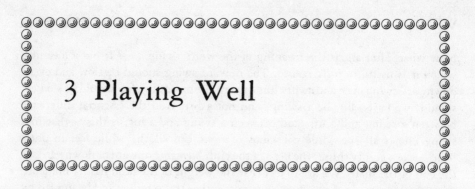

3 Playing Well

EVERY golfer has had a day when things have gone astonishingly well, though he will probably afterwards try hard to see it as a time when he just happened to play his 'normal' game. For the 24–handicapper, this means hitting a few shots from more or less the middle of the club. The 12 man, however, would not be satisfied with anything much worse than a 75 on his card. Nicklaus, Miller, Player, Weiskopf and their kind want, once in a life time, to break 60. Amongst a very few others, Gary Player did this in 1974 in the Brazil Open to complete in just about as fitting a way possible his own *annus mirabilis*.

However, although it is what score you did and whether or not you won your match that seems to count for most, there is that other factor that gives more joy to the inner man: not how well you *scored*, but how well you *played*.

WHAT IT OUGHT TO LOOK LIKE   Patrick Campbell

I was playing in the Bowmaker Tournament at Sunningdale, partnered with Leopoldo Ruiz from the Argentine, who is popularly known as 'The Thin Crust of Bread'.

The Thin Crust is very tall, with shoulders a mile wide and a seventeen-inch waist. He's incomparably the healthiest man I've ever seen and was feeling so healthy, indeed, on this occasion that he took to playing a 2-iron off every tee, in the interests of being able to find the ball again after he'd hit it.

He took his 2-iron off the fifth and with a punch so savage that his hands were over the ball while the club-head was still about shoulder high he hit it 300 yards, almost beyond the pond, pulverizing the divot. There was a military-looking gentleman, retired, standing beside me. 'By God,' he said in a low voice, 'I've been playing golf for fifty years and I never knew it was supposed to look like that.'

from *Patrick Campbell's Golfing Book*, Blond & Briggs (UK)

GETTING THAT CERTAIN FEEL R. T. Jones

To determine just how hard to try to hit a golf ball in order to get the best results is often a perplexing problem. Everyone knows the dangers of pressing and the troubles one can encounter when trying to hit too hard. But the shoe can rub the other way, too, and the fellow who tries to swing too easily is often just as close to disaster. Somewhere between these two extremes is the happy middle ground the golfer must tread.

I cannot recall that I ever accomplished any really good scores or won any matches by trying to knock the cover off the ball. Good driving has been a part of all the really fine rounds I ever played. It is true that, except for those occasions when a putter goes phenomenally hot, a man must be driving well to score well. But all that is needed is ordinarily good length and a good deal of accuracy, the latter feature being by far the more important of the two.

I got as much fun as the next man from whaling a ball as hard as I could and catching it squarely on the button. But from sad experience I learned not to try this in a round that meant anything.

But there is the other extreme that is just as bad. Whenever one becomes too careful and begins to steer his shots, he can get into just as much trouble, and his trouble may be found a lot farther from the green than if he had taken a good, healthy swing. Easing up almost always leaves the left side in the way—there is not enough pull to get it around where it ought to be—and when the swing finds itself blocked, there is no way for it to go through cleanly and smoothly.

Of all the times that I have struggled around the golf course, there are a few easy rounds that stand out in my memory. These are the ones I should like to play over again, and it would not take long, for there are not that many. One at Sunningdale, England, one at East Lake in Atlanta, two at Augusta, Georgia (both in one day), one at Interlachen in Minneapolis, and that's about all. Other scores were as good, but no other rounds were as satisfying.

Strangely, perhaps, one thing stands out about all those rounds; I had precisely the same feel on each occasion; I was conscious of swinging the club easily and yet without interruption; my left side was moving through without hindrance, yet I was making no special effort to get it out of the way; in fact, I had to make no special effort to do anything.

Sunningdale came first. I did not recognize the symptoms, because I had never had them before. Then, the next year, we had an open tournament at East Lake. In warming up before the second round, I suddenly realized that I had the same feel I had had at Sunningdale—and it worked again. It is not unnatural that I tried to get it every time I went out on the course, but only a few times did it come.

from *Bobby Jones on Golf*, Doubleday & Co (US), Cassell & Co (UK)

POSSESSED   Michael Murphy

The growing exaltation I was feeling possessed me then, crowding out questions, problems, anything that seemed not to fit. I felt the land as we climbed the hill, the sea breeze, the grass beneath my feet. A film had dropped from my eyes, from my hearing, from all my senses. The smell of the sea and the grass, of leather and perspiration filled the air. I could hear a cry of delight in the distance, then tiny cheers. Something had broken loose inside me, something large and free ...

I looked out from our vantage point; we could see for miles now. The sun was dipping behind the western hills, while purple shadows spread across the water and arabesques of grass below. The curving fairways and tiny sounds arising from them, the fields of heather, the distant seacaps were all inside my skin. A presence was brooding through it all, one presence interfusing the ball, the green, MacIver, Shivas, everything.

I played the remaining holes in this state of grace. Specters of former attitudes passed through me, familiar curses and excuses, memories of old shots, all the flotsam and jetsam of my golfing unconscious—but a quiet field of energy held me and washed them away. I can think of no better way to say it—those final holes played me.

from *Golf in the Kingdom*, The Viking Press (US), Latimer New Dimensions (UK)

THE IDEAL COUPLING   Jack Nicklaus and Herbert Warren Wind

Quite early in this book, when I was discussing the great pleasure I got in playing the last two rounds of the 1960 U.S. Open with Ben Hogan, I mentioned that during that tournament I had a wonderful feeling whenever I set up to play a shot: my right knee seemed right under me, so to speak, and I could pivot very easily on the backswing and move into a strong hitting position on the downswing with equal ease. I also mentioned that countless times afterward I tried to recapture that particular feeling before the ball and was never able to. In a later chapter, when I was recalling the second World Amateur Team Championship (for the Eisenhower Trophy), which we played at Merion in 1960, I remarked that my hands felt absolutely marvelous on the club that week: my left wrist formed an almost straight line with the back of my left hand. Having the sense that I was perfectly aligned on my target, I stopped thinking about how I was executing my swing and devoted all my attention to playing each shot as well as I could. No wonder I had such a fine tournament! Naturally, I tried to establish that same ideal coupling of the left wrist and hand on many subsequent occasions, hoping to rediscover the sense of correctness, comfort, and confidence I had at Merion, but I never managed to. I bring up these two incidents—it would be no trouble to add a dozen more—because they serve to point up the recurring problem I've had holding onto a position, a move, or just a feeling which worked wonders for me and which I wanted to make a permanent part of my game.

There are, thank goodness, some phases of golf technique that a man can master (change to *almost master*) through hours and hours of repeating a certain action. However, looking back, I would guess that one of the principal themes of this book would be how elusive golf is even for those of us who have made the game our profession. I remember, for example, reading how Henry Cotton, after a putting session in which he had holed everything in sight, tacked some brown paper around the grip of his putter and had a friend trace with a pencil the exact position of his hands. The idea behind this, of course, was that Cotton was hoping that if he placed his fingers in precisely the same position the next time he went out, he might perhaps be able to summon up again the same astonishingly effective stroke and touch. The following day he tried it out. With the brown paper still tacked around the grip of the putter, he carefully positioned each finger where the guide lines indicated. And what happened? It didn't feel the same at all. The stroke he had wanted to re-create had entirely vanished.

from *The Greatest Game of All*, Simon & Schuster (US) Hodder & Stoughton (UK)

DIVINE FRENZY   R. T. Jones

I can still see the awesome figure made by Compston towards the finish of his round. One of the British writers said that he was playing 'like a frenzied giant'. A tall, powerful man, Compston was truly striding after the ball as though he could not wait to vent his fury upon it. Watching from the clubhouse as I saw him sweep past the sixteenth green, I had the feeling that spectators, tee-boxes, benches even, might be swirled up into his wake. As he left the eighteenth green after his great sixy-eight and made his beaming way to the clubhouse through a myriad of well-wishers, he was about as happy a figure as I have ever seen.

from *Golf is My Game*, Doubleday & Co (US), Chatto & Windus (UK)

MAKE WAY FOR THE SENIOR GOLFER   Alistair Cooke

Do you want to hear about my 39 on the tough back nine at Noyac, a fairly new—but, as we oldsters like to say, a 'testing'—course at the end of Long Island? Well, you're going to, because Donald Steel [editor of *The Golfer's Bedside Book*] asked me to put down 'whatever comes to mind'. And this is what comes to mind with more poignancy than anything in these twilight years. (I am speaking, you understand, as a golfer. As a boulevardier, a martini mixer, a wag when I play with the secretary of Women's Lib off the back tees, I am indistinguishable from the college cut-up.)

I will make the account of this masterful round brief, but only out of consideration for those lobster-tanned veterans who took up the game at the age of eight, progressed by kangaroo stages to a two handicap and have deteriorated so alarmingly with each decade that when asked to exercise total recall and recount the history of some of their triumphs they reply, like Bing Crosby, 'Total recall? I can't even recall when I last broke 80.'

Well, sir, it was a glittering Sunday afternoon in the late fall. I was sitting out on our terrace on the North Fork of Long Island facing the deep blue waters of Peconic Bay and feeling pretty hot under the collar, I can tell you. We had had three people to lunch. We were still having them to lunch and it was twenty-five minutes to four, a whole hour past the time when I normally have bussed my wife with resounding gratitude, torn off to a links course twelve miles away and started to lace long drives and cunning little pitches—alone, of course—into the declining sun. I had already given rather gross notice to these dawdlers of my intentions by retreating to my bedroom and going through my normal medical routine as a senior golfer (we shall come to that a little later on).

Our guests—my lawyer, his wife and sister—would have been, at any other time, enchanting company. In fact, until they started on their third lobster at three p.m. I was convinced that no more amiable guests had ever wolfed our vodka or darkened our towels.

Far off, across the old Colonial meadows at our back, a church clock struck three-thirty. The old Colonial churches still have their uses, not the least of which is to toll the knell of parting guests. My lawyer turned to me and said: 'A beautiful time of day, this, especially in the fall.' In a flash, I saw my opportunity for a cliffhanger's cry. 'Yes, indeed,' I said, 'you know, a friend of mine now pattering towards the grave told me that when he gets to Heaven—he is what they always call a *devout* Catholic and he has no anxiety whatsoever about his destination—and is asked by St Peter what, if he had lived longer, he would most wish to have prolonged, he will reply—"later afternoon golf".'

'That's right,' said my lawyer, 'you usually play around this time, don't you?'

I furtively leaned over to him while the ladies were still slurping up the repulsive butter and lemon sauce. '*Around* this time,' I said with a meaningful ogle. '*By* this time I am usually recording my first par on the very difficult fourth hole whose green recedes invisibly into Long Island Sound.'

He is a guileless man—except in all matters pertaining to residuals and cassette rights—and he started as if a fox had started out of its burrow on our fast-eroding bank or bluff. 'Listen,' he whispered beseechingly, 'don't let us stop you . . . .'

I stopped him right there and begged the ladies to round things off with a liqueur. 'A dram of cognac, a soupçon of kirsch?' I suggested. 'Goodness, no thanks,'—thank goodness—they said.

'Really,' he implored.

'I tell you what,' I said, now in complete control of a situation not even imagined by the late, great Stephen Potter, 'we are going to dinner on the South Shore not far from you. Why doesn't Jane drive your ladies over an hour or so from now, *when they are ready to leave*? You and I will take your car, whisk around a fast eighteen holes at Island's End, and then we'll meet them all back at your place?'

I anticipated his next line, which was: 'You know, I'm ashamed to say I don't play, but I love to walk around. D'you think I could just amble along?'

The trajectory of our departure was never matched by Bugs Bunny. Fifteen seconds later we were on our way, leaving the women to surmise, 'Did they go for a swim? Irving doesn't really care for swimming.'

Island's End is a semi-public course, which means that at unpredictable times it is likely to be infested by a couple of busloads of the Associated Potato and Cauliflower Growers of Long Island. It was such a day. 'No way,' said the young pro, 'there are seventy-five of them out there and you wouldn't get through five holes before dark.'

'Too bad,' said my honest lawyer.

'I retain,' I said 'an escape clause for just such emergencies. I am a member at Noyac on the South Shore, and on Sundays not even guests can play.'

We snorted off to the ferry, trundled across the Bay, roared the five miles to the North Haven ferry, made it, and thundered up to the pro-shop at Noyac on the stroke of five. To all such jocularities as 'trying out a little bit of night golf, eh, Mr Cooke?' I turned a contemptuous ear. We were in an electric cart in one minute flat. (I hasten to say to snobs from the Surrey pine and sand country that no invention since the corn plaster or the electric tooth-brush has brought greater balm to the extremities of the senior golfer than the golfmobile, a word that will have to do for want of a better.)

A natural and chronic modesty, which I have been trying to conquer for years, forbids my taking you stroke by flawless stroke through the following nine holes. ('I think we'll take the back nine,' I had muttered to my lawyer, 'it's a little more testing.') Suffice it to say that when we approached the dreaded eleventh—an interminable par five with a blind second shot up to a plateau three yards wide between two Grand Canyon bunkers—my friend was already goggling in the car or cart stammering out such memorable asides as, 'I don't believe it, it looks so goddam easy'.

An imperious drive had put me in the prescribed position for the perilous second shot. I was lining myself up, with the image of Nicklaus very vivid in my mind, when I noticed two large gorillas disturbing my peripheral vision. I paused and looked up in total, shivering control. Happily, on closer inspection, they turned out not to be gorillas but two typical young American golfers in their late twenties. They were about six feet three each, they carried the dark give-away tan that betokens the four-handicapper, and they waved at me nonchalantly and said, 'Go ahead, grandpa, we've got all the time in the world'.

Again I went through my casual Nicklaus motions. My three-wood followed the absolutely necessary arc and the ball came to rest precisely midway between the two bunkers. 'Many thanks,' I said briskly and waved back at the aghast gorillas. They marched fifty yards or so to what I was crestfallen to realise were their drives. Gallantly I indicated that no matter what the humiliation to me they should proceed. They banged two stout shots, one into the right bunker, the other on the edge of the pine woods.

By the time I came up to my ball, I was sitting upright with a commanding expression, worthy of Adolf Hitler arriving in Vienna in his hand-made Opel. The gorillas paused again, and waved again. 'Go ahead,' they said.

"Enks vemmuch," I said. I took a five-iron with all the slow calculation of Geronimo Hogan. Ahead lay a great swale, another swirl of bunkers, a plateau and the bunkers guarding the sloping green. I heard in my ears the only sentence I have ever heard at the moment of address from George Heron, my old Scottish teacher of seventy-eight summers, springs and winters: 'Slow along the ground, big turn, hit out to me.'

It rose slowly like a gull sensing a reckless bluefish too close to the surface, and then it dived relentlessly for the green, kicked and stopped three feet short of the flag.

'Jesus!' cried one of the gorillas, 'd'you hit the ball this way all the time?'

'Not,' I replied, 'since I left the tour.'

We left them gasping. And, to be truthful, I left the ninth hole gasping.

'You never told me!' shouted my beloved friend and lawyer.

'I never knew,' I said.

from *The Bedside Book of Golf*, (ed. Donald Steel) B. T. Batsford (UK)

HOW IT OUGHT TO BE DONE   Patrick Campbell

In January, 1961, an exhibition match took place between Sam Snead and Harry Weetman, to celebrate the opening of Israel's first golf-course at Caesarea.

It also marked the first occasion upon which a match was followed by a gallery of 2000 people only twelve of whom—by my own personal estimate—had ever seen the game played before.

A brisk breeze was blowing up the first fairway, touching at times, I should say, fifty miles an hour, as Snead and Weetman tossed for the honour.

Snead won, teed up his ball and then stood looking at the audience with an appearance of patience which anyone knowing him would not have trusted an inch.

What the audience was doing was commenting in Hebrew, German, Polish, French, Spanish and a variety of Scandinavian languages upon the force of the wind, the magnificence of the new club-house, the political situation *vis-à-vis* Jordan, Colonel Nasser and half a hundred other matters including Snead's Palm Beach straw hat. The babel of sound was tremendous, and only partially dissipated by the gale.

None of those present, of course, could have been expected to know that death-like silence should have been their portion, that Snead had been known to threaten legal action against people dropping pins half a mile away while he was trying to hole a four-foot putt.

As the Master continued to remain inactive, save for an ominous tapping of the right foot, the noise became even greater. I was able to identify enquiries in English, French and German as to whether he had already, perhaps, done it and if so where had it gone, and if he hadn't what was he waiting for and would it be possible for him to get on with it now?

Snead then made a suggestion which some of the stewards carried out in part, waving their arms and asking politely for silence. This had the immediate effect of redoubling the noise, people asking one another in genuine bewilderment how silence on their part could possibly contribute to whatever Snead was trying to do. In the end a comparative hush was achieved, Snead stepped up to his ball and with that long, beautifully timed, power-packed swing slashed one straight down the middle, quail high into the wind and all of 280 yards.

Death-like silence fell upon the gallery, for the first time. They'd seen him hit it, but no one was prepared for the result. No one, in fact, had seen where the ball had gone. It had simply passed out of their ken and so they remained silent, rather than to appear at a disadvantage by applauding where, perhaps, no applause had been earned.

They were more ready for Weetman, as he stood up to it. Word had gone round that perhaps the ball went rather farther than anyone could have a right to expect. They saw every inch of Harry's tee-shot, an obviously apprehensive right-handed bash that took off like a bullet, turned sharp left and finished on the far side of the ninth fairway, about 150 yards off the line.

A great roar of applause went up, a thunderous clapping of hands. Snead's expression, never too sunny in action—or even in repose—would have frightened the lives out of a platoon of armed Algerian terrorists in broad daylight.

Subsequently, there was even worse to come. Many of the stewards got tired of the labour of lugging ropes around, seeing that the gallery paid little attention to them, and knocked off, leaving the ropes where they lay. At one moment, round about the seventh, Snead found himself trying to play a wedge shot over or around three splendidly bearded old gentlemen who stood directly in front of him, watching whatever he was trying to do with lively interest. Later, a pretty girl in khaki shorts picked Harry Weetman's ball out of a bush and helpfully placed it in his hand.

But how, as I say, could anyone who had never seen golf played before know any better? And how can anyone who has never seen Snead hit a golf ball guess that that is the way it ought to be done?

from *Patrick Campbell's Golfing Book*, Blond & Briggs (UK)

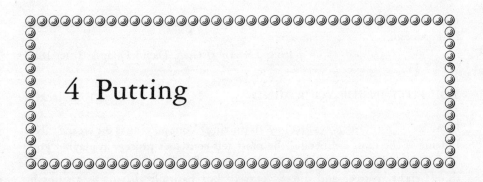

4 Putting

THERE is no chapter in this book devoted to driving, the long iron or approach play, but putting insidiously sneaks into any writing about golf.

My selections begin with a few thoughts about the psychology of the thing, continue with how it ought to be done—note the opposite laws set down with such authority—and conclude with pessimism about the whole process.

ATTRACTIONS OF PUTTING   Sir Walter Simpson

To the beginner putting seems the least interesting part of the game. It feels mean to go dribbling and creeping up to a little hole, whilst a teeing-ground, from which you may drive the ball unknown distances into space, is ready close by. Like other things, essentially foolish in themselves, such as preaching, pleading, feeling pulses, etc., putting becomes attractive in proportion to the skill acquired in it.

from *The Art of Golf*, David Douglas (UK) 1887

WAITING TO PUTT   Sir Walter Simpson

When a putter is waiting his turn to hole-out a putt of one or two feet in length, on which the match hangs at the last hole, it is of vital importance that he think of nothing. At this supreme moment he ought studiously to fill his mind with vacancy. He must not even allow himself the consolations of religion. He must not prepare himself to accept the gloomy face of his partner and the derisive delight of his adversaries with Christian resignation should he miss. He must not think that it is a putt he would not dream of missing at the beginning of the match, or, worse still, that he missed one like it in the middle. He ought to wait calm and stupid till it is his turn to play ... and putt as I have told him how—neither with undue haste nor with exaggerated care. When the ball is down, and the putter handed to the caddy, it is not well to say, 'I couldn't have missed it.' Silence is best. The pallid cheek and trembling lip belie such braggadocio.

from *The Art of Golf*, David Douglas (UK) 1887

YOU PUTT INSIDE YOUR MIND   Tony Jacklin

If you are off form, it shows first in your putting. Your putting is the escape valve. Putting is the most deliberate, the most self-conscious process in playing golf. When you drive, you've got to think what you are doing—study yourself, put things right, correct and direct yourself; but basically driving is an unself-conscious action. There's the fairway, here's the ball, hit the damn thing. It's what you might call a 'free' situation.

But you putt in a 'closed' situation. Your ball is only a few feet from the hole, perhaps. It's not a case of getting as far as you can hit. There's something natural, elemental, about taking a damn good smack at a ball when you drive: when you putt, you're being artificial.

You take in all the conditions of the putt—distance, gradient, whether the ground breaks a bit to the left or to the right, wetness or dryness, type of grass and so on. You feed all this into your brain. You register these facts and, out of that, you develop a sense of how it will *feel* in your mind if you putt correctly. Then you putt. When you putt, you play to what you think you should feel. You move your club in relation to a procedure you've set up in your mind. You putt inside your mind, and if you putt properly in your mind, you sink it.

Now, if that's so, your concentration, which means your capacity for living entirely inside your own mind, must be at its very best. Nothing must interfere. For those few seconds the outside world must cease to exist. *You* have got to cease to exist, except for experiencing that one single sensation of knowing exactly what it is that you're going to do—of knowing how it is going to feel to do it properly.

from *The Observer* (London) 14 July 1974 (interviewer: Kenneth Harris)

SHORT PUTTS   Sir Walter Simpson

Although every golfer theoretically accepts it as politic to play for the back of the hole, yet few putt as if they thought it was. The majority treat the hole as a place more difficult to get into than it really is. They seem practically to believe that a putt one ounce too strong, or one hair's-breadth off the line, must be out. Consequently many short putts are played so timidly that they are six inches off the line, or within six inches of the goal. Now the fact is, that (from short distances) the hole is pretty big, and from all distances it is capable of catching a ball going at a fair pace. I admit that more putts of over two yards must be missed than are held, because a putting-green is not a billiard-table; but many more would go in than do if players credited holes with a little of that catching power which they really possess.

from *The Art of Golf*, David Douglas (UK) 1887

BE PAST THE HOLE   Walter Hagen

Putting has won many a match for me. My penchant for holing the ball has made up for my wildness on the fairway in match after match. Much of the indifferent putting I've seen is due to the shaky, uncertain way a ball is hit. I like to hit a ball firmly. Banging the ball recklessly isn't going to help, of course, because mechanically it is as difficult to hole out from beyond the cup as it is from short of it, distances being equal. But at least you've had one try when you go past the cup.

One of the best putters I've ever known, not a man who figured prominently in tournament play but who won a lot of matches from players who were a stroke better than he from tee to the green, made a special point of hitting every ball at least as *far* as the hole. The way he acquired this practice was to penalise himself every time he failed to give the ball a chance to reach the hole on any green during a round of play.

There is a favourable psychology, as well as logic, working for the player who consistently hits the ball hard enough to reach the hole. I've made it a point to note how often poor putters are short and I've been amazed at how much more frequently the good ones are beyond when they miss.

from *The Walter Hagen Story*, Simon & Schuster (US), William Heinemann (UK)

TOUCH IS THE KEY   R. T. Jones

I regard the putting stroke as so truly a miniature golf stroke that I think it is a mistake to try to exclude any members of the body from participation in the action. In other words, I do not believe in trying to hinge the stroke upon either wrist, or in trying to restrict the movement to any sort of fixed base. Naturally, the shortest putt requires only the gentlest tap, actuated only by the hands; a putt slightly longer may require that the arms should swing a bit; and the long approach putt may need a stroke long enough to induce a little movement in the hips and legs.

In putting, and in chipping, too, it is important that the backswing should be long enough. Nothing can be worse around the greens, than a short, snatching stroke. I have had some of the real masters of the short game tell me, and I heartily agree, that it is most helpful to swing back a little farther than needed on the first few chips or putts of any round. In this way they can be certain of attaining that feeling of a smoothly-floating club so necessary for a delicate touch.

Actually, this touch is the key to good putting. Very few putts of any length are dead straight, so that no line is right except for one speed; and the player who tries to straighten even the shortest putts by charging the hole will miss a lot of those coming back.

I will guarantee that more putts under twenty feet—the kind you like to hole—will go in, and three-putt greens will pop up less often, if the player will forget about the precise alignment of his putter and learn to adjust his touch so that he may always keep his ball above the hole and always reach the hole with a dying ball. A ball dying on a slope above the hole often topples in, and always stops close by; nothing is more disheartening than to watch a ball barely miss the lower side of the hole and then curl down the slope some five or six feet. And remember, even on the short putts, that the hole is of full size for the touch putter, while it presents only an inch or so to the charger who has to hit the exact centre of the cup.

I like to think of putting as very much like rolling a golf ball from my hand across a green towards a hole. I know I should then not worry too much about the backswing of my arm. I think it would instinctively take care of itself. So in putting, I don't like to worry too much about the alignment of my putter at address or about my backswing, except that it be long enough. The picture I want uppermost in my mind is of the line I want the ball to travel on, and of how hard I want to hit it.

from *Golf is My Game*, Doubleday & Co (US), Chatto & Windus (UK)

GAME WITHIN A GAME   Henry Longhurst

The art of putting at golf resembles that of goalkeeping at soccer, in being 'a game within a game'. Furthermore, as I remember so often reflecting as I leant nonchalantly against the uprights—having played in goal since the age of eight—both are games which enable a fellow with a certain crafty cunning to neutralize the efforts of stronger, braver men, and this in any walk of life is a source of much inward satisfaction.

On the other hand, both putting and goalkeeping may lead to an embarrassing immortality not to be endured in other departments of the game. The poor wretch who lets it trickle slowly between his legs in a Cup Final is remembered long after missers of sitting goals have sunk into a merciful oblivion. A yard putt missed on the last green may also live for ever.

Thoughts of putting comes to my mind because I have recently mentioned the four secrets of putting, as outlined to me one day years ago by Bobby Locke, who was presumably the greatest holer-out in the world in the post-war years, and one or two people have asked to be let in upon them.

I hope that I am not poaching on Locke's professional preserves in revealing them. A good agent, I should have said, could have got him £1,000 for them.

ONE: You must hit the ball clean. This does not involve any nonsense about 'top spin' or 'trying to make it roll'. If you flick a ping-pong ball off a table, you take aim with your finger-nail and flick it cleanly. Touch the table and you 'smudge' it. It is the same with brushing the putter along the grass.

'You can tell a good putt,' says Locke, 'by the noise it makes'—and very remarkable it is to hear him demonstrate, interspersing clean hits with an odd one just touching the grass. Ping, ping, PUNG, ping, ping, PUNG, they go—and so on. It occurs to me that Locke was probably the loudest putter in golf.

TWO: Every putt you will ever have in your life, on any course, in any country, of any length, is dead straight. Elementary, when you come to think of it—but had you thought of it that way? Of course, on a sharp slope the ball may roll almost in a semi-circle—but you did not make it do so. All you can do, time and time and time again, is to hit it dead straight—not necessarily, of course, straight at the hole. A bullet fired in a high wind at Bisley will travel in a slight curve. The man who gets a bull with it adjusted his sights and aimed straight. The mental relief on grasping this simple conception is unbelievable.

THREE: Hold the putter very loosely. 'Ha!' I remember saying, 'and what about when you have a four-footer to tie for the Open?' 'Hold it looser still!' he said.

FOUR: Any fool can putt through a hoop four feet wide from ten yards or more. In other words, you take three putts through getting the distance wrong, not the direction. So when Locke wanders slowly between ball and hole, he is not, as one might suppose, pondering on the infinite or looking for leather-jackets. He is making up his mind how far it is. See also Rule One.

If you sometimes hit it clean and sometimes touch the grass, it may make a difference of four or five feet in distance—the difference between two putts and three.

FIVE: This is my own, based merely on observation. Locke evolved a 'drill'. Never mind the details—we can all evolve our own. In other words, for every putt he ever made, irrespective of distance or circumstances, once the machinery was set in action he went through the same motions. No extra waggle, no extra look at the hole. For better or for worse. Which is yet another reason, I fancy, why it was almost inevitably for better.

from *The Sunday Times* (UK)

PUTT IN COMFORT   R. T. Jones

Up until 1921, my putting was about as bad as one could imagine; I had experimented with it for years, but most of my experiments had taken the form of attempted imitations of some of the good putters I had seen, notable among whom were Walter Travis and Walter Hagen. I had studied the styles of these men, particularly that of Hagen, and would always try to assume the same posture at address, and attempt to swing the putter in the same way. The result of these efforts—and it was a result that should have been expected—was a tension throughout my whole body that would not otherwise have been present, so that however accurately I might reproduce the stroke that had been successful for the man I was imitating, the effect of it was destroyed because I could never relax. After all these experiences, I determined to putt naturally.

The putting stroke is the simplest of all because it is the shortest; once a person has developed a fairly good sense of what it is all about, and once he has developed a rhythmic stroke that can be counted upon to strike the ball truly, the only thing he should worry about is knocking the ball into the hole.

From day to day, I found that my putting posture changed noticeably. I always employed the same grip; I always stood with my feet fairly close together, with my knees slightly bent. Always, too, I saw to it that my back stroke was ample; but sometimes I felt most comfortable facing directly toward the ball; at other times, perhaps a quarter turn away in either direction. Again, there were times when my confidence was increased by gripping the club a few inches down from the end; at other times I liked to hold it at the very end of the shaft.

There are, of course, good putters among the so-called average golfers who by patience, study, and practice have developed putting methods they follow as they would a ritual; on the other hand, these instances are rare.

Anyone who hopes to reduce putting—or any other department of the game of golf for that matter—to an exact science, is in for a serious disappointment, and will only suffer from the attempt. It is wholly a matter of touch, the ability to gauge a slope accurately, and most important of all, the ability to concentrate on the problem at hand, that of getting the ball into the hole and nothing more. I think more potentially good putters have been ruined by attempting to duplicate another method than by any other single factor; by the time they can place themselves in a position they think resembles the attitude of the other man, they find themselves so cramped and strained that a smooth, rhythmic stroke is impossible.

from *Bobby Jones on Golf*, Doubleday & Co (US), Cassell & Co (UK)

YOU PAYS YOUR MONEY   Henry Longhurst

Having declined last week* to reveal for threepence a recently discovered secret of putting to end all secrets of putting, I received numerous requests, some even

* In a newspaper article.

offering to forward postal orders. But I regret to report that the formula appears to have been temporarily mislaid. It no longer works.

Turning to more accepted sources of inspiration, the master golfers, we find, alas, that they speak with many voices. A symposium of their advice might well be entitled, were it not already the copyright of Sir Osbert Sitwell, 'Left hand, right hand'. However, there is comfort in this. Whatever one's own method, one is bound to find some great man who says it is the right one, even if the rest, as is likely, list it under 'Common faults'.

In no department are the experts so much at sixes and sevens as in the realm of ballistics. 'The ball,' says Alfred Padgham, writing in 1936 when he was as good a putter as any man in the world, 'should never have over-spin as it reaches the hole, because with over-spin or top-spin it is liable to run round the rim.'

'Most good putters,' says Hogan in 1949, 'have the ability to make their ball start rolling directly it leaves the club-head. . . . The more roll you give the ball, the farther it will travel. . . .'

'No ball,' says Longhurst in 1950—knowing nothing whatever about it, but calling the ballisticians to witness and remembering an experiment on the sand greens of Lagos—'has ever reached the hole *without* top-spin, and no ball has ever started rolling directly it left the club-head.' It you don't believe it, try on sand, where the ball leaves a track. Hit upwards, downwards, sideways, or with the end of the shaft like a billiard cue; you still see a gap where the ball has jumped on starting.

'Never mind about top-spin and all that,' says Locke. 'Hit the ball clean. Don't let the club touch the grass.' In the same vein Padgham declares that you must look not merely at the ball but at the precise spot on it that you mean to strike—which reminds me of the man who teed up his ball so that, while striking, he could read the maker's name, and later observed: 'The trouble is, I'm such a —— quick reader!'

From prolonged study of the masters one may extract certain useful and positive hints. Sarazen uses what he calls the 'over-forty finger', i.e. the right forefinger pointing as a guide down the shaft. Locke, again, says, 'Grip very loosely.' When I said, 'That's all very well, but what about the four-footer to win the championship?' he replied, 'Grip it looser still.' He also maintains, graphically, that every putt in the world is straight: it may be aimed off to allow for borrow, but is still in itself a straight putt.

The timid putter will take comfort from Johnny Palmer, the American, who was an air gunner over Tokio—an experience hardly calculated, one would have thought, to make a man dead from two feet on returning to earth, though Palmer is said to be dead from ten. He maintains that one's ball should only just reach the hole, thus giving it three chances to topple in.

The composite perfect putter might, I fancy, combine steel putter; weight on left foot; eye over the ball; straight back and straight through; no bodily movement—and a good deal more. After which, he would probably yank the ball to the left as often as the rest of us.

Only one man really had the secret. He was the member of the Oxford and Cambridge Society, held by some to be eccentric, who, after long study of a crucial putt on the last green at Rye, remarked at last, 'It isn't on!' With that he pocketed the ball, turned on his heel, and marched into the club-house.

from *Golf Mixture*, T. Werner Laurie (UK)

THE YIPS   George Plimpton

One evening in San Francisco I heard for the first time about the 'yips'—a phenomenon talked about rather uneasily by the pros, and with wary respect, as one might talk about a communicable disease ravaging the neighboring township. The yips (a name invented by Tommy Armour, who had them) was the term given the occupational malaise of golf—a nervous affliction that settled in the wrist and hands, finally, after the years of pressure and the money bets and the strain. It was what ultimately drove the pros out of the game to the teaching jobs at the country clubs, setting the balls on the tees for the girls in the Pucci pants who came down for their two free gift lessons of the summer.

The legs don't give out, as in so many other sports, or the wind, or the sense of timing, or the power, but the *nerves*, so that one could see the hands of great golfers beset by the yips tremble visibly on the putting greens, the greatest names in golf completely at the mercy of short putts of 4, 5, 6 feet.

I said I had never heard of such a thing.

Dave Marr told me that he had seen Byron Nelson stand over a 4-foot putt at Florida's Seminole golf course, and, finally, after swaying back and forth several times, he had stabbed at the ball desperately and sent it *40 feet* past the hole.

At that same club, Seminole, Craig Wood had them so badly during an exhibition match, which should have relaxed the pressure, that he hit the first nine greens right on target in regulation strokes, but then putted so badly that his first-9 total was 44. His dismay was such that he refused to putt out at all during the second nine; when he reached the greens he stooped and picked up the ball and stuffed it in his pocket and walked on to the next tee. The rest of his foursome, sympathetic, allowed him double gimmes, the regulation two putting strokes, and marked him down as such.

There was someone, a curious youngster, unaware of the ravages that the yips are capable of committing, who had gone up to the golfer and had the temerity to ask: 'Why aren't you putting out like the others, Mister Wood? I mean, I don't understand . . .' and then he had stopped in mid-sentence because Wood had such a murderous look on his face.

It seemed to get them all. Leo Diegel had an awful time with nerves. He fussed around with a pendulum stroke with his putter but most people thought he was afflicted with a spastic tic. A great golfer, he never had the right mental equipment and he knew it: 'They keep trying to give the championship to me,' he once said, 'but I won't take it.' In the British Open in 1933 at St Andrews he faced an incredibly short putt, just a foot or so, and he wandered up to it shaking like a leaf and stubbed it past the hole to lose the championship.* Vardon, at the end of his career, in 1920, when he was in his fifties, got the yips. They were blamed on two attacks of tuberculosis. He called them the 'jumps' and recommended putting in the dark as effective treatment. Apparently it didn't work. Gene Sarazen (he eventually got them, too) recalls Vardon as the most atrocious putter he had ever seen. 'He didn't 3-putt, he 4-putted.'

Rod Funseth . . . said that one of the saddest examples of the yips he had seen were those infesting the person of Jon Gustin, who was known for owning one of the prettiest swings on the tour. Funseth went on about him at some length. Apparently, he was a great dresser—he had been a former flag-bearer in the Honor Guards in Washington. Very snappy. 'So you had,' Funseth said, 'the fine combination of a great swing, smooth and pretty as Snead's, and a guy who *looked* great as a golfer, like he stepped out of the advertising pages of *Esquire*, and yet what would happen, because of those yips, was that he would stand over the ball to swing—his irons, drives, putts, any shot—and his hands would come back, but the *club head wouldn't*. It would stick there right behind the ball like it was cemented to the ground.'

'Lord Almighty,' I said.

'He had to give up the tour.'

'Well, I would think so.'

'Worst case I ever saw.'

'No cure, I don't suppose, for the yips.'

'Golfers who have the yips *try* to cure them, God knows,' Funseth said. 'Gene Sarazen found one—at least one that worked for him. Watch him in the Senior tournaments. He steps up to the ball and hits it all in one motion—almost like he's hitting a shot off a polo pony. He doesn't dare stand over the ball, because he knows he'll freeze. Snead had the idea you could drift into a sort of "pleasant daydream" to get back to the fundamentals of the practice swing. And then I recall that Bobby Locke had an idea that the yips could be cured by holding the club very loosely.† If the yips had him bad, why you wouldn't be surprised to see his club just slip out and fall on the grass. Really no thing to have,' Funseth said. 'There's no sure cure. The yips can get so bad that you hate the idea of being in the lead in a tournament—where the pressure can bring on an attack. You begin to crave for a fair round, even a mediocre one, where the pressure isn't so stiff.'

---

* Others have reported that poor Leo missed the ball altogether—perhaps it was the next one he stubbed past?
† But Locke at his best also felt that the putter should be held as gently as possible so as to maintain the maximum of 'feel'.

The great distinction to make was that there was no similarity between the yips and 'choking'—though every once in a while the younger pros, who looked on the yips as something that couldn't possibly happen to them, would say that yips was just a fancy word that the older pros thought up to hide the fact that pressure get to them too.

'Who told you that?'

'Oh, one of the younger professionals.'

'That figures. If you want to see choking on a vast scale—I mean, what the caddies call the Apple Orchard for the big lumps that turn up in the throat—and if you want to see the eye-staring and those clammy foreheads, then you got to take in the qualifying tournaments that the rabbits play in. Ludicrous. Or you'll see one of those kids play in the high 60's for a round or so in the Open, and then what happens to him? The pressure gets to him. He skies to an 80. He chokes. He's so scared he damn near closes his eyes when he swings.'

Someone said: 'PeeWee Reese, the shortstop, used to have a good phrase for the choke. He'd say, "I know I'm choking when I'm chewing and can't work up a spit".'

'Sometimes a particular hole will cause a choke—a choke hole,' said Marr. 'Like the 18th at Cypress. It's like walking into a certain room in a big dark house when you were a kid—you get this fear that hits you.'

Johnny Pott said: 'That's why we spend so much time on the practice tee. You're down there trying to groove the shot, to tone up the muscle memory, so that when you get out on the golf course and the pressure's really on—the choke at hand, and you can sense your eyes popping, and the jaw shaking—the muscles can still perform in their usual groove and you can get your shot off. You practice to get the muscles moving almost automatically.'

'Doesn't that work for putting as well?'

'No, because muscle memory doesn't have anything to do with putting. Take Sam Snead. He's got the most famous swing in golf—you wouldn't find a differential of a millimeter in the circle of his swing if you took a thousand stop-action films of the guy. Perfectly grooved. Great on long putts, where the demands on muscle and swing are slightly more. But short putts! Give me someone out of kindergarten! His hands come back fine, but then the blade seems to go out of control just at the stroke. Sometimes he hits the top of the ball so that if it drops, it bounces every which way to get in there. Snead has had the yips for years. That's why he took that pro's job at Greenbrier way back in 1937. He thought he was going to have to quit the tour because he had the yips so bad. Or take Hogan, the most tragic case. Best tee-to-green player there ever was. Ever. I mean he puts the ball *there* off the tee, then *there*, just where he wants, then *there*, right on the green. You might as well *give* him those shots. But once on the green his troubles begin. He had those two holes to go at Oak Hill—just par-par, that's all he had to do to tie for the 1956 Open, but the yips got him. You know the guy got ten thousand letters from people trying to help him.'

'Ten thousand!' I said.

'That's right.'

I once asked Claude Harmon about those ten thousand letters, and whether he thought I would get an answer if I wrote Ben Hogan and asked him what the most ridiculous of the suggestions received had been—I thought that might be interesting.

'You wouldn't get an answer,' Harmon said, looking at me sharply. 'Because I'll tell you one thing. Hogan would have *tried* every damn one of them—I don't care how "ridiculous"—to rid himself of those things.' He repeated what I had heard so many people say: 'If only Hogan could have putted—Jesus, he'd've made every record in the book look silly.'

Hogan's miseries with the yips reached a climax in the 1954 Masters* when, leading the field, he went to pieces on the final holes of the tournament. He 3-putted the 13th, missed a 4-foot putt on the 15th, 3-putted the 17th, and then came to the 18th needing a 6-foot putt to win the tournament. Claude Harmon said that Hogan went off to the side of the green and he made about one hundred practice strokes with his putter, all markedly different—changing his grip, the position of his hands on the club, the stroke itself. When Harmon asked him about it later, Hogan said that he had been trying to find a stroke, any stroke at all, in which he felt comfortable—a last-minute desperate search—and after the experimenting at the edge of the big crowd around the green, he had taken one of the styles back out on the putting surface and, perched over the ball, he used it, and not unsurprisingly he missed the putt.

Claude Harmon had an interesting notion that a golfer's control over those shots, putts especially, which were conducive to the yips, was at best fragmentary since the ball traveled over the *ground*, and was at the mercy of irregularities and worm casts and the rubs of the green and beetles sticking up their heads to look round and minuscule pebbles and so forth.

'Even a machine will miss half the time from six feet. It's been tried,' Harmon said. 'Golf is really two games. One is the game in the air. The golfer can lick that part of the game. It sounds like quite a feat—I mean, you've got to get all those parts of your body moving absolutely correctly to send that ball off the tee at over 200 miles an hour. But once the ball is up in the air, there's not much that can happen to it. The air is a medium a golfer can control, as easy as fish in water: he can move the ball in it just where he wants to—fade it, or hook it to his liking, if he's good enough—and he's never going to be surprised unless he makes a mistake himself. Or unless he hits a bird. But the other part of the game is across the ground. It sounds easy. You hardly move a muscle to hit a putt. A child can

---

* It's doubtful that Hogan had the yips this early. I think his final 75 was merely a poor last round—by Hogan standards. He went out in 37 and came back in 38, so there was little difference in his play on the last nine holes and missing a final 6ft putt to win is standard procedure for most golfers!

do it easier than nothing. But the medium controls the ball, that's the difference; the golfer can get the ball moving, that's all. After that, the ball moves and turns and dies by reason of the ground surface. What you can't control gets the best of you after a while—death and taxes, the old song—and that's what the yips are.'

Harmon's story reminded me of Bernard Darwin's anecdote about the famous billiard professional who saw his first game of golf and remarked on it as interesting enough, but wondered why (as he said) 'do golfers on the green first knock the ball up to the hole, and *then* put it in.'

Some golfers felt that any prolonged absence from the game resulted in such a loss of confidence that an infestation of the yips would result. Bobby Cruickshank remembered that when his great rival* Bobby Jones returned to competition in 1934 after a four-year layoff, his putting had deteriorated to such an extent that he wandered around the Masters that year asking his fellow golfers if they could spot what was wrong. 'It looked the same,' Cruickshank said. 'I mean you'd see him address the ball, then set the putter in front of the ball, and then at the back of the ball again, and then the stroke—that was the famous procedure he went through. But you could see he had no confidence.'

Claude Harmon told me of a more recent example of the damage a layoff could do—the decision of Mike Souchak to take his family for a month's vacation on the beach after he had a remarkable succession of wins and near-wins on the tour. 'I told him he was crazy. You got to keep at it. When he came back it was gone—it had floated away on him, and what he had was like the yips.'

Occasionally, though, one heard of cures. Roberto de Vicenzo, at one time afflicted with the yips so badly that he had the reputation of handling the spookiest putter on the tour, had been able to do something about it. It had not been easy. In the throes of the disease he had changed putters every week, picking out a new putter every time he went into a pro shop. He looked in a closet at home in Argentina not long ago and found fifty putters standing there, a total not counting many he had given away. No one of the putters seemed better than another. Each seemed utterly unreliable. In 1967 in Australia he blew an eleven-shot lead in the last fourteen holes because of his putting and lost to Alan Murray in a play-off. He talked about an occasion in England when his putters had let him down—his accent heavy, his big hands moving artfully in the air to describe his meaning, his chair squeaking under him, his face expressive under the white baseball-style golf hat he wears to cover his thinning hair.

'In the British Open, in 1965, I think, we are playing the final day, which is thirty-six holes, and in the morning I am leading. I have had one bad green, number 9, which I three-putt in the morning, but I still in very good position. So we come to number nine in the afternoon and I say to myself, "Roberto, you no three-putt this green this afternoon, do you?" I didn't. I make *four* putts. I was so

* No one was Jones's rival: he was too much better than any of his contemporaries—including even Walter Hagen, who seldom won if Jones was in the field.

mad I wanted to break all my clubs and quit the game and never play again. I had no confidence. I look at the cup and she look like a little spike mark. I tell myself, "Roberto, you no can put the ball in there." So I lose my confidence and I lose the tournament right there.'

Vicenzo's cure turned out to be a matter of self-application—finding the right type of putter, the correct style of hitting a ball with it, the regaining of confidence, and practice, endless practice. Many golfers go through an equivalent regimen of experiment and practice without finding the answer: Snead had tried a number of putters and such grotesque putting styles—the 'sidewinder' in particular, in which he faces the hole and strokes the ball just off the outer edge of his golf shoe—that only his great grace as an athlete keeps him from looking ludicrous. Vicenzo was lucky. He found his putter two years ago. A mallet putter that he says is appropriate for his big hands. He watched other golfers' putting styles and decided that all the good putters (with the exception of Billy Casper and Doug Ford) use their *arms* primarily in the putting strokes, not the wrists, which had been his style. So he changed his style and found his sense of 'feel' increased immeasurably. His confidence began to return. He practiced endlessly—especially to get what he refers to as the 'head in rhythm . . . to work the head and the hands at the same time.' He began to collect some tournament wins—notably the British Open, and then a close run at the Masters which he would have taken to a play-off had he not handed in a mistotaled score card. But he was phlegmatic himself about the future. 'The putt is a funny game. You can't think you got it for always. You can lose it tomorrow. But for the moment,' he said, 'I feel better when I step onto the golf course. I no feel scared to step onto the green. Not any more. Or maybe for the time being, eh?'*

Another older player I talked to about the yips was John Farrell, once the great rival of Bobby Jones and now a teaching professional in Florida. He said that if you play in competition long enough you're sure to get the yips. 'Walter Hagen,' he said. 'If you had to vote for the player with the best temperament, well you'd *have* to vote for him. Hell, he had such confidence that there wasn't a shot that held any terror for him: they used to say that when he had a particularly tough shot to make, and he'd stepped up and made a great one of it, why then he'd whisper at his caddy, "Did I make it look hard enough?" and give him a wink, y'see. Well *he* got them. The yips. He got them so bad that he tried strokes and grip styles you could scarcely *believe*: cross-handed putting; or sticking the elbows way out so that the wrist action was throttled down and his whole body moved as stiff as a derrick. He even tried putting in the dark—thought that might cure him. Nothing did. . . .

I asked the question I had put to the others—if there was any connection between the yips and losing one's nerve.

* It was. Roberto 'retired' early in 1976. Poor putting was the reason for his decision. However, he is still competing.

'It's that you lose *nerves*, not nerve,' Farrell said. 'You can shoot lions in the dark and yet you can quiver like a leaf and fall flat over a two-foot putt.'

'I would think,' I said, 'that years of experience standing over two-foot putts, and gaining all the know-how of reading greens and distance, and the competition—that all of that would be to a golfer's advantage . . . confidence.'

'Oh, I wouldn't want to be so sure as that,' Farrell said. 'I always remember Waite Hoyte, who pitched for the Yankees, you'll recall, and what he used to say about "experience". He said experience *punishes* you. A veteran player *knows* what can happen to him: he comes onto a pitcher's mound and he knows the batter waiting for him can pop the ball right back to the bullpen where he's just come from for a home run. He's gone through it before. So he's something of a fatalist. It's the same in golf. "Experience" punishes you as you continue with the game. That's why in golf we speak of someone being "competitively young" or "competitively old". Craig Wood, you see, he was "competitively young" at forty-three because he started playing serious golf when he was well into his thirties. Then on the other hand Bobby Jones was "competitively old" at twenty-three—he had started at fifteen, you see, which gave him early "experience" but it aged him good and quick as a golfer.'*

'Experience,' Farrell went on ruefully. 'I won the Open in 1928 at Olympia Fields, and then in 1929 I missed the cut at the Open at Winged Foot. Dropped from the tournament I had *won* the year before! D'you think *that* experience did me any good! Well, I'll tell you. The next year at Interlachen, Minneapolis—in the 1930 Open which Bobby Jones won to fetch himself the Grand Slam—I stepped up on the first tee with the "experience" gained from those bad rounds the year before, and what did I do but get myself an 8 on that first hole. I managed to pull myself together after that and I finished eighth behind Jones, but don't talk to me about *experience*. Snead can't win the Open because of his memories—missing that two-footer in the 1947 Open. Palmer won't win the PGA. He has that block. No; it's the kids, the strong young golfers who have it all. They make great big errors—I mean, a kid like Marty Fleckman coming up with an 80 after leading the Open into the last day in 1967—but he's at the age when mistakes are easily forgotten; those kids' imaginations aren't jumpy with crucial flubs—y'know, disaster, that's what they don't know about. Not yet. It'll come. They'll get there. Experience will come. Oh yes.'

from *The Bogey Man*, Harper & Row (US), André Deutsch (UK)

---

* Not so. Jones retired at the age of 28, having won the British and US Open and Amateur Championships in a single year—1930. In 1925, when he was 23, his greatest achievement (including winning each of the three British Opens for which he entered) lay ahead.

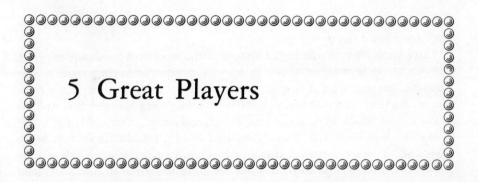

5 Great Players

In this chapter I have not tried to include a piece about each of the outstanding champions—many make an appearance elsewhere in the book—but I did want to cover the long sweep from Young Tom Morris, Willie Park, Harry Vardon to the millionaires of the 1970s.

No one can say who was the greatest of them all, for all a golfer can do is beat everyone who is there in his own era. Vardon, Jones, Nelson—though for rather too short a period to judge—Hogan and Nicklaus all did this. And Gary Player now cannot be denied full status after his achievements in 1974 and the spread of time he has won major championships. Even so, Taylor, Braid, Cotton, Snead and Palmer are being left out of consideration on the grounds I have mentioned: not having beaten everyone *often* enough for *long* enough. And what of Hagen? Would he have thought it worth the effort to train himself to the consistent precision of the modern player? Probably not, but he would still have had enough tricks up his sleeve to beat anyone at matchplay.

However, is the amassing of championships everything? If not, has anyone swung a golf club better than Sam Snead, Ted Dexter and Joyce Wethered? And if 'grace under pressure' is the supreme attribute then our choice would have to be Bobby Jones. Perhaps indeed golfing ability alone, should not be the sole criterion. As a man Jones stands alone. In his youth, he was the supreme athlete of a great decade and bore adulation without feeling that it implied anything more than that he just happened to be an excellent player of a game. Despite worship that would unbalance most, I don't think he valued his golfing achievements as being worth more praise than should go to anyone who happens to have a talent for anything. And then in middle age he was physically destroyed by a spinal disease and, as his body wasted, he bore that too with grace.

Enough. Here are a group of very good players and what some writers thought of them.

When noticing the scores mentioned in the first passage, bear in mind that a course did not always consist of 18 holes; that the fairways were rough, the rough was left to grow as it willed and greens were not carefully tended carpets. These things the modern professional could have dealt with successfully but I doubt that he would have done much better than Young Tom if he had to play with the ball and clubs of that time.

YOUNG TOM MORRIS   H. S. C. Everard

Born in 1851, the first we hear of him outside the family circle was in a match at Perth, in April 1864, when a sum of about five pounds was subscribed by some gentlemen there, during a tournament, to be played for by him and a boy of the same age named Greig.

Three years later, at the age of sixteen, came his first win of importance at Carnoustie, in September 1867. Prizes to the value of twenty pounds were competed for and sixteen couples entered; three rounds or thirty holes were played, the result of which was a triple tie between young Tommy, Bob Andrew of Perth, and Willie Park, score 140. Bob Fergusson was next, 144; and Jamie Anderson, Bob Kirk, and Willie Dow tied at 145. On the tie for first being played off, Tommy won by a stroke or two, Andrew being second. It will be admitted that it was no small triumph for a lad of sixteen to distance a field wherein such leading exponents of the game as those above mentioned were arrayed against him. His father was also playing, but did not back him for the tie, as he thought him 'ower young': events, however, proved he might well have done so, for in the matter of nerve and determination, as was afterwards abundantly shown, he was unrivalled. In the open championship of this year he occupied the good position of fourth, with 175, his father winning with 170, Willie Park second, 172, and Andrew Strath third, 174. The succeeding year saw him to the front at Leven, with a score of 170 for 36 holes, being one stroke better than Bob Kirk, and seven in front of Davie Strath, who in his turn was seven better than the fourth prizeman, Bob Andrew. This same year (1868) also saw him champion at Prestwick, and that too with the then unexampled score of 154, no less than six strokes better than it had ever been won at previously, his father in 1864 holding the next lowest record with 160—the sire on this occasion running second to his son with 157; Bob Andrew third, 159, and Willie Park fourth, with 162. The following year (1869) he absolutely spread-eagled the field, winning with 157 at Prestwick, no less than eleven strokes better than Bob Kirk, 168, and twelve better than David Strath, 169. Not content with these laurels, he added another and crowning victory in 1870, eclipsing his own brilliant play by a still more extraordinary score of 149, this last performance entitling him to the absolute custody of the champion belt, which he had thus secured three times in succession. The trophy so brilliantly won remains an heirloom in his father's family.

He was a very strong driver, with a rather forcing style, not with quite so full an all-round swing as some of his brother professionals, but every ounce of strength went into the stroke, and as for a bad lie, he seemed positively to revel in it. There was one particularly disagreeable ball, his control over which never failed to fill the writer with admiration, and that was when the position of the ball was so very much below the level of the ground on which the striker had to take his stance that he could with difficulty reach it at all, and that only by almost sitting on the ground; this sort of ball he could, and generally did, drive with a wooden club as far as his best shots from the tee. In a gale of wind he was particularly good, as the height of ball he generally drove was eminently adapted to travelling well in the teeth of it; his iron play was magnificent, and he also made frequent use of the iron niblick in approaching out of bad places. His power with this rather prosy and unpromising sort of instrument was also remarkable; his father states that never will he forget a shot he saw him drive up to the gas hole at Musselburgh, out of a hole, with this club. In length it was about equal to a very fine long spoon shot, and quite straight up to the hole. As a partner to any beginner or abominably bad player, of whatever golfing age, he was a tower of strength; he always accepted the situation *à merveille*, whilst, if his ally could play at all, it was astonishing how strong the opponents had to be, if amateurs, in order to make a match of it. With men who would now be handicapped at from fourteen to eighteen strokes, he was never afraid to play combinations, any, or all of them, good enough to win the St Andrews or any other medal.

from *Golf*, The Badminton Library (UK) 1893

WILLIE PARK   J. H. Taylor

Willie Park was a most deceptive player. To see him swing a club was to form the conclusion that he had not troubled to learn even the most elementary notion of what had to be done. It was ungainly, laboured and, as was often seen, treacherous in its control. Violent hooks were as frequent as the ghastly push outs, and it was always a source of wonder that a man who had played all his life could have retained such crudity; and this was the opinion of others besides myself. There are golfers who seem incapable of developing a good style, try as they may with years of practice. They appear to have but one conception of how the club should be swung. I cannot offer an explanation, but it is there for all to see, and in this category of ugliness I do not exclude the writer. This inability to swing the club without grace or precision must have haunted Willie all his life, but the merciful Providence who comes to the aid of struggling golfers gave to Park a splendid compensation. Admittedly he was a bad wooden club player. He was content to poke and squeeze the ball somewhere on the desired line, content, I feel sure, in the comforting knowledge that 'what he lost on the swings would be more than made up on the roundabout near and on the green'. His work on the green was pure wizardry, and a genius for running in long putts from all distances hardly explains the mystery. I have seen all the good putters, Americans and others, and give it as an honest opinion that Willie Park had them all beaten, in the language that our American friends will understand, to a frazzle. If the rest of his game were anything like the deadliness of his putting, Willie would have been the world beater of his time.

from *Golf: My Life's Work*, Jonathan Cape (UK)

HARRY VARDON   J. H. Taylor

In his early days Harry Vardon had a most ungainly style. A lift in his back-swing violated the principle of accepted orthodoxy. One expected to see, as a result, the ball slung away far to the right or sharply around to the left, but, as if in defiance of all accepted standards of what was right and proper, nothing of the sort happened. True, as the days went on, Vardon's lift became embodied into a style that was as graceful and perfect as any golf swing one is ever likely to see, which resulted in the perfect golfing machine. Little did I guess when playing him at Ganton that I was playing a man who was to make golfing history and develop into—what is my solemn and considered judgment—the finest and most finished golfer that the game has ever produced. I have seen and watched every player of eminence during the past fifty years and taking into account everything they have done I still hold that my opinion is sound, and I am willing to uphold it even if the world should be against me. The test of who should be considered the best golfer, as I see it, must conform to this formula. He is one who over a length of years has played fewer bad or indifferent strokes than any other aspirant, and in addition has shown, during this period of time, consistent brilliancy. If this is conceded, and its logic appears to be irrefutable, then Harry Vardon stands alone in all the glory that his performances testify.

from *Golf: My Life's Work*, Jonathan Cape (UK)

ONE HERO   Paul Gallico

The sports-writer has few if any heroes. We create many because it is our business to do so, but we do not believe in them. We know them too well. We are concerned as often, sometimes, with keeping them and their weaknesses and peccadillos out of the paper as we are with putting them in. We see them with their hair down in the locker-rooms, dressing-rooms, or their homes. Frequently we come quite unawares upon little meannesses. When they fall from grace we are usually the first to know it, and when their patience is tried, it is generally to us that they are rude and ill-tempered. We sing of their muscles, their courage, their gameness, and their skill because it seems to amuse readers and sells papers, but we rarely consider them as people and, strictly speaking, leave their characters alone because that is dangerous ground.

Also, we grow up with them and see them change from pleasant and sometimes unspoiled youngsters into grievous public pets, boors, snobs, and false figures. I am, by nature, a hero-worshipper, as, I guess, most of us are, but in all the years of contact with the famous ones of sport I have found only one that would stand up in every way as a gentleman as well as a celebrity, a fine, decent, human being as well as a newsprint personage, and who never once, since I have known him, has let me down in my estimate of him. That one is Robert Tyre Jones, Jr., the golf-player from Atlanta, Georgia. And Jones in his day was considered the champion of champions—in other words, better and more perfect at playing his game than any of the other champions were at theirs. He was the best golf-player the world has ever known, and still is, because no one has yet appeared capable of challenging his record.*

Probably no celebrity in sport ever attracted quite so much attention or was so dominating a figure and yet remained completely unspoiled. Jones even had his own personal Boswell, Mr O. B. Keeler of the Atlanta *Journal*, one of the better sports-writers. For a great many years Keeler reported on Jones almost exclusively. Jones was hero-worshipped by Atlantans and the golf public generally nearly *ad nauseam*, and yet he never lost his head or permitted it to swell. In Scotland and England, where he played in tournaments, the natives practically made a god out of him. He remained unaffected. He was exposed to the attacks of the most ill-bred and ruthless pests in the world, the curiosity-seeking golf nuts and autograph-hunters, and his privacy was assailed from morning until night. He never in all his career could engage in a friendly golf match (except on his home course) without being followed and swamped with attention and, more often, annoyance. Yet I never heard of his being deliberately rude. The only thing I think he ever permitted himself to do when chivvied and harassed beyond human endurance, particularly during an important tournament, was quietly to turn and walk away.

He has a record of some ten years' contact with press and public and the golf world, in which, to my knowledge, he never once said the wrong thing in any public utterance or interview, never insulted anyone or hurt the feelings of any sect, organization, or people. I have never known him deliberately to lie to the press, the common fault of every newspaper celebrity. He had a gorgeous instinct for doing the right thing—such as asking to be permitted to leave the trophy representing the British Open Championship in the keeping of the Royal and Ancient Golf Club at St Andrews, Scotland, where he won it. He made the Scotch love him as one of their own.

He was a good loser, but even a better winner. And he had the almost unbelievable intelligence and grace to quit after his greatest accomplishment, his grand slam of 1930, when he won the amateur and open championships of Great Britain and the United States, the four major tournaments of the golf world.

He was born Robert Tyre Jones, Jr., but millions of people knew him merely as Bobby—Bobby Jones. And he hated the name Bobby. If he knew you well, he would sometimes dryly request that you call him Bob, and not Bobby. From the crowd he accepted the Bobby as it was meant, a diminutive of affection. This is a

* Written in 1937 and before the arrival of Jack Nicklaus.

trivial and unimportant item until you try to picture yourself going through life eternally being hailed by a name that you thoroughly detest.

Before I knew Jones well, early in my sports-writing career, I was sent down to Atlanta by a national magazine, assigned to play a round of golf with him and report what it was like to play with the great one. Bob agreed to a game. (I was still a cub then and quite unknown as either a writer or columnist, but it made no difference to Jones. Later, on a similar assignment, Helen Wills refused to play with me.) He invited two of his friends and we went out to East Lake, his home course. Nervous, self-conscious, and badly frightened, I blew up on the first tee and stayed blown for the entire eighteen holes except that I went higher each hole. I doubt whether I ever suffered so acutely in all my life. But I learned something about Jones in that round. Towards the end, after taking nine to get close to the green, I botched my niblick approach, cutting the legs out from under the ball instead of hitting it properly, but with astonishing results, because the ball rose into the air, dropped two feet from the pin, and stayed there. Jones sneaked a great sigh of relief and said: 'Fine shot, partner. Well played.' And then we looked at each other. His face was all properly regulated respect and mingled admiration and serious pleasure at having been permitted to witness such a miraculous demonstration of a difficult game, but there was something funny going on at the corners of his mouth. I guess I must have had a strange expression too, because suddenly we both fell down on the green and howled with laughter, and after that everything was all right.

I suspect that the Jones humor has been what has really got him through all these trying years—and if you don't think it is trying to be a celebrity in our country, wait until you manage to chin yourself four hundred times or outsit everyone else on a flagpole—when at times the assaults on his nerves, good nature, and good manners would otherwise have been unbearable. It would not be fair to say that Jones never took himself seriously. When he entered a tournament he entered to win. He was quite willing to admit that he did not like to lose. But his sense of the eternal ridiculous lay very close to the surface and I think he often saw himself as a slightly comic figure that did things that amused him vastly. People who are able successfully to laugh at themselves are able to take a great amount more of punishment and abuse than the humorless crew. It takes much more to snap the temper of a man who can read something funny into any and every situation. Well, what more can I say for my hero? He was a gentleman and there was laughter in his heart and on his lips, and he loved his friends.

from *Farewell to Sport*, Alfred A. Knopf (US)

JAMES BRUEN   Pat Ward-Thomas

Of all the golfers I have watched down the years there was one whose game had a quality of excitement that was incomparable. Hogan and Cotton could stir the imagination and command attention by virtue of their presence alone; Thomson and Snead could create an awareness of beauty, and all the other great ones in their different ways made a powerful demand on the senses, but the golf of none of these men had a greater dramatic appeal for me than that of James Bruen, citizen of Cork.

Although few of the present growing generation saw him play, and many indeed may scarcely have heard of him, those that did could never forget. The image of his swing, surely the strangest that modern first-class golf has known,* remains clear in my mind to this day. There can never have been a style quite like it. He drew the club back outside the line of flight and turned his wrists inward, to such an extent that at the top of the swing the clubhead would be pointed in the direction of the tee box. It was then whipped, no other word describes the action, inside and down into the hitting area with a terrible force. There was therefore in his swing a fantastic loop, defying all the canons of orthodoxy which claim that the back and downswing should, as near as possible, follow the same arc. There must have been a foot or more between Bruen's arcs of swing.†

The first sight of him was positively startling—and anyone, unaware of his identity, must have been inclined to scoff, but not for long. In this method of his Bruen had an instrument of tremendous power. The action of his hands was identical to that of wielding a whip, and one has but to try this to realize how much greater is the acceleration into the hitting area, whether it be with a whip, a club or throwing a ball.

I certainly would not recommend anyone to loop deliberately in the quest for power; few if any of the greatest golfers have found it necessary, but with Bruen it was; and wisely at the time no one attempted to change his style. Cotton has said that he has made Bruen try a normal method and that he hit the ball well—but without the great length that his own swing produced. To what extent, if any, his swing was responsible for the injury to his right wrist that hastened his departure from tournament play can never be known. Bruen denies that golf had anything to do with it. Soon after winning the amateur championship in 1946 he was lifting a tile in his garden when he felt a sudden pain. Thereafter it was always liable to be troublesome, and none of the expert advice and treatment he sought could cure it. Whatever the cause there was no doubt that the wrist had to withstand a considerable shock every time he hit a full shot, such was the force of impact.

Bruen, an only child, started golf when about eleven years old and pursued his own natural way of hitting the ball. He was fat in those days and weighed something like 14 stones. At sixteen he murdered all opposition in the boys'

* Well Miller Barber and Gay Brewer are odd, to say the least, and Trevino hasn't the prettiest of swings but this piece was written before their advent.
† Even Jones had a loop in his swing, as have all great golfers but Bruen's was undoubtedly at the ultimate extreme.

championship. It was obvious that an extraordinary talent had arisen. Two years later he was in the winning Walker Cup team at St Andrews and, aside from halving his foursome with Harry Bentley, there was no doubt that his presence and the formidable golf he played in the practice had a strong psychological influence on the outcome of the match. The following summer he led the qualifiers in the Open, also at St Andrews, finished thirteenth in the championship—and was narrowly beaten in the last eight of the Amateur. He was only just 19.

There was no limit to what he might have achieved had the war not come, and had he so desired. His power was prodigious—he hit the ball enormous distances with a vast, soaring flight that gave him a great advantage on heavy courses, and his powers of recovery and strength from deep rough and sand were almost incredible. The nature of his swing brought the club into the hitting area at a remarkably steep angle and he could cut the ball huge distances out of places where normal men simply heaved and prayed. This ability to recover was essential, for his swing could not be expected to repeat with absolute consistency. Suddenly a drive would boom away towards extra cover into country where others neither ventured nor reached, but invariably the ball would emerge. The deadly willow scrub of Birkdale must have shrunk at his approach when he beat Robert Sweeny in the final of the first Amateur after the war.

All this was terribly exciting to watch; there was an unexpectedness and a variation to his golf that has not been surpassed on such a high level. Yet it would have been unfair to describe him as erratic, in the usual meaning of the term, and certainly in no sense was he crude. There was an almost hypnotic quality about his play; its very strangeness was compelling, its power and unusual beauty fascinating. Bruen had a wonderful rhythm that concealed the explosive violence of the club's impact on the ball, and this was most noticeable in the lovely, soft, slow action of his pitching, and in a beautiful, delicate touch when chipping and putting. Several of the strongest golfers, like Carr and Weetman, have been similarly blessed and Bruen at his finest was a great putter.

Thus, as a very young man, he had everything. No course, whatever its length or difficulty, was safe from destruction, and how terribly disconcerting he must have been to play against. It was sad that his career should have been so brief, for he might well have won an Open championship. As it was he appeared but little after 1946. Three years later he played in the Walker Cup and in 1950 won the *Daily Telegraph* foursomes with W. D. Smithers. I often think that this was the most attractive tournament of its time, with leading professionals and amateurs paired out of the hat and no strokes involved. Bruen and Smithers made a perfect combination that year at Formby, for Smithers revelled in the challenge that some of his partner's driving would set him. I shall never forget how Bruen, three times out of perhaps five attempts, carried the range of dunes that crosses the tenth fairway, with no great wind to help. This was huge hitting. The following summer he played again in the Walker Cup match at Birkdale but his wrist betrayed him in the foursomes and competitive golf saw him no more, save just once for an hour or so at Portrush nine years later.

Bruen was there as an Irish selector; he had been playing well and had entered the Amateur. His wrist had begun to hurt in practice but, after some hesitation, he decided to play. His golf was still impressive, even though its old power had gone, and he was soon in a winning position; but the wrist was swollen and he withdrew from the match, rather than scratch after winning. This glimpse, brief though it had to be, was infinitely worth while for it stirred memories of the most fascinating golfer I have ever seen, or probably ever will see. There will never be another quite like him.

from Masters of Golf, William Heinemann (UK)

THE MAESTRO   Henry Longhurst

When anyone asks me who is the greatest striker of a golf ball I ever saw, my answer is immediate. It is Henry Cotton. I am just old enough to have seen Harry Vardon play, but was not old enough at the time to make a fair assessment of his powers. Whatever they were, I cannot believe them to have been greater than Cotton's in the 'thirties. He lifted up the nation's golfing spirit after eleven long years of American domination and, with it, the status of his own profession.

For this the Americans themselves were largely responsible. In 1928, when he was twenty-one, he set sail for the United States under his own steam, buying his own ticket and taking with him a letter of credit for £300, which incidentally he brought home intact. He soon appreciated that the great sporting figures of the day were regarded in America almost as the aristocracy, whereas at home sport carried with it no special standing. When Walter Hagen came to England to win our championships, he stayed at the Savoy and drove up to the course in a hired Rolls-Royce. He was already 'one up' on the rest of the field. Cotton decided that what Hagen could do he could do.

I think it is fair to say that Cotton regarded himself, in his competitive days, as a kind of 'property', to be taken the greatest care of and kept in the best possible condition if it were to give the desired results. For this reason he took it to the best hotels and at lunch time, having no desire for the smoky air and, for the celebrated, the inevitable attachment of bores and sycophants to be found in the club-house, he changed his clothes in the car and retired to the hotel. Naturally enough, there were those who thought he regarded himself as too good for the common herd.

He developed an immense strength in his hands, and they became the focal point in his essentially simple swing. As the ball flew straight at the flag, you felt that, if you hit it in that fashion, it could hardly do anything else. He could do almost anything with a golf ball on purpose and would have made a great trick-shot artist. We often used to challenge him to take his driver from a bad lie on the fairway, simply for the aesthetic pleasure of seeing the ball fly away as though fired from a rifle, and I remember once at Bad Ems seeing him knock a shooting stick out of the ground with a 1-iron shot at a range of 20 yards. We christened him the Maestro, and he deserved it.

At the same time he developed a flair for getting himself into the news, sometimes, but not always, on purpose. With all this he was naturally the centre of attraction wherever he played, and became probably the first professional golfer to be recognizable at once to the man in the street.

In 1929, now aged twenty-two, Cotton played in his first Ryder Cup match at Leeds, where he beat Al Watrous by 4 and 2, and it now seemed only a matter of time before he won the championship. He had his chances, but on at least two occasions let them slip, mainly, as he now thinks, through listening to the rumours that used to fly about the course before the present walkie-talkie system came into use, and not appreciating what he needed to do.

It was against this background that the championship opened at Sandwich in 1934. Cotton had with him four sets of clubs—why, I do not know—and for once could not hit his hat with any of them. He practised on Saturday till darkness drove him in, and had never been in such discouraging form. He settled on a set of clubs, for better or for worse, and on Monday morning, in the first qualifying round, was drawn to go out first, accompanied by a marker. He played what remains in his own opinion the best round of his life. He hit every green in the right number—33 shots, 33 putts; total 66. Such is golf.

The magic lasted. He opened the championship proper with a 67, and in such a way that one saw no reason why he should ever again take more. On the second day he arrived on the 17th tee needing only two par fours for another 67 and the then fantastic total of 134. At each hole he hit a tremendous drive. His second to the seventeenth ruled the flag and finished about 12 feet from the hole, and he holed the putt for a 3. He hit another magnificent iron shot to the last hole, though he cannot have seen it finish, for he was at once enveloped by a stampeding multitude determined to see history being made on the last green.

I remember the shot perfectly. It bounced a couple of times and came quietly to rest about four feet from the stick. He made no mistake with the putt and history had indeed been made. Sixty-five! A total of 132 and the nearest man, Alfred Padgham, nine strokes behind.

On the morning of the final day Cotton turned in a 72 in harder conditions, a more than adequate score which was beaten by only three players, and now he was out on his own by 12 strokes. He returned to his hotel for lunch in the usual way, and I do not believe it entered the head of a single person present that they might be about to witness in the afternoon the most agonizing golfing spectacle any can remember to this day.

Things went instantly wrong. He timed his arrival for the start but found it postponed for a quarter of an hour owing to the immense crowd which had assembled to watch the triumphant formality of his final round. In his own words: 'Like a fool, I went and sat in a small tent all by myself. Lack of experience again. Today I should go out and hit balls, go for a walk, anything bar sit and brood. Already I had been undermined by people congratulating me before I had won. The editor of one of the golf magazines seemed to think he had appointed himself my official manager and kept popping in and out of lunch telling me not to sign anything without consulting him when I had won. I had been humbled by golf too often. I sat and thought how anyone could take 82 in a championship, and anyone else could do 69, and there is the whole thing gone. Why, it was only a mile or two away, at Deal, that poor Abe Mitchell took 83 to George Duncan's 71 and lost 12 strokes and the championship in a single round.'

The start was a foretaste of what was to come, and I hardly like to write of it even now. His first drive was skied and his second with a 2-iron hit a lady, standing at cover point, on the knee. Through the green it is no exaggeration to say that a competent 12-handicap player would have given him a good game and, if he had not putted, considering the circumstances, miraculously, he might have taken 90.

There was much talk at the time of his having eaten something that disagreed with him or having failed to digest his modest lunch. The latter, I am sure, is true or he could not speak of it with such feeling to this day. 'I played in a cold sweat and wanted to be sick. I ought to have gone off and vomited in the nearest hedgerow, but I didn't, partly because I was too ashamed and partly because there aren't any hedgerows at St George's anyway. I could not get anything but fives. I could not get a 4 even at drive-and-pitch holes where all the week I had been looking for threes.'

At the long thirteenth—'another b—— 5 coming'—the course of the round, and with it, he now agrees, probably of his life, was changed. He holed a four-yard putt for 4. It broke the spell and he coasted home to win by five shots from Sid Brews, of South Africa. He missed a short putt on the last green but it did not matter now. A British player had won the championship at last and they carried him shoulder high off the green.

from *The Sunday Times* (UK)

BEN HOGAN   Frank Beard

After my round, I ran into Ben Hogan in the clubhouse, which, from my point of view, is like an average big-league baseball player coming face to face with Babe Ruth. In my opinion, Hogan is far and away the greatest golfer who ever lived, and there isn't anybody in second place.

I was glad to see Ben, even just to say hello and wish him well. He told me he's recovering from a shoulder operation and hopes to start playing a little golf soon. I first met Hogan when we were paired together in the U.S. Open in San Francisco in 1966. He was already fifty-three years old, but he could still stroke the ball; the following year, he shot a 66 in the Masters, the lowest round of the whole tournament.

Later, I played an exhibition with Ben and spent an evening sitting and talking with him, and I found that the image I had of him, the image that had been built up by the press and by the players, too, was all wrong. He was full of warmth and humor, eager to talk about his days on the tour, easy to listen to. He had mellowed, I'm sure, in the years since he'd stopped winning tournaments regularly.

I've got my own theory about Hogan. I think that one day, when he was in his twenties, he flat decided he was going to be the greatest golfer that ever lived, and for the next twenty years, he shut everything out of his life except golf. I don't think it was his natural way, but he put himself in a box, from the moment he approached a golf course until the moment he left, and nobody and nothing could penetrate that box.

Hogan paid a big price to be the best—he gave up social life, friendships, everything; he dehumanized himself—and I think he always knew how big the price was. Now, with everything proven and competition behind him, I think he's trying to make up for all the years he lost. He's returned to his natural, friendly ways.

He was my first hero in golf, and he still is.

from *Pro: Frank Beard on the Golf Tour*, Thomas Y. Crowell (US)

PALMER AT TROON   Pat Ward-Thomas

The basis of Palmer's game in its formative years was power of a tremendous order. In achieving the command of accuracy and flight that now are his nothing of this power has been sacrificed; he is one of the few great long drivers of all time, and no one has ever matched his strength with long iron; he is a wonderfully bold pitcher and as fine a putter in moments of truth and crisis as there is, but there is much more to Palmer.

First there is the unswerving dedication to the business of winning, without the cold inhuman intensity of a Hogan, for Palmer wisely appreciates the virtue of being able to relax, and to condition his concentration to its finest pitch when the dies are cast. He has also the precious trait in his character of being immensely responsive to challenge, and this, as much as anything else, was the driving force behind the massacre of Troon.

Naturally he would want to defend his title successfully; the presence of

Nicklaus, Snead, Rodgers, Littler, as well as the great Commonwealth players, made the strongest field since Cotton beat the whole American Ryder Cup team in 1937. The beating of them must have been a great incentive. In an age when the making of money dominates the thinking, and sometimes the manners, of most professional players of games, Palmer is rare in his appreciation of a title for its honour alone. Then there was the Old Course itself.

Any golfer whose game is conditioned to the superbly groomed and watered fairways, and holding greens of America must find the adjustment to British conditions, and the smaller ball, extremely trying. Of all the great American players who have competed in Britain, only Hogan and Palmer have mastered the conditions in a short time.

Fortunately Troon had been lengthened since the last Open there in 1950 or heaven knows what Palmer would have done to it, and it was not without irony that the two holes most altered played a significant part in Palmer's triumph. The fourth, with its diagonal drive between guardian bunkers, and full second shot, was out of range for almost everyone but Palmer. Yet in four rounds he had two sixes and two fives, and I am certain that the sixes were fuses that lit the destroying fires within him. In the second and third rounds he played the remaining holes in five and seven under fours respectively. The last nine holes measured 3,645 yards; in each round Palmer played them in 32—golf that, in its power and control, has never been surpassed.

Long before the Championship began Palmer said that the eleventh would be the key hole. It was difficult, dangerous, and greatly dependent on the bounce of the ball. The tee shot had to be played on a line crossing the fairway towards thick gorse on the left, with rough and gorse on the right as well. An unkind kick could mean any number of strokes. Even if the tee shot was safely contrived the long second to an uphill green, hard against the railway wall, was fearsome indeed. In five rounds, including the qualifying, Palmer had three threes, a four, and an unlucky five when his ball finished inches through the green in thick grass. Never will I forget the sight of Palmer's rifling second shots, with a one or two iron, that subdued the hole as no one else in the world could have done.

It is difficult not to devote the whole of this piece to Palmer. All else was in such a minor key, save for the unyielding courage and splendid golf of Nagle. He alone made the remotest challenge, and he had the strain of being at the scene of execution throughout that last long summer day. He had the crowds and the pressure and twice played the course in 70; what an admirable person he is. Young Huggett showed determination and a brave heart to a degree that none of the other British could match; Alliss and Thomas were highest of all the Ryder Cup players, a mere seventeen strokes behind. There was a powerful lesson that week for British golfers, if only they will take heed.

There were lessons too for the organisers, one in the behaviour of part of a huge crowd at the end, that at best was the grossest discourtesy to Palmer and Nagle, but these can wait. There was much in the background to remember: the wonder of the golf of Snead who, at fifty, finished sixth; the beauty of Littler's swing and the pity that he did not reach the last day; the remarkable performance of Rodgers, that ebullient young man from California, in his first British event; and an invaluable, if painful stage in the development of Nicklaus, which he accepted with fortitude. It was fitting that the rosy little figure of F. McLeod, the oldest living American champion should be present, that Walter Hagen should telephone felicitations to Palmer from New York, and that the champion himself, such is the balance and modesty of this exceptional man, should talk of many things but golf far into the night.

from *The Long, Green Fairway*, Hodder & Stoughton (UK)

NICKLAUS – AN IRRESISTIBLE FORCE   Pat Ward-Thomas

Nicklaus is as near to an irresistible force as amateur golf of this generation has known, and naturally people have started making comparisons. Is he a greater golfer than Harvie Ward was in the middle fifties, or Lawson Little a quarter of a century ago, or Jones in the imperishable twenties?

When Ward won the Amateur at Prestwick in 1952, his golf embodied a perfection of style and technique that were unsurpassed in his time. It did not seem possible that anyone could play with greater charm, grace and deadly effect, and then the unhappy suspension, that was more the fault of others than himself, brought a sunlit world crashing about his ears. His swing now is by no means what it was, and, although he can still play superbly, the continuity of concentration for lasting competitive effort seems beyond him. Nevertheless it was good to hear that his life has become settled once more.

Ward certainly has a place among the great ones, but he never had the power of Nicklaus, and, whether one likes it or not, controlled power is the foundation of success in the modern game. One of the earliest examples of power play on this level was Lawson Little, who lives beside the first fairway at Pebble Beach. It was fascinating to talk with him awhile, although difficult to believe that this middle-aged man, who has suffered a little from the ruthless passage of time, was once such an immense golfer. He still, however, plays uncommonly well. That he should be watching Nicklaus was somehow appropriate because, concerning these two, comparison between past and present is permissible.

In his great years, Little, then almost as massive in build as Nicklaus although finer proportioned, was enormously long from the tees. Thus much of the rest of his game was reduced to pitching. In those days the number of clubs was unlimited and he carried a positive battery of lofted irons. The wedge had not become a dominating influence in first class golf, and it is unlikely that Little

WINNERS OF THE OPEN CHAMPIONSHIP TROPHY

1   Max Faulkner, 1951, Royal Portrush
2   Ben Hogan, 1953, Carnoustie

3 Arnold Palmer, 1961, Royal Birkdale
4 Bob Charles, 1963, Royal Lytham and St Annes

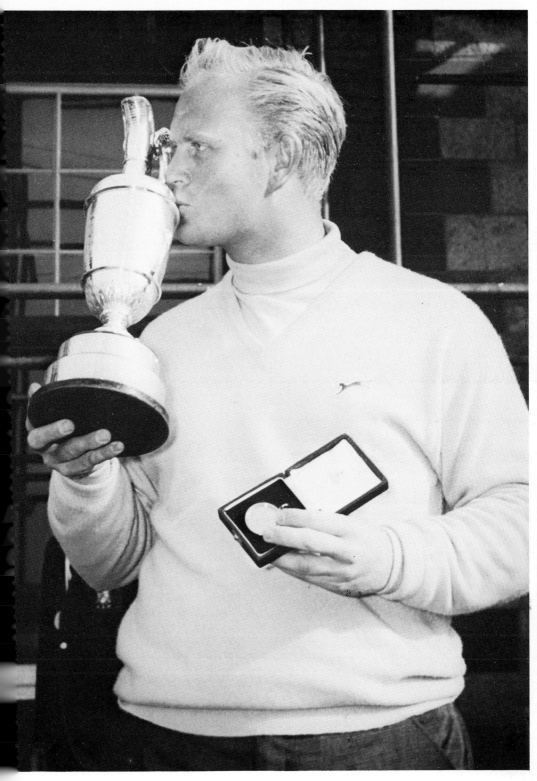

5 Jack Nicklaus, 1966, Muirfield

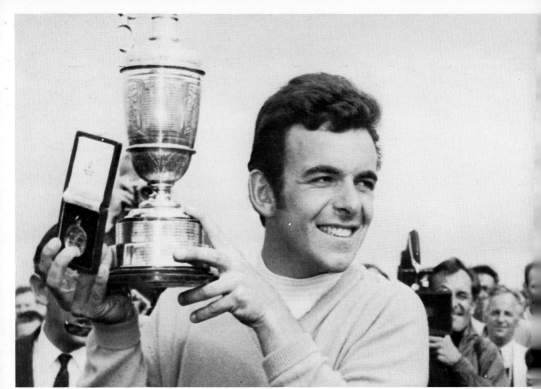

6 Tony Jacklin, 1969, Royal Lytham and St Annes
7 After a tie, Jack Newton (left) and Tom Watson, who won the play-off,
1975, Carnoustie

8 Before the 1970 Open at St Andrews, past – and future – winners meet the camera: (*back row, left to right*) Arthur Havers (1923), Gene Sarazen (1932), Dick Burton (1939), Fred Daly (1947), Roberto de Vicenzo (1967), Arnold Palmer (1961, 1962), Kel Nagle (1960), Bobby Locke (1949, 1950, 1952, 1957), Henry Cotton (1934, 1937, 1948), Peter Thomson (1954, 1955, 1956, 1958, 1965); (*front row*) Densmore Shute (1933), Bob Charles (1963), Max Faulkner (1951), Jack Nicklaus (1966, 1970), Tony Jacklin (1969) and Gary Player (1959, 1968, 1974)

WINNERS OF THE US MASTERS

9 Previous year's victor, Jack Nicklaus (left) helps 1976 US Masters winner Ray Floyd into the traditional green blazer

THE PLEASURE OF HOLING A GOOD ONE

10 (*Top left*) Peter Thomson, 1963, Leeds
11 (*Left*) Gary Player, 1968, Wentworth
12 (*Above*) Tom Watson ties for the 1975 Open at Carnoustie
13 (*Right*) Nick Faldo birdies the last to tie for the 1977 Uniroyal at Moor Park

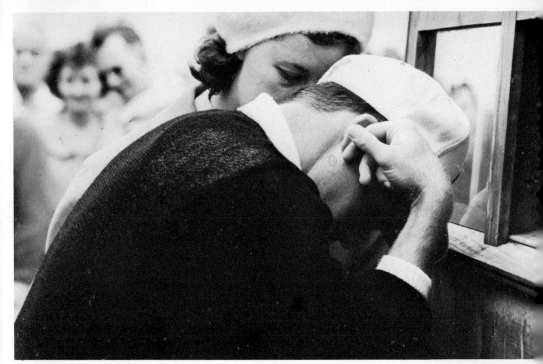

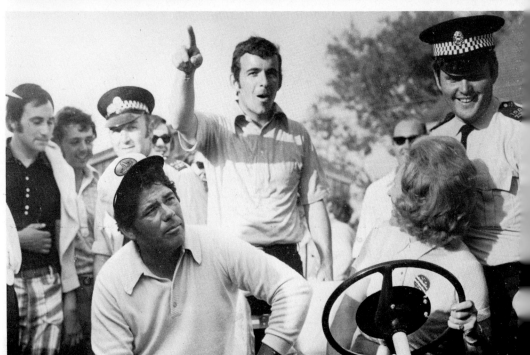

WHO'S THE WINNER?

14 Gary Player breaks down in tears after taking a 6 on the last hole of the 1959 Open. But all was well, the others faltered too

15 Lee Trevino just after winning the 1972 Open; Tony Jacklin (*pointing*), defeated, tells the driver what to do with Trevino

could command, or ever needed to command, the accuracy into the greens that Nicklaus has.

The constant watcher of tournament golf nowadays may be excited, but is no longer surprised, at the velocity achieved by the mighty from the tees. The British have seen Hogan and Palmer, and although Nicklaus has not quite their control he drives about as far as Palmer, and with that same rifling flight that seems to bore a hole in the air.

Mention was made in an article from Pebble Beach of Nicklaus at practice, and of how drive after drive flew down the precise line to a caddie in the remote distance, with an unwavering regard for the shortest distance between two points. The impression was not so much of a ball driven by a swing, which certainly is true of Palmer for all that he hits so hard, but rather as if it had been propelled by a hammer blow from some mechanical device.

Nicklaus is so strong that he does not require a full swing, and at the top of it the club never reaches the horizontal. The backlift is simple with no break in the wrists until the widest possible arc away from the ball has been achieved. Then, from a stance which makes clearance of the left side after impact as easy as possible, and an anchorage so solid that it might well be cast in concrete, so massive are his legs. Nicklaus lets fly. There is no suggestion of a slash. Considering the force involved, the whole method is remarkably balanced and controlled.

The same strength is revealed in his long irons, and, like Palmer, Snead and J. Hebert, among the few leading golfers who do, Nicklaus carries a number one. In one round he was green high in two at the eighteenth, well over 500 yards, using this club for the second shot in still air.

It was interesting to examine his clubs, for their comparative lightness, and to see how low on the blade the beautifully compact mark of impact was, compared to that made by most other golfers. This was evidence of an abnormal precision and purity of striking but, all these considerations of strength aside, much more is required to have reached the peak of achievement already attained by Nicklaus.

On the second hole after lunch in the final, his ball lay on sandy grass. A wide bunker was between him and the pin, which was placed just beyond, and yet, with a swing so delicate in rhythm that it concealed the firmness beneath, he played the shot perfectly to within two feet of the hole. He has a remarkable sensitivity of touch in the short game, and his pitching with wedge or short irons is wonderfully exact. Time after time he would finish within a few feet of the hole, invariably leaving himself with a putt for a birdie. This standard is unapproached by the British, which is one of the principal causes for their failure in competition against Americans. Nicklaus always attacks with this shot to the pin, and with the putt that follows. Never has one seen a golfer whose whole appearance on the greens suggested a greater degree of determined concentration.

His putting method is similar to Palmer's except that the knees are not locked inwards to the same extent. The body is crouched over the ball, with the head well down; and the stroke is the usual crisp American tap, the right hand pushing the club through low along the line. The sight of Nicklaus on the green, the chunky body absolutely motionless save for the quick turns of the head as he checks the line with those clear blue eyes of his, the ash-blond hair peeping from beneath his white cap, and the set lines of his face, remain an enduring picture, but there is another besides.

Nicklaus is intensely deliberate in the playing of his shots. He takes a while to rock into his stance and has several waggles before swinging, but otherwise he moves briskly. I can see him now, alert, confident, striding down the fairways, far ahead of his caddie, Gonzales, a quaint figure, round, swarthy, Portuguese, with cigar in holder, who carried for H. R. Johnston when he won the Championship at Pebble Beach in 1929. This year was memorable not for his victory but for the defeat of one man in the first round.

R. T. Jones came to Monterey an overwhelming favourite, as he was for every championship he entered in those years. He had won this one four times in the previous five attempts, and the shock of his defeat on the first day by Goodman can be imagined. Jones was two down early in the game, but squared the match. Then at the long fourteenth, his pitch failed to carry the bunker guarding the green; the saving putts thereafter would not fall, Goodman held on until the end, and the world of golf turned dark for many people. Later that day, Goodman was beaten by Little, aged seventeen, but four years later he became the last amateur to win the American Open.

It would be absurd to compare Jones and Nicklaus as to style and personality, although they have many qualities in common. The big question that rises now in the minds of American observers is not whether Nicklaus is as good as Jones, but whether he can approach his record. For the present, the 'quadrilateral' is quite safe, because the British Amateur and the American Open are played at roughly the same time, and no one could compete in both. In terms of age, Nicklaus has made as good a start as Jones, who did not win the Amateur until he was twenty-two, but had won his first Open the previous year.

Soon there will be the opportunity to ask Jones himself for an estimate of Nicklaus. The train is bearing one ever nearer to Georgia, and as these words are written it is hurrying through the darkness across the land of Hogan, who gave more energy and thought to the business of winning than anyone. In the years to come it will be fascinating to see what Nicklaus makes of it all: if his ambition remains boundless, there is no telling what he may achieve.

from *The Long, Green Fairway*, Hodder & Stoughton (UK)

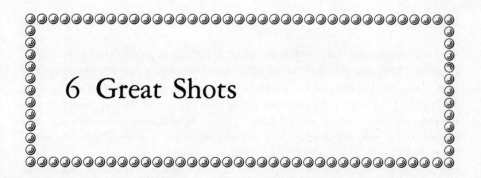

6 Great Shots

COMING to the last hole in the club annual knock-out we stood all square. The last was a par-3, uphill, into the wind and about 220 yards. My 2 iron bored low and straight at the flag and that was that.

Perhaps this is the essence of a great shot: it should be struck with precision and, if need be, power; it must be played at a crucial point in the game. Long putts on the practice green and fine drives on the driving range do not live on in the memory. There must be a sense of occasion. This is true of the most famous of all: Jones's long iron from sand to the 17th green at Royal Lytham and St Anne's that won the 1926 British Open. The same is true of most of the shots described in this chapter. Few of these come from the modern era for I suspect that we now demand that *every* shot a champion makes is near perfection. Indeed, why not? They are quite well rewarded for doing just that.

THROUGH THE TEETH OF THE STORM   Bernard Darwin

Vardon's driving when he beat Massy in playing off the tie at Sandwich was, I think, the most beautiful display of wooden club hitting I ever saw; but for sheer thrilling quality give me Taylor at Hoylake in 1913. There was no great excitement since, after qualifying by the skin of his teeth, he won by strokes and strokes; but I have seen nothing else in golf which so stirred me and made me want to cry. The wind and the rain were terrific, but not so terrific as Taylor, with his cap pulled down, buffeting his way through them. There are always one or two strokes which stick faster in the memory than any others, and I noticed the other day that my friend Mr Macfarlane recalled just the one that I should choose. It was the second shot played with a cleek* to the Briars hole in the very teeth of the storm. I can still see Taylor standing on rocklike feet, glued flat on the turf, watching that ball as it whizzes over the two cross bunkers straight for the green. There never was such a cleek shot; there never will be such another as long as the world stands.

from *Out of the Rough*, Chapman & Hall (UK)

* The present-day club would be a 1 iron with a narrower face.

BRIGHT MEMORY   Michael Murphy

We now come to the thirteenth hole, which is famous in golfing circles. It is a par three up a hill, to a pin that stands silhouetted between a pair of twisted cyprus trees. Between the tee and the green lies Lucifer's Rug, a field of clotted gorse, 200 yards of it to catch any shot that is less than perfection. Along the left runs a steep ravine, from which several boulders rise. It was fortunate I thought as I looked to the pin, that I had come to this concentrated state of mind by now. Every Monday the caddies of Burningbush and other links came here to hunt for lost golf balls, some trained their dogs for the task. At various points in the history of the club there had been efforts by members to have the hole enshrined as a golf museum, thus prohibiting further play upon it. It was even said that a body had once been found 'under the rug'.

The tee shot had to carry to the green but not roll down the other side, for another ravine dropped off there. Few players could reach it with an iron, so in effect a wood was required to do the work of a pitching wedge. To make matters worse, there was usually a wind across the rise—witness the twisted cyprus trees—so the shot had to be played to the left, to the ravine side. It was a hole in all respects suited to test the powers of 'true gravity'.

The wind was now blowing from left to right, hard enough to lift the distant flag. I took out a two iron and gazed at its sweet spot, as if it were an icon . . . .

. . . I slowly marched to the firing line, praying to my golf club icon and looking intently for that mystical joining with the ball. I teed up. As I did there was another bloodcurdling cry, Shivas was wailing again behind my back. I was so startled I jumped. He shook his head apologetically, but said nothing—his attention seemed to be focused somewhere else.

Whether from the many holes of high concentration or from this incredible performance my mind seemed blasted empty. It was impossible to summon any image. I swung without thinking and the ball flew like a bullet on a low trajectory, a white streak against the yellow, rising into the sky before it fell to the green. The picture of it is still painted brightly in my memory.

from *Golf in the Kingdom*, The Viking Press (US), Latimer New Dimensions (UK)

BUZZING LIKE A PARTRIDGE   R. T. Jones and O. B. Keeler

On the twelfth hole of the afternoon round at East Lake, Ted Ray made a shot which stands out in my mind today as the greatest I have seen.

Our boys had finished the morning round 2 down but had started brilliantly after luncheon, especially Stewart, and had got in the lead. Then, beginning with the twelfth hole, the visitors executed four birdies in succession and went back in front. Vardon got the birdie at No. 12, but Ray, in getting his par 4, produced this astonishing shot. His drive was the longest of the four, as usual, but right behind a tree. The tree was about forty feet in height, with thick foliage, and the ball was no more than the tree's altitude back of it, the tree exactly in line with the green. As Ray walked up to his ball, the more sophisticated members of the gallery were speculating as to whether he would essay to slice his shot around the obstacle to the green, 170 yards away, or 'pull' around in on the other side. As for me, I didn't see anything he could do, possibly; but accept the penalty of a stroke into the fairway. He was out of luck, I was sure.

Big Ted took one look at the ball and another at the green, a fair iron-shot away, with the tree between. Then without hesitation he drew a mashie-niblick, and he hit that ball harder, I believe, than I ever have seen a ball hit since, knocking it down as if he would drive it through to China. Up flew a divot the size of Ted's ample foot. Up also came the ball, buzzing like a partridge from the prodigious spin imparted by that tremendous wallop—almost straight up it got, cleared that tree by several yards, and sailed on at the height of an office building, to drop on the green not far from the hole . . . . The gallery was in paroxysms. I remember how men pounded each other on the back, and crowed and cackled and shouted and clapped their hands. As for me, I didn't really believe it. A sort of wonder persists in my memory to this day. It was the greatest shot I ever saw.

from *Down the Fairway*, George Allen & Unwin (UK)

THE GREATEST SHOT I EVER PLAYED   Walter Hagen

On the twelfth green I played one of the finest stymies* of my entire career. On his second shot Abe's ball was on the extreme back edge of the green. My shot was short and to the left. I played the third shot up and left myself eight feet from the hole. Abe had a thirty-foot putt and he all but holed it, just missing the cup and stopping on the very edge to the right, leaving me a dead stymie, blocking the hole.

Things looked extremely black for me right then—having a dead stymie at eight feet and knowing if I didn't make it I'd be 3 down with only six more holes to play. I could putt around his ball, but I could see no possible chance to hole my ball. I decided to use a seven-iron. I looked the green over . . . back and forth, back and forth. Then I hit my ball just short of Abe's, which lay delicately poised on the very rim of the cup. My ball hit a breath of an inch behind his, jumped it and stayed in the hole! We halved the hole and I was still in business. And that stymie shot of mine disturbed Abe so much he hooked his next tee shot badly, and

---

* Until 1952 you had to play around or over an opponent's ball on the green. A 'stymie' meant that an opponent's ball lay between your ball and the hole. Nowadays, of course, you would ask him to mark his ball.

lost the hole, leaving me only 1 down. I finished the match by winning 2 and 1. That stymie, the greatest shot I ever played, paid off.

from *The Walter Hagen Story*, Simon & Schuster (US), William Heinemann (UK)

IRON SHOTS WIN CHAMPIONSHIPS   R. T. Jones and O. B. Keeler

... it was an iron shot won me the British open championship.

Curious thing, now I come to think of it. In the winning of three national open championships, one British and two United States, there has invariably been one single iron shot that did the trick. You see, the boys never let me get away with anything like a lead. When I managed to win the British open with a two-stroke margin, I felt I had spread-eagled the field; the result was never in doubt after the 72nd hole! I had to play off with Bobby Cruickshank to win the United States open of 1923, and I had to play the last dozen holes at Scioto in 1926 in ten 4's and two 3's to nose out Joe Turnesa by a single stroke.

And in every case an iron shot stood out most obtrusively.

The one against Cruickshank at Inwood is mentioned rather fully in a preceding chapter. It was with a No. 2 iron. The following year I sent that iron to a dear friend, the late Mr J. S. Worthington, who was going home to England—to die, as it turned out. He wrote me not long before he sailed and asked me for one of my discarded clubs, as a sort of keepsake. There was only one that I thought enough of to send him; the one that got me my first big championship.

This shot at St Anne's, and the one at Scioto, were each with a mashie-iron, but not with the same one, as I gave the first one to Charlie MacFarlane right after the tournament. Charlie was very kind in what he said about that shot. It was at what might be called a crucial juncture.

The seventeenth at St Anne's is a hole of 411 yards,* with apparently acres of sand along the left side of the fairway, all done out in dunes. The hole bends to the left and the sand is not a good place to play your second from. Added to the native disadvantages of a sand lie, from the position in which I found my ball after a slightly pulled drive I could not see the green at all. Al Watrous, with whom I was paired, had lost a lead of two strokes and we were level with two holes to play. Here he had a good drive and his second was on the green. As suggested, it was a critical position.

The only way I could get a good look at the green, and what lay between it and my ball, was to walk far out to the right, nearly across the fairway. I did this. The prospect was not precisely encouraging. I had to hit a shot with a carry of close to 175 yards, and hit it on a good line, and stop the ball very promptly when it reached the green—if it reached the green. This, off dry sand, though the ball

_____
* 453 now.

luckily lay clean, was a stiff assignment. You know, an eighth of an inch too deep with your blade, off dry sand, and the shot expires right in front of your eyes. And if your blade is a thought too high—I will dismiss this harrowing reflection.

Anyway, I played the shot and it came off, and the ball stopped closer to the pin than Al's and he took three putts. This gave me a stroke in hand which was tremendously needed, and I had some luck at the last hole on both my drive and my second shot to get a par 4, Al losing another stroke by visiting a bunker which I missed by a couple of feet, at least.

The same type of club—do you wonder I'm fond of the mashie-iron?—came out for the final shot to the green at Scioto fifteen days later, on the last hole of the United States open championship. As I stood on the last tee I was told that Joe Turnesa had finished with a birdie 4 on a hole of 480 yards. I had a stroke in hand and a birdie would keep me in front of Joe; and there was better than a fair chance that I would win the championship, as the closest competitors were not going any too well.

I hit that drive as hard as I could. There was a cross wind off the right but it did not seem to affect the shot. When I got to the ball, near the left edge of the fairway, I needed a poke with the old reliable mashie-iron, a bit more than a half swing, to get home. It was about 180 yards, but I did not want to play a shot that carried to the green, which was slightly domed; what is called a turtle-back. It was a dangerous business, banging the ball firmly to that type of green, and I decided on another kind of shot. I hit a rather low ball, aimed to carry to ten or fifteen yards in front of the green, it being perfectly open, and run the rest of the way. The line was good and the range near enough right; the ball ran about 20 feet past the pin. I had two putts to finish in front.

from *Down the Fairway*, George Allen & Unwin (UK)

SHOTS THAT WON THE 1966 BRITISH OPEN

Jack Nicklaus and
Herbert Warren Wind

Saturday. Wind from the west, blustery but subsiding. Five of us in contention. Rodgers and myself out last, Palmer and Sanders playing just in front of us, Thomas paired with Henning just in front of them. After the first hole, I was back in a tie for the lead: Phil bogeyed it and I holed from 25 feet for a birdie. I turned in 33 after two more birdies and six pars, and after getting my par on the tough tenth, I was comfortably out in front again—three strokes ahead of Thomas, four ahead of Rodgers and Sanders. Palmer was out of it. On the eleventh, a short 4, I was in a position to add another stroke to my lead after punching my approach seven feet from the flag. I jerked the putt, though, and it broke off a foot before the cup. I took pains with the 15-inch tap-in I had left for my par. I thought I hit it the way I wanted to, but the ball rimmed off the left corner of the cup and stayed out. That shouldn't have shaken me—I still had a two-shot margin on the closest contender—but it did.

I began to worry and I began to play jittery golf, exactly as I had on the second nine the day before, I got my par on the twelfth, a short 4, but only because I hooked my drive so badly it cleared the heavy rough and finished under the gallery ropes in rough the spectators had trodden down—I had a very playable lie. I didn't get my 3 on the short thirteenth, though. I was weak with my iron off the tee and way strong with my running, uphill chip. I couldn't pull myself together. I played the fourteenth poorly. There I pushed my tee-shot into an awkward spot in the bunker off to the right of the fairway and took a bogey 5. I'd lost three shots on four holes—my entire lead. Thomas, I learned, was in with a 69 for 283. Sanders, playing the eighteenth, was headed for 283 if he parred the home hole, which he did. I would have to par the last four holes to tie them. I wasn't at all sure I could.

On the fifteenth, 407 yards, I got my 4 but it was a wobbly one. A mediocre approach left me 40 feet short of the hole, and I had to putt over the humpy contour in the middle of the green called the Camel's Back. I managed to get down in two by holing from four feet.

The pin on the sixteenth, a 198-yard par 3, was at the back of a slippery green which slopes up from the front. The wind was behind me and I played a 7-iron. I had the ball on the pin but it was short, a good 30 feet short. And then I came through with the first good attacking stroke I'd played since the eleventh. I didn't hole that 30-footer but it was hit squarely, it was dead on line, and it couldn't have stopped more than an inch or two short of the cup. (I didn't want to go by the cup and leave myself a downhiller.)

Golf is not at all a logical game. There was no reason, really, why I should have lost my composure so completely after I had three-putted the eleventh from seven feet. There was no reason either why I should have suddenly regained it just as completely because I had made a firm putt and firm par on the sixteenth. That is what happened, however. I walked onto the seventeenth tee full of confidence, a different man. I was no longer thinking about how I might lose the championship, I was thinking about how I could win it. I thought I could. All I needed was a birdie and a par. The seventeenth—why, that was a very birdieable hole. The eighteenth—that was a tough 4 but I could make it.

A par 5 that measures 528 yards, the seventeenth is a rather unique hole. The tee-shot is semi-blind. The fairway slopes slightly up for 200 yards or so, and this cuts off your view of the landing area. After the fairway reaches the top of its rise, it twists to the left and continues on a relatively straight line to the green. About 100 yards from the green a high bunkered ridge thrusts itself into the fairway from the right, but a golfer doesn't have to concern himself with this ridge if he's hit a good drive—his second will carry it with plenty to spare. Beyond this ridge the fairway becomes very tight as it moves between a high mound of rough on the right and broken rough ground on the left, and it is nothing much more than a channel as it tumbles toward the left side of the flat circular green set in a hollow and banked by rough. From where you play your second after a good tee-shot, the left side of the green is visible, but most of the right side is hidden by that high mound of rough. An easy par, yes, but no giveaway birdie.

On Wednesday, when we had that east wind blowing against us on the seventeenth, I had used my 3-wood off the tee. On Thursday and Friday, with the west wind behind and right-to-left, I had used a 1-iron, aiming down the right side of the fairway and letting the wind take the ball in a little. No percentage attempting the shortcut over the corner: there was a series of bunkers along the left edge of the fairway but none on the right. On Saturday, as I stood on the seventeenth tee, it seemed to me that the wind was a bit stronger than it had been the two previous days. To be on the safe side I decided to play a 3-iron off the tee: there was always the danger, if you aimed down the right, that you might get the ball out past the corner and into the rough. The 3-iron proved to be almost too much club. My tee-shot finished in the fairway but only two yards short of the rough. I looked across the fairway at my yardage marker, the last bunker on the left, and consulted my yardage chart: since I was out equidistant with the front edge of that bunker, that meant I was 238 yards from the center of the green. Now to get the right club. With the big ball and no wind, 238 yards—that's easy: that's a 1-iron. Downwind with the small ball, 238 yards—that's more difficult to figure. I settled on a 5-iron. Not that I was able to go about things this scientifically, but I made my allowances more or less this way: one club less for the small ball; one and a half clubs less for the following wind; one club less for the run on the ball (it would have to be played to land on the fairway short of the green); and a half club less for the extra distance you get when you're charged up and the adrenaline is flowing. I could see the flag. It was in about the middle of the green, a little to the right. From where I stood, the flag was almost directly in line with the left edge of the big bunker in the face of the ridge jutting above the fairway. I took my line a shade to the left of the left edge of the bunker. I was going to try to play a straight shot but the kind of a shot which, if it slipped off, would slip off to the right.

My first reaction after I'd made contact with the ball with my 5-iron was that I had played as good a shot as I was capable of. I saw the ball fly over the ridge on the line I wanted and I saw it land on the fairway about 15 feet short of the green, and then—it seemed an awful long time later—a loud roar went up from the gallery packed around the green. The ball had gotten an ideal bounce onto the green, and as I saw for myself as I came hurrying up the fairway, it had finished about 16 feet from the flag, short and to the left. What a beautiful sight that was! By the time I walked onto the green, I felt comparatively calm. The important thing was not to go for the putt, just to get the ball as close as I could. I lagged it to within inches of the cup and holed the tap-in for my birdie. Now a par on the last hole would do it.

Muirfield's eighteenth is a 429-yard par 4, a straightaway hole from tee to green. It's a well-designed hole. To begin with, it demands an extremely accurate tee-shot. The fairway, a slim one, is bunkered on both sides, but you must particularly avoid the left side where three bunkers cut progressively deeper into the fairway. The green is bunkered front, left, and right, and you're playing a fairly long approach into it, so that's not an easy shot either. But the key to the hole is the tee-shot. In a west wind a left-to-right player like myself had a definite advantage, for that kind of wind blows across the eighteenth from the right and gives you a perfect bank to hit into. On my three earlier rounds I had taken a 1-iron off the tee. I went with the same club again, aiming down the middle and counting on the wind to cushion my fade. The ball ended up in the very center of the fairway, 208 yards from the heart of the green, according to my yardage chart. A 4-iron or a 3? I chose the 3. I didn't want to hit the shot hard, I just wanted to hang it in the wind, the way I had my tee-shot. Besides, the flag was set only 20 feet from the back edge of the green, and I wanted to be up. I'd be past all the trouble then. If my approach went over, there was nothing serious to worry about—just a little upslope and I could putt off of it. I hit that 3-iron well, my fourth good iron in a row. I cut it into the wind and it carried past the middle of the green and sat down softly about 25 feet to the right of the flag, absolutely hole-high. I read the putt to break a foot and a half from right to left and reminded myself that the green was fast and that this was no time for hero stuff—just get that putt up close. I had the speed correct and the ball stopped seven or eight inches to the left of the cup. I lined up that little putt and carefully tapped it in . . . . I had won the British Open.

from *The Greatest Game of All*, Simon & Schuster (US), Hodder & Stoughton (UK)

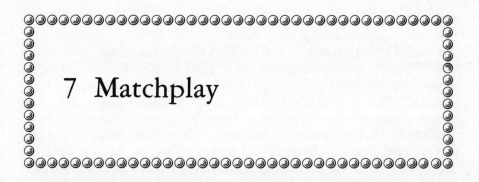

7 Matchplay

I REGRET the comparative passing of matchplay golf. Today, there is really only one event for professionals that commands attention—the World Matchplay held at Wentworth, England each year. But the entry is by invitation only, some of the great ones do not come, and the field is extremely limited, so the event lacks the drama brought by the crash of the mighty at the hands of unknowns. Nevertheless it is followed with great interest—in the UK particularly—and could come to rank as a fifth major championship if the entry were open and most top players took part.

But apart from this there is only the Ryder Cup, whose result is not often long in doubt, and in which, under the present format, there are probably too many matches. True there are a variety of Amateur Championships but in the 1970s it is the professional who dominates interest in the world of golf.

I suppose the matches between professionals just about deserve a mention but more often than not they are little more than exhibitions with prize money fairly equally divided and have little effect on a player's reputation.

Though the selection that follows draws mainly on the modern era, it is dramas of the past which perhaps most remain in the memory.

JONES v HUNTER   R. T. Jones and O. B. Keeler

But I got another lesson in 1921—the amateur championship at St Louis, when we had a further flavor of international competition in the entry of Willie Hunter, who had won the British championship that same season at Hoylake, where Mr Allan Graham so conclusively exterminated me in the fourth round. Willie came over to play in our national amateur championship at the St Louis Country Club, and, gosh, how I pined for a chance to get at him! Now (thought I) we've got some regular greens that will hold a pitch and not skid a putt off into a bunker. Now (thought I) we've got some regular turf, and Willie can't run his drives a hundred yards or so after they hit the ground. Just let me at him, I reflected, more or less fatuously.

But most of all I wanted to win this championship. I was getting along. I'd been to Britain. I'd played in three national open championships and four national amateur championships. I was now a veteran, at the age of 19 years. It was time to win something that counted.

I started blithely enough, qualifying in 151 for the two rounds, seven strokes back of Francis Ouimet, who was medalist, and a dozen strokes ahead of the top score. I beat my first man, Clarence Wolff, 12–11, and my second, Dr O. F. Willing, 9–8, and everybody, including myself, fancied I was set to kill off the British champion when I met him in Round 3.

All in all, I suspect I got more education out of that match than from any other I ever played. I could outdrive Hunter freely from the tee. And the rest of my game was working well enough to suit me. But he stuck to me like a bulldog. I was playing well in the morning round and was 2 up at the luncheon intermission. I found myself saying (to myself), 'Only 2 up!' I worried a trifle about that, and changed my pants for luck, donning a pair of long flannel trousers with a pin-stripe. I was beginning to think a little about my sartorial appearance on the golf course, and I liked those pants and also fancied they were lucky, since I had won a couple of matches in them.

Willie picked up a hole at the third in the afternoon. We battled on to the eighth tee and I had got the hole back and was still 2 up, with eleven to play.

The eighth at St Louis is called the Cape Hole, and it is a dog-leg to the right, giving you a fair pitch after a straight drive out the fairway. If you want to carry the tall trees in the angle you may get much nearer the green, even on the front of it, if you are bold and have sufficient *gluteus maximus* in your stroke. I decided to carry the trees—indeed, I had been doing that all week—and pick up another hole (possibly) and break Willie's obstinate back right there.

I went for the carry over the angle, and the ball, for the first time all week, caught the topmost branch of the tallest tree, and dropped in a ditch full of stones and weeds, with at least one rabbit in it—he came bouncing out as my first blast failed to extract the ball.

Willie won that hole with a par 4. He won the next hole, a par 5, while I was still reflecting on the mutability of fortune. I went 1 up at the long thirteenth; he sank a thirty-foot putt to square at the fourteenth. I blew the fifteenth on a short putt after a convenient spectator had saved me from going out of bounds, and he sank a long putt again to go 2 up at the Redan Hole. I had a five-yard putt for a win at the next hole, the thirty-fifth of the match, to stay in it, but I missed, and we shook hands.

That night O. B. Keeler, who is working with me on these memoirs, came to my room at the hotel . . .

He told me I had lost the match, and very likely the championship, on the eighth hole in the afternoon round, when, with Hunter 2 down, I had taken the chance instead of making him take the chance.

I told him he might be right but I could not play match golf that way. I had to play every stroke for all there was in it. I could not play safe. He said that was a laudable frame of mind, but it would cost me a lot of tournaments. And still I don't know. It is true that since I started playing match golf as near as I can like medal golf—shooting for par and letting my opponent shoot what he can—I have managed to win a couple of match-play national championships. And three open, or medal-play, championships. Old Man Par after all is the toughest opponent you can have, and if you play him and play him close he generally will look out for the other fellow. But there's that old maxim: 'When you get him 1 doon, get him 2 doon; when you get him 3 doon, get him 4 doon!' I sort of like that, too. Even if it did kill me off, against Willie Hunter, at St Louis.

from *Down the Fairway*, George Allen & Unwin (UK)

HAGEN v COMPSTON   Walter Hagen

Our match of seventy-two holes was scheduled thirty-six for Friday, April 27th, and the final thirty-six for Saturday, April 28th. My pal, the big Scotland Yard detective, got me out of a comfortable bed about six in the morning of the first day. After a leisurely breakfast, the limousine placed us on the first tee shortly before nine. As our Daimler pulled up in front of the club-house, out stepped the Scotland Yard giant, followed by Bob Harlow, then me. A crowd of some several thousand people had already gathered and at the sight of our little group they burst into shouts of laughter. The British have a keen sense of the ridiculous.

That first round was an amazing one for me. I found myself swamped by a flood of Compston's superb shots. He started by winning four holes of the first six; we halved two. His every shot was masterful. On those first nine holes he consistently outdrove me by twenty yards. He holed an eight-yard putt on the ninth for a 3, giving him a lead of five holes. He had gone out in 32 and I had taken 38.

On the tenth he holed a putt of ten yards for a 2, going 6 up. We halved the next two and at the thirteenth I finally won my first hole with a 5 to his 6. And please note that he had to take a 6 for me to win. He took the fourteenth, I won the fifteenth by one stroke. We halved the next two and I won the eighteenth when Compston was short with his tee shot. He failed to negotiate a half-stymie. He became 4 up on me at the end of the morning round.

I've talked a lot about liking to fight when the pressure was on. Believe me, I certainly felt that pressure when I stepped on the first tee for the afternoon round. Having played only practice shots on the Moor Park course, I'd been handicapped during the morning round by not being familiar with the course. And Compston was very careful not to show me a shot. He didn't even resort to my well-publicised strategy of picking the 'wrong' club as an indicator for me. Perhaps because I automatically picked the wrong club anyway. Compston just let me get around by the Braille system.

I started a bit more comfortably on the second eighteen holes, but my feeling was short-lived. Compston was not quite as sharp in the afternoon, for he pulled his drive at the fourth and sliced into the rough off the tee. He recovered from this first mistake with a good run-up shot and won the hole, as I three-putted on the green. I got one hole back with a 4 on the fifth. At the turn I was 7 down, a serious but to me certainly not a hopeless situation. I was over the tenth green with my drive. I got a 3 with a pitch and a long putt. But it did me no good, for he came up with a 2.

He got greedier as the round progressed. Outside of the twelfth and the seventeenth, he took every other hole from me. I was suffering from mild discomfort from a blister on my right hand . . . but suffering far more over the fact that at the end of this first day's play I was 14 *down*.

Compston had come home in 30 on the afternoon round to give him a 66 to my 76. Only four wooden club shots were played through the greens in the entire thirty-six holes and all of those on the seventh hole. On each round he had holed the third and tenth in 2. He missed only one putt of four feet or less in the entire thirty-six holes. He had me over the well-known barrel!

My Scotland Yard detective earned his money the next morning, for it took him some twenty minutes to roll me out. I had slept the dreamless sleep of an exhausted kid. The day was beautiful, warm and sunny . . . just like Long Island in July. I enjoyed the drive up from London to Moor Park. I felt like playing golf and I expected to do well. However, I had no brilliant golf in me and Compston kept right on with his remarkable run.

He won first blood in the third round with a 3 at the big hole, the third, where I took three putts—a fault I was guilty of five times the day before and four times on Saturday. By the time we reached the ninth I was 17 to the bad. At least I was being consistent! At the eighteenth green I was faced with a putt of twenty feet or the match was over, for I was then 18 down. It was high noon . . . a balmy day. The drive up to the club-house, passing the eighteenth green, was bordered with colourful rhododendrons and busy with cars bringing more fans to see the afternoon round. If I don't make the putt, I thought I'm beaten 19 and 18 to go. And all those beautifull shillings must be paid back to customers at the gate. As luck would have it, I made the putt and guaranteed at least a start of the afternoon round.

That last round of our match consisted of a single hole. We fought to the end, however. I had to putt from a foot and I made Archie putt from six inches. We halved the hole for him to take the match, 18 and 17 to play. We shook hands and proceeded to play an exhibition match for the remainder of the round. I'd invited some friends out to see the match and they did not arrive until noon . . . just in time to see me get knocked off by an expert. I thought they and the other late arriving spectators deserved to see some golf in return for making the trip up to Moor Park . . . although I may be facetious in terming what I had played in the Compston match *golf*.

Several incidents of the match amused me . . . even while Archie was piling up his lead. The Moor Park officials conceived the idea of having a tall caddie carry a big blackboard around with us, on which they marked the standing of the match, after each hole. Not *once* did my name appear on the board. Another sight that really got me was Compston's caddie toting a large toy black cat . . . Archie's mascot and good-luck piece.

That gallery threw me, too. Never in my long career of competitive golf have I been conscious of getting the *kind* of applause I received at the fifteenth hole when I made a fair recovery shot from a trap. I realised for the first time in my life I was getting 'sympathy applause'.

Compston was a great golfer and he'd worked hard at his game. He did everything right. He gave me the worst beating of my career and I had only one statement to make to the British Press: 'When you are laid out good and flat, you must not squawk!'*

from *The Walter Hagen Story*, Simon & Schuster (US) and
William Heinemann (UK)

JONES v TOLLEY   R. T. Jones

From the start, and even before play commenced, everyone around St Andrews seemed to be looking forward to the possible meeting of Cyril Tolley and me on Wednesday afternoon.† Of course, we both had to win two matches in the interim, but this had seemed quite likely of accomplishment when we expected Mr Roper to shoot fives. Cyril, too, had a narrow escape in the first round, but he also managed to make it.

This was very definitely one eighteen-hole match into which I went with the complete realization of its vast import and difficulty. I had won from Cyril by a very wide margin over this same course in the Walker Cup Matches of 1926, but that had been over thirty-six holes. Jimmy Johnston had also beaten him in the singles of the Walker Cup recently completed at Sandwich.

But no one had any illusions about Cyril. He had always been a fearsome competitor in this championship. He had won it for the second time the year before, and so would carry with him the very considerable prestige and responsibility of the defending champion. He was a big, powerful player with an exquisite touch in the short game, and in my opinion the most dangerous man I could possibly meet in an eighteen-hole match at St Andrews.

---

* Shortly after this massive defeat, Hagen again won the British Open. Compston was among those he beat. Later the same year, there was a repeat match, this time on American soil. Hagen won handsomely.

† Bobby Jones found the British Amateur more difficult to win than any other and did not succeed until near the end of his competitive career when in 1930 he achieved the 'Grand Slam' or 'Impregnable Quadrilateral' of the British and US Opens and the British and US Amateurs. The British Amateur gave him the most trouble once more and this was the toughest match.

Added to this, on the dawning of the day upon which the match was to be played, the conditions of nature were precisely those to cause me greatest concern. The greens were hard and fast and the wind was blowing towards the sea at something more than half a gale. Sand was being whipped from the bunkers, and spectators and players alike were seeking refuge behind the dunes and whins whenever a lull in the play developed. St Andrews was in real truth St Andrews on such a day, and the test was more of resourcefulness in manoeuvring than of regularity in playing standard golf shots . . .

Nor have I any real recollection of how good the golf was—that is, in total—but I have graven on my soul, I think, the completely brutal ferocity of that man-to-man contest. Cyril and I had been very good friends for many years before that day, and we have remained fast friends ever since. I know that that match still stands in his memory, as it does in mine, as an afternoon when each of us called upon every resource in an all-out effort to beat the other. There was nothing of the dilettante in either one of us. I think we both have found at other times something of the aesthetic in golf, but we would have none of it that day. I know I felt the same exultation and desperate urgency I should expect to feel in a battle with broadswords or cudgels. And after it was all over, when I said I felt six years older, I was perpetrating a masterpiece of understatement. It was the kind of match in which each player plays himself so completely out that at the end the only feeling to which he is sensitive is one of utter exhaustion.

As for the golf, I have the score cards before me. They are not exciting. They are as follows:

Jones	4	5	4	5	5	4	4	3	5	39		
Tolley	5	4	4	4	5	4	5	4	3	38		
Jones	4	4	5	3	4	3	5	4	4	36	39	75
Tolley	4	5	4	4	3	5	4	4	4	37	38	75

Yet I also have the cards of other leading matches played at the same time. The figures of our match look very good in comparison. The truth, I think, is that our golf from a match-play standpoint, under the harrowing conditions, was fully as good as could have been expected. There is no way to exaggerate the difficulty of the Old Course on that Wednesday afternoon. As the match itself was primitive, I think the playing conditions must have been also.

As a few examples, Tolley drove the ninth green, 306 yards; we both overdrove the twelfth, 314 yards. With the gale at our backs, neither was able to hold the green with the tee shot at the short eighth, the ground being just as hard, in another sense, as the wind. Playing the short eleventh, in the opposite direction, Tolley hit a strong iron which at one time was hovering above the green, yet was blown back to the fairway short of Strath bunker, where he found it half-embedded in wind-blown sand. In my effort to avoid a similar fate I played too strongly over the green on to the bank of the Eden River. I remember watching

Cyril playing from this loose sand-on-turf and thinking how simple it would be for him to fluff the ball into Strath bunker. Actually he fluffed it only a few feet, and then into the bunker, whence he emerged with a great shot to get a five but lose the hole to my four.

The putting, too, was as difficult as could-be imagined. The greens were as keen as glass and had been somewhat scarred by the heavy traffic of players. On every putt, account had to be taken of the wind effect, as well as of the breaks and irregularities in the putting surface. In consideration of all circumstances, I think neither Cyril nor I have reason to be ashamed of the figures we produced.

In sixteen holes the match had been brought back from one down to even six times, with the two players alternating in taking the lead. The play on the seventeenth, the famous Road Hole, is still being discussed. That it was a break for me is undeniable. Just how colossal a break it was will perhaps never be known. The facts, as agreed by Cyril and me, along with all observers known to me whom I consider to be competent because of their opportunities, are as follows:

The two drives, with the wind behind, were long, with Cyril out in front. My ball lay near the left side of the fairway, his about centre, or maybe a little right-centre.

The hole was cut behind the road bunker, so that it was entirely shut off from my position and only barely open to Cyril.

Playing the odd, my second was an iron to the left of the road bunker which bounded into the mass of spectators, and dropped on the apron at the back of the green, a few feet off the putting surface.

Tolley's second was short and curled off the slope at the front of the green, stopping in a position leaving the bunker between his ball and the flag.

I, being furthest away, chipped to a distance of approximately eight feet from the cup.

Tolley's little pitch dropped exactly on the only possible spot, barely over the bunker, at the top of a slope running down to the hole. His ball stopped within two feet of the cup.

I holed the eight-footer and Cyril, of course, holed his for the half.

The point of controversy was and is: Where would my ball have finished had it not been stopped by the crowd? Would it have finished on the eighteenth tee or in the rough beyond the eighteenth tee, or would it have gone into the road? No one knows, or ever will.

If the ball would have gone into the road, the stopping of it definitely saved for me the hole and the match. If the ball would have stopped either on the eighteenth tee or in the rough beyond, I think in all reason I could have approached as well as I had chipped.

I think, though, that the really interesting part of the situation lies in having a knowledge of the mental processes of the two players.

Long before this fateful afternoon I had gained a great respect for the famous Road Hole. In the Open Championship of 1927, when in every round it had been within range of the second shot, I had four times played short, relying on a chip and a putt to get a four and refusing to take any risk with the road or the bunker. This time two circumstances were different. A gale of wind was blowing and the ground was quite hard and fast.

With my long tee shot, in order to reach a spot in front of the green from which I could chip to the hole clear of the bunker, it was necessary to play very close to the road and almost directly at it. A small error in judgment or a little extra run on the ball would surely put it into the road. A little less, and I would not have a clear shot at the hole.

I had never heard of anyone playing intentionally past the Road bunker on the left, but after more study than I normally give to a shot I concluded that this was my best chance. At least I should not be playing directly towards the road. If I should succeed in merely sneaking the ball past the Road bunker, I should have a very short, easy chip; and I expected to have an adequate margin for error on the long side.

At least one observer thought that I had played directly into the crowd, knowing that they were packed so densely that the human barricade must stop my ball. This was very definitely not the case. I should never have been so heedless of the possibility of inflicting injury upon a spectator. I made completely audible requests to the stewards to move the crowd back on the left side, and even mounted a high piece of ground to motion them back myself. I played only after several minutes, and after it had become apparent that the crowd could be moved no farther.

I attempted to play a soft shot with a number-four iron, designed, as I have said, barely to pass the bunker. I have a very distinct recollection that as I swung the club I was acutely aware of the prime necessity that the ball should pass the bunker. If it did not, my situation would be hopeless. I know that I gave the shot a little extra nudge. I saw the ball land about even with the bunker and take a bound forward. I know it was strong, but I don't know by how much. Yet I did see it strike a spectator and drop near the green.

Tolley, seeing my ball so well located, decided that in order to save a half, he must go for the flag. This was a more reasonable prospect for him, because he was playing more nearly down the length of the green. But I think as he was swinging, an unwelcome thought intruded. I think he must instinctively have flinched from the road, and so his shot, being a bit weak and with a little curl to it, did not finish as he had intended.

It cannot be stated as a fact, but it is nevertheless my conviction that Tolley's third shot on this hole has never been surpassed for exquisitely beautiful execution. I shall carry to my grave the impression of the lovely little stroke with which he dropped the ball so softly in exactly the right spot, so that in the only possible way it finished dead to the hole. Tolley himself, after the passage of twenty-eight years, confirmed to me that this was the finest shot of his life. I am sure that it was.

It certainly put the seal of necessity on my eight-foot putt. If I had not holed this one, I would not be writing this story. Although it had been as tense a hole as I had ever played in my life, the result only served to increase the pressure. Coming now to the eighteenth all square, there was no room for either of us to make a mistake.

Two long drives down the big wind left us both some ten yards short of the green, with Tolley ahead, as he had been all day. Being a bit on the left side, I had to play a run-up through the Valley of Sin; since pitching was out of the question under the conditions, I made too certain of getting through the big swale, which is the Valley, and overran the hole some twenty-five feet. Tolley played up to within a little more than half my distance. I missed my putt but left the ball very close, and then I went through, I think, the most agonizing moments of that entire year.

Tolley was one of those players who had a flair for the spectacular. Although he did it in a different way, he played the game, like Hagen, in the grand manner. As I watched him putt, I remembered that he had holed one longer than this on the thirty-seventh hole at Muirfield to beat Bob Gardner for the 1923 Championship. I fully expected him to hole this one, and there was nothing I could do about it. But he missed, to relieve my agony, and we headed for the nineteenth.

I have always regretted that such a splendid, exciting match should have been decided by a stymie, yet the stymie was an accepted and important part of match-play golf in those days, as indeed I think it should be today and always. And as Tolley himself said, generously but truly, he had left himself wide-open to it. A slack second to the left of the green and a weak chip had left his ball seven feet short of the hole in three, whereas mine in two lay only ten feet away. Since the two balls were on the same side of the hole, when my very careful putt stopped only a couple of inches short, the hole was completely shut off to anything but a miracle.

The great battle had ended and the release from the tension was almost unbearable. I was neither exultant nor elated, just very, very tired.

from *Golf is My Game*, Doubleday & Co (US), Chatto & Windus (UK)

CAMPBELL v O'SULLIVAN   Patrick Campbell

In 1949 the British Amateur Championship was played at Portmarnock, Eire— an interesting occasion in view of the fact that the British competitors had to submit to the rigours of passport examination and Customs inspection before being allowed to play in their own championship.

It was—making the situation slightly worse—won by an Irishman, Max Macready, from an American, Willie Turnesa, but what causes the event to linger in my memory is the fact that I got as far as the fifteenth hole in the fifth round—a 300 per cent improvement on previous endeavours.

Having emigrated, like 920,000 other Irishmen, to England I was drawn to return home for this particular Amateur by the enormous advantage of being able to stay with my parents while it was in progress, and not in an hotel.

Hotels are murder during a championship week if you're not a member of the regular tournament mob. Unless you know—as the English, whose spiritual home is the Armed Forces, say—the drill, you're liable to find yourself shacked up with seven old ladies in a temperance guest house ten miles away from the course on which the championship is being played.

On all these occasions there is always one hotel in which the knowledgeable boys are gathered together, and if you're not in it it promotes an emotional climate in which you're already three down.

There are no means of assessing—say from the A.A. book—which this hotel is likely to be. Choose the four-star one and you find that all the boys are staying at half the price in a charming road-house immediately opposite the course. If the four-star hotel is the right one you can only get into it by booking a month ahead, before you've seen the draw. When you do see the draw, and find you've got Joe Carr in the first round, a reservation for five days at £5 per day bed and breakfast looks like being an unnecessary expense.

The night life of hotels can draw you out very fine, too. After dinner you can sit in the lounge on the outskirts of the knowledgeable boys listening to them talking about Amateurs they have taken part in in the past. There is no limit to the scope or the accuracy of their reminiscences. They can recount, shot by shot, the details of every round they've played over the last five years, with sidelights on the exceptional good fortune, in moments of crisis, enjoyed by other distinguished players who beat them at Deal, Troon, Hoylake and everywhere else. Attempts by the non-tournament man to introduce subjects of a more general nature, like the plays of Ionesco, Picasso's ceramics or the convoluted literary style of Henry James meet with no success.

The alternative is to go to bed and get a good night's sleep, to be alert and fresh for the morrow. But before retiring it's obviously a good idea to get out the putter, and knock a few balls up and down the carpet.

There's a design of stripes on the carpet which, by a happy coincidence, clearly demonstrates whether or not the club-head is being taken back, and brought forward, square to the line of the tooth mug which has been placed on the floor in the opposite corner of the room. But, according to the stripes on the carpet, the club-head is coming back *outside* the line, while the follow-through finishes several inches to the left of the tooth mug, and must, indeed, have been doing so for years. It's still, however, only 9.15. There's ample time to work on it—

By 10 p.m. you're getting only one in six into the tooth mug, against a previous average as high as three. Also, the carpet is much faster than the greens are likely to be. You achieve the conviction that you're practising a putting stroke which will not only push it six inches to the right of the hole every time, but also leave it at least two yards short. Throw the putter back into the bag and get into bed and try to forget all about the stripes. Try, indeed, not to think about golf at all—

Five minutes later you're up, in bare feet and pyjamas, in front of the full-length mirror in the wardrobe, trying to see what it looks like if you really do pull the left hand *down* from the top of the swing, instead of shoving the right shoulder round. Suddenly, it feels right so you get the driver out of the bag and have a swish with it in front of the mirror and it demolishes an alabaster bowl concealing the light fitting in the ceiling. Clear it up and back into bed and try to think of some reasonable explanation for the chambermaid in the morning—

By midnight there's been another putting session—disastrous—and a spell of short chips into the wastepaper basket two of which, striking the door high up with an incredibly loud bang, provoked a thunderous and outraged knocking on the wall from the man next door. Back into bed—the feet are frozen—where you lie with the sheet up to the eyes wondering if the whole hotel has been roused and the manager, in his dressing-gown, will soon be in with a policeman, and they'll find you've smashed the alabaster bowl and knocked all the paint off the door and there's no explanation. None, except perhaps that you're playing in the Championship—or at it.

To sleep, perchance—except that it's an odds-on certainty—to dream. It's that very special nightmare, unhinging in its grinding frustration, of being on the first tee in the British Amateur Championship, except that the tee is enclosed by a small wooden shed and you're inside it and there's no room for your back-swing and in any case the tee-shot, supposing you could hit it, har got to emerge through a tiny window high up near the roof—

Stark, staring awake and the time is five to five. Get up and have a bath? It might be so weakening that the driver will fly out of your hand and blind Willie Turnesa. Read? The more interesting passages in *Lady Chatterly's Lover* would have the impact of *Eric, Or Little By Little*.

Perhaps the greens are as fast as—much faster than—the carpet. Has anyone, in the Amateur, ever taken four putts on each of the first nine holes?

If the quick hooking starts will six new balls be enough? Has anyone, in the Amateur, ever had to *buy* a ball off his opponent as early as the third hole? Is it allowed by the rules . . .?

The waiters are still laying the tables when you come down to breakfast, and the papers haven't arrived. To spread the meal out—it's only 7.30 a.m.—you order grapefruit, porridge, a kipper, bacon and eggs, coffee, toast and marmalade. Each item goes to join the previous one in what feels like a hot croquet-ball, lodged at the base of the throat.

The chambermaid does want to know what happened to the alabaster light fitting.

The car, left outside all night because the hotel garage is full, won't start.

The contestant for the British Amateur title is ready to—and does—go down without a struggle to a nineteen-year-old medical student from Glasgow University, pulling his own trolley, six and five.

For the 1949 Amateur, however, I not only had the comforting presence of my nearest and dearest around me after dark, to say nothing of free board and lodging, but also the benefit of the advice and counsel of Henry Longhurst, who was staying with us.

He was early in the field both with counsel and advice. Before going over to Portmarnock for the first round I had an hour loosening up at a course near my father's house, with Henry in attendance to see, even at this eleventh hour, if something couldn't be done to put things right.

At the end of the first fusillade he said, through clenched teeth, 'It's like watching a man scraping a knife against a pewter plate.'

Put out—some of them had finished on the fairway—I asked him to be more precise about his discomfort.

'You're trying to hit them round corners,' he said. 'It's agony to watch it.'

We conducted an interesting experiment. I stood up to the ball. Henry laid a club on the ground behind me, pointing in the direction which my stance suggested might be the eventual line of flight. When I came round to have a look I found to my surprise that I'd been aiming at a small shelter in the distance, perhaps fifty yards to the right of the true objective. 'Swivel the whole gun round,' said Coach, 'and try firing one straight.'

It seemed madness to tamper with the system now, and specially to try hitting one straight after years of hooking it back from the rough on the right. I tried it, however, just once. Aiming, it seemed to me, diagonally across the fairway to the left, I hit one straight down the middle, quail-high and all, perhaps, of a quarter of a mile.

'Right,' said Coach. 'We'll leave it at that. You've probably only got four more of those left.'

It looked as though four would be enough. My section of the draw was infested with Americans, mostly from Winged Foot—a distinction which suggested that they were all probably well above Walker Cup standard. I'd drawn someone called Udo Reinach, a threatening set of syllables presenting a picture of a crew-cut, All-American tackle weighing 210 lb. with a tee-shot like a naval gun. To remain with Udo for as many as twelve holes would surely see duty done.

I met him. He turned out to be Willie Turnesa's patron and protector who, as he said himself, had just come along for the ride. He was small and elderly and noticeably frail. In a ding-dong struggle, with no quarter given or asked, I beat him on the seventeenth by holing a long, up-hill putt which went off some time before I was ready for it. If we'd completed the course both would have been round in the middle eighties.

Next day I met another American, also from Winged Foot. I'd never been able to remember his name, but he was a friend of Udo's . Indeed, he'd known Udo for nearly forty years, which put him in the late sixties. He confessed to me that he had no serious intentions about the Championship at all, having merely come along on the ride that Udo was on, and—owing to latent heart condition—rather doubted his capacity to get round the whole of Portmarnock's 7000 yards.

He very nearly had to. I beat him with a four on the seventeenth by putting a 5-iron absolutely stiff after hitting my tee-shot straight along the ground.

It was gratifying to see a line in one of the Dublin evening papers: 'In the lower half of the draw Campbell, a local player, is steadily working his way through the American menace.'

By the following evening I'd got through another round. I can't remember his name either, but I know he was a Dublin man who was about half my size and capable of playing, on the very top of his game, to a handicap in the region of nine. Coach summed up the situation at dinner that night. 'No one,' he said, 'since the inauguration of the Amateur has ever had it easier for the first three rounds. It's a pity, in a way, it's over now.'

He was referring, graciously, to the fact that I was to meet Billy O'Sullivan in the morning, in the fourth round.

Billy, who was well known to me, had been Irish Amateur Champion so often that it didn't seem possible he hadn't turned pro. With a two-handed, black-smith's grip he hit it farther off the tee than anyone in Ireland. A Killarney man himself, he'd brought two-thirds of that fiercely partisan area with him, to assist in the laying waste to the city of Dublin which would automatically follow his almost certain victory in the final on Saturday afternoon.

I was devoid of hope. My coach—creator with Valentine Castlerosse of the Killarney Golf Club—had transferred his loyalties without equivocation to the local man, even inviting me to share his pleasure in contemplation of the beating that Billy, with his fine, free, slashing Killarney swing, would hand out to the plodding, mechanical, American methods of Willie Turnesa. 'We want him fresh,' were my coach's last words of advice, 'so don't keep him out there too long—not that you will.'

By the eleventh hole it looked as though Billy would be back in the club-house for a long and leisured lunch. He was four up, and on a loose rein. I was aiming the gun right out over the head of mid-wicket and hauling it so far back around the corner that time after time it finished up in the sandhills on the left. We were unattended by an audience. Even the camp-followers from Killarney were drink-ing stout in the bar, preparing themselves for the rigours of the O'Sullivan-Turnesa final.

Abruptly—and I can't remember how—Billy came to pieces. I got two holes back, so that on the fourteenth tee he was two up with five to go, a margin still sufficiently large, it seemed to me, not to leave the result in doubt.

Then something extraordinary happened. The fourteenth is a long, narrow green sloping up into the sandhills, with several cavernous bunkers in front. You couldn't play short and if you were over you'd a vile, slippery chip all down-hill on a green burnt brown and ten miles an hour faster than any hotel carpet. On the left, however, pin-high, was a patch of short rough into which I'd hooked all three previous second shots, by accident. They had remained there, however, leaving a comparatively simple scuffle up to the hole.

It would, if nothing else, be interesting to see if I could put it into the rough on purpose. For the first time—not having dared to try the innovation before—I swivelled the gun, played left of the green and it stayed there, a combination of almost unbelievable circumstances.

Billy, outside me as usual, played a beautiful iron shot which hit the middle of the green, ran up the slope and disappeared over the top edge. His chip back slid eight feet past. He missed the putt. I holed a shortish one for a four, to be only one down. Even in the white-hot glow of having played a hole with the loaf, and having seen Billy making the obvious mistake, I still regarded it merely as a postponement of the inevitable three and two defeat that was coming my way—particularly in view of the nature of the fifteenth.

It's a short hole—about 170 yards—from a raised tee on the edge of the beach to a green sunk in sandhills, with jungle country all round and a deep hollow on the left. A brisk breeze was blowing off the sea, straight across. A further assurance of disaster was provided by the presence of Laddie Lucas and, I think—my eyesight was beginning to go—Gerald Micklem, an expert audience ready to enjoy to the full, a high, looping hook which would not be seen again or, alternatively, a furtive, defensive socket on to the beach.

One—or both—of them remarked that they were glad to see I'd got so far, in view of the fact that rumour had it we'd been back in the club-house for quite some time. No disarmingly modest response occurred to me. An uncontrollable but still faint trembling had started in my legs, more or less guaranteeing a shank. I struck at it quickly with a 3-iron. It travelled low and straight into the cross-wind, and finished six feet from the hole. Incredulous laughter, instantly and graciously muffled, broke from Messrs Lucas and Micklem. Billy, holding his too far up into the wind, finished on the right-hand edge. His putt was short. Playing for a certain half from six feet, I put mine into the hole, and we were all square. As we walked down to the sixteenth tee Billy, possibly echoing a thought put into his mind by Lucas and Micklem, made his first remark for some time, 'I don't know how you do it,' he said.

I couldn't have told him, even if he'd really wanted to know. I was too busy trying to think of a method, based upon past experience, which would put my tee-shot on the fairway, and at least 200 yards away. The sixteenth is a long par-5, and grouped around the distant green were something like five hundred people, waiting for the close finishes. For reasons of personal dignity and self respect I had no desire to intrude into their company, having already played four.

The knee-trembling was becoming more acute, very similar, in fact, to the time when as a child of ten I was menaced by armed members of the I.R.A. My only desire was that the match should be over, one way or the other. No trace of the killer instinct had established itself, although I'd won four holes in a row.

It felt like a fairly good one, though the follow-through was curtailed because long after I'd hit it I was still looking at the ground. It turned out to have been low and rather hooky, but on the hard ground it had gone quite a long way. Billy hit a rasper right down the middle.

Then, as we walked off the tee, we saw an extraordinary thing—a spectacle like an infantry regiment, charging towards us. It was the five hundred people— probably two hundred of them from Killarney—who'd been waiting round the green. Instinct seemed to have warned them that a Homeric struggle—I was thinking like a golf correspondent—was in progress, and they wanted to be in on the kill.

They engulfed us. I lost sight of Billy, over to the right. I became conscious of an excited steward, dragging a length of rope. 'Jaysus—' he cried—'I never thought I'd be doin' this for you!' He put down the rope and I stepped over it. 'Get back there!' he bawled at the crowd. 'Back there now, an' give him room!'

The ball was lying just on the edge of the rough, but nicely cocked up. People were standing round it in a semi-circle, five deep, craning in death-like silence to see over one another's heads. Hundreds more, lining the fairway, made it look like a long, solid tunnel to the green. It had the curious effect of promoting confidence, so many people expecting to see it go straight.

I took a long, slow swing with a 3-wood, making it look right for the audience. There was a lovely whip off the shaft, but I never saw where it went. They were after it, almost before I'd hit it. All I saw was a mass of backs running away from me. My caddy and I were left alone. He was a young and inexperienced lad, as staggered as I was that we'd got so far. 'I never seen a t'ing,' he said.

Billy and I were both short, left and right, though I only knew where he was by the crowd around him. Someone told me it was my shot, and asked me the score. I found I didn't know.

I'd a fifty-yard chip, up to the hole. Again the crowd, pressing in, seemed to narrow down the possibilities of error. I left it two feet from the hole. Then the running backs hid it from me again, forming a solid, brightly coloured wall round the green. I'd quite a job to push through them, to find that Billy was about four feet away. Both of us holed our putts. Before mine dropped the gallery were running for the next tee.

It was still my honour. The ball was looking dingy and scuffed, after the hard, sandy fairways, but in a peculiar way I felt it was part of me, that it knew what we were trying to do. Nothing could have made me change it for a new one. We were both in this together, and what we were trying to do was to beat hell out of Billy O'Sullivan, for whom I'd suddenly conceived such a hatred that I could scarcely wait to bash one down the middle so far that he'd jump at his and please God leave himself with an unplayable lie in a bush.

We were both down the middle. As I walked slowly and shakily after the running backs, now seemingly multiplied by four, I was accosted by a well-spoken stranger. 'Are you all right?' he asked me. He appeared strangely concerned. 'Yeah,' I said. 'Yes.' He looked at me for a long moment. 'You look,' he said, 'as if you're going to faint.' I saw for the first time that it was my father. 'I'm all right,' I told him, and walked on.

We were both on in two. We both got our four. We walked in silence to the eighteenth tee—all square and one to go.

It took a long time before the stewards were able to clear the course. It was round about lunch time. People were pouring out of the club-house and the beer tents, running for positions of vantage. In a championship all square and one to go will cause any true golf enthusiast even to put down his bottle of stout, and come out and have a look.

The eighteenth at Portmarnock is a nasty one. A long, high mound on the left means you've got to keep your tee-shot well out on the right, to get a view of the green, and even then there's a rise in front of it which stops you seeing more than the top half of the pin.

I stood up to the ball, still having the honour. All hatred of Billy O'Sullivan had subsided, having given way to a bone-cracking weariness in which whatever mental processes were still alive were focused upon the immediate warming and soothing after-effects of two large Irish whiskeys in one glass.

I was shifting the club-head about, trying to get a grip with the left hand which would push the ball out to the right, away from the mound on the other side, when someone let out a roar that froze me solid. 'Fore—' he bawled—'ya silly ole bitch!'

I looked up—and saw an elderly woman, her wits deranged by scores of shouted, contrary instructions, scurrying about in the middle of the fairway, like a rabbit fleeting from two thousand dogs. A friend or relative fell upon her, and dragged her away to safety. I started all over again. A moment later, playing with the greatest care and concentration, I hooked my tee-shot straight into the base of the mound.

'Bad luck,' said Billy. It seemed to me that his rugged features were irradiated by an expression of gentle, brotherly love. The swine hit a beauty, a mile long and out on the right, giving him an easy 6-iron to the green.

I was sloping after the running backs again, trying to calculate the minutes that remained between me and the two large Irish, when I found myself confronted by H. Longhurst, my patron and coach, of whom I'd seen nothing during the heat of the day. 'You're doing well,' he said pleasantly. 'Why not try winning, for a change?'

'Go,' I told him, 'and set them up inside. Plain water with mine.' Knowledgeable man that he is, he walked away.

It wasn't lying too badly but, being under the mound, I couldn't see the green. I took out a 5-iron and hit it high into the air. It felt fairly all right, but the gallery put me straight. They let out a great cry of, 'Oooh—!' on a descending scale, indicating beyond doubt that we were up to the ears in radishes, for the first time for six holes.

I'd no idea where it was and still hadn't when I reached the green, which was hemmed in by the largest crowd I'd ever seen. There was no trace of the ball or, indeed, of anyone who seemed to know where it might be found. I pushed through the people massed in front of me and then heard a disordered shouting away to the left. Someone over there was waving a small red flag on the end of a long pole. I was in a deep bunker so far off the line, and so little used, that it was full of scattered stones and weeds growing up through the sand.

I went in after it. It was lying all right, clear at least of the stones. It was only then that I remembered Billy, and the important part that he was playing in the proceedings. I asked someone what had happened to him. He didn't know. General conjecture and speculation broke out. Several people thought he'd put it stiff. Others believed he was out of bounds, in the garden of the club-house. In the middle of all this a man, carrying a ham sandwich and a cardboard glass of stout, came running over the hill, his face suffused with excitement. 'He's up to his doodlers in the pot bunker!' he bawled. 'Ye've got him cold!'

For the second time, in this last, vital hole, I was about to play a shot without being able to see the pin—a fair commentary, I had time to remark, upon the accuracy of my method under pressure. I climbed out to have a look and saw Billy, already standing in the deep pot bunker cut into the right-hand edge of the green. The pin was only a few yards away from him. He'd have to play a miraculous one to get his four. If I could scuffle mine out and take only two putts, we'd very shortly be starting off down the first again, drawing farther and farther away from the healing malt in the bar.

I climbed down into the bunker again. The only unforgivable thing would be to leave it there. Expelling every breath of air from my lungs that might build up unwanted pressure, I swung the club-head slowly back and equally slowly forward. It nipped the ball rather sweetly. It disappeared over the brow of the hill.

When I pushed through the crowd and walked on to the green I knew at once which was mine. It was four feet from the hole, a not impossible, dead straight putt, slightly uphill. Billy was three or four yards past it. No one could have got any closer out of that pot bunker, with a burnt-up green.

He had a horrible curly one with a six-inch borrow all down the side of the hill. He missed it.

I can remember exactly how I holed mine. I gripped the putter so tightly that it was impossible to break the wrists, and shoved it straight in. So incalculable are the workings of the human mind that I knew, even under that nerve-crinkling pressure, that I couldn't miss.

I don't remember anything at all about the next half-hour. There must have been a great deal of pleasure in assuring people in the bar that I had, in fact, beaten Billy O'Sullivan. The opportunity must have arisen for the extra pleasure of telling them, in part, how. There must also have been the extreme physical joy of the corrosive malt, slowly seeping through the system shaky and dehydrated by tension, fear and the need to discipline muscles jumpy and wayward as jelly. It's all a blur, but I do remember the thing that suddenly gave it edge and shape. It was the reminder, by someone who'd just bought me another large one, that I had, within the hour, to go out and do it again.

from *Patrick Campbell's Golfing Book*, Blond & Briggs (UK)

THOMSON v LOCKE   Peter Thomson

There is a great deal of monotony about four days of stroke play. For one thing it doesn't get really tense and exciting until the last hour or two of the fourth day. Matches are entertaining from the first ball hit.

I have enjoyed the matches I have been fortunate enough to play and many others too that I have witnessed. I would like to see much more of it scheduled. Promoters and spectators alike would get more from it.

A match as distinct from a round of stroke play is a much more personal clash between the two that are engaged. Assuming the form of both is somewhere near similar, the stronger personality will invariably come out on top.

Of course there are variations and accidents, but in principle in a match your opponent has a big influence on the way you perform. Unless you can somehow exclude him from your attention.

I received a great training in matchplay by learning the hard way. I had played some amateur golf which in those days was always matchplay, but in 1951 Bobby Locke invited me to South Africa for the summer. It was a marvellous opportunity for a young professional like me to sit at the feet of the great man, for at that time he was undisputed champion of the British world and it could have been strongly debated whether Hogan or Locke was the master.

Indeed he was very very kind to me and apart from getting an insight into the mind of a big winner, it was also possible to study his technique.

By the time I got back home I was a much wiser boy and by 1954 I had won the Open myself. In the summer of 1956 he invited me back again, this time for a head to head series of 47 matches that took us all over South Africa and Rhodesia. Some matches were long but most were one-day games over courses strange to me.

I will never forget some of the finishes we had. For a start I would strain so hard to win I would tie myself in a knot. Out of the first fourteen matches he won eleven of them and at that stage I had to take stock.

With nothing more of my reputation to lose I began to sit back and watch what was happening, and suddenly it all became clear. I was trying to beat him and he just sat back and let me beat myself.

I was trying to outdrive him, out-approach him and out-putt him. It was all too much of a strain and I succeeded in nothing.

At that stage I took up a new attitude and relaxed and tried nothing except to keep out of the trees and stick to par. *I struck oil.*

Locke always played in a 'uniform' of white shoes, plus-fours, a white dress shirt with the sleeves rolled up and a club tie.

It was most impressive and he always looked the complete professional to his fingertips. He also looked a superior figure which destroyed a good many of his opponents by annoyance.

Normally he was completely unflappable even in the crises but our matches took a new twist.

I gave away no holes to him by impetuosity. I made him earn every one he chalked to my deficit, and suddenly I found myself being generously served with 'presents'.

I won the next eleven matches or tied them and at last we were equals. In the end of the tour he won 22 to my 21 and considering his home ground advantage I felt it was a good result.

I had learned a great deal about matchplay.

from *This Wonderful World of Golf*, Pelham Books (UK)

PATTON v JACK   Pat Ward-Thomas

In 1957 I spent six weeks in North America. It was an endless pursuit of golf, much of which has now receded into memory's remotest corners, but there was one unforgettable day. The Walker Cup match was played at Minikhada, deep in the land of Hiawatha where all the names have the sound of running water. The course was poised in woods by the edge of a handsome lake and on the second day sunshine poured mercilessly down, humidity was fierce and the warmth beneath the trees exhausting. At lunch-time I had little inclination for food; a hamburger and a cup of coffee, when the morning play was done, were all that I could face because, apart from the heat, there was an extraordinary feeling abroad—that the British Isles could win the match. I could not bear to miss any of the afternoon play, and waste the time in idle talk or unwelcome eating, so I hastened through the trees once more to join the leading match in which Reid Jack had lunched five up on Billy Joe Patton.

The overall position was that the British needed five points from the eight singles for their first victory in the United States. Jack had given a magnificent start with his lead over Patton; Carr, Thirlwell, Wolstenholme, and Bussell were within a hole of their opponents and Sewell and Scrutton were recovering. It seemed too good to be true that Britain could win, and one hardly dared let the thought linger in the mind, but as I hurried on I felt the stirring of rare excitement. Before any possibility of victory could become a probability Jack and Carr, in the first two matches, had to win. Surely Jack could not fail after being five up on a man who had been at variance with his game all morning, and as I caught up with the match on the third green I hoped that Jack would still be at least five up. I was just in time to watch him take three putts, and lose the hole, and then heard that he had lost the first two as well. This was frightening news, and my heart sank as I watched Patton, with his sudden quick stride, walk from the green as if his body had been charged with an electric current.

If ever there was a golfer of inspiration it is Patton. His golf, as inevitably it must be with his lightning swing, often undergoes the most remarkable variations. Sometimes his game is indifferent, even poor, but once let him feel the quickening of inspiration, then everybody can watch out. For many years he has finished high in the Masters at Augusta, playing against the finest golfers in the world. His temperament responded to the great occasion and in these moods he was capable of beating anyone, and was not afraid of doing so. In 1954 he went into the last round several strokes behind Hogan and Snead but on the sixth holed his tee shot, and then was away on a tremendous challenge to the two great golfers. Had he not chosen to go for a long carry over water at the thirteenth, and played safely for a five, he would probably have won or at worst joined the tie in which the next day Snead beat Hogan by a stroke. But safety play was alien to the heart of Patton. He tried boldly for his four, the ball dropped into the water and he took a seven, but he finished only a stroke behind. The same year he was sixth in the Open championship.

Augusta suited Patton because there is room there from the tees, and he could unleash that whipping explosion of a swing of his without the feeling of restraint that other courses impose. Minikhada was different. The holes wind their way through avenues of trees, and there is little margin for the errors that Patton was almost incapable of avoiding. And yet on this August afternoon the trees did not matter for he gave one of the most lethal, and in the circumstances diabolical exhibitions of recovery play that I ever expect to see. In the art of emerging from seemingly impossible places he must rank with the greatest of all; with Ted Ray, Hagen, Bruen, Carr and the rest. This ability is undoubtedly valuable in stroke play; in a match it can be terribly disconcerting to an opponent in whom hope and fear are kept in constant conflict. This can undo the finest concentration, and Jack that afternoon endured one of the cruellest experiences a golfer could have on such an occasion.

Admittedly he was at fault in allowing Patton to win the first three holes after lunch and give that dangerous man hope of a reprieve. Two indifferent second shots and a missed putt did the damage, but in spite of these mistakes Jack never allowed the rhythm of his beautiful swing to falter, nor his composure to be disturbed, and still could have won the match. Two halves steadied him and then Patton struck, with a superb iron shot to the sixth and a good putt. Now Jack was only one up but British eyes were joyful once more when Patton cut his shot from the seventh tee into the woods, and Jack hit a perfect drive to the centre of the narrow dog-leg fairway. Patton found his ball playable, and in this he was fortunate for it might have been hard against a tree, but it did lie in heavy rough and at first there seemed to be no possible way in which he could reach the green. Meanwhile Jack had hit a long iron shot to within fifteen feet of the flag and must have felt, while waiting for Patton to prospect the situation, that he would become two up again. This was the kernel of the whole match.

If Jack did win the hole the relentless stream of Patton's recovery would have been dammed, and perhaps the light of inspiration would have gone from his golf. In any event Jack then would have been able to attack his man once again, knowing that he had a hole in hand as precious insurance against losing the lead. Patton, too, with his quick intelligence must also have appreciated how important it was not to lose a hole at this tense, psychological point of the match. His only line to the green, some 180 yards distant, was between two trees, one close to him and the other a few yards away, and the ball lay in clinging, lush grass. He took a four iron, his swing flashed, and the ball drilled through the gap and finished just over the green. I have never seen a greater recovery shot but, and this was not unlike Patton, he fluffed the little chip from behind the green and was still outside Jack. Then cruelly he holed the putt. Jack just missed his for the win; Patton had escaped with an outrageous half, and most important of all his confidence was unimpaired, even increased. Two holes later the match was square after Patton had hit two cracking wooden club shots up the hill of the ninth. It was about then that I passed Charles Coe, the American captain. He is not a man of great outward expression, and there is a coldness to his face that belies the quiet charm beneath, but this time there was a bleak anxious look as well, and with good reason.

Whilst the handful of British supporters had been suffering the agonies of the damned watching Jack, great things had been happening behind. Philip Scrutton, after trailing all day, had drawn level with Rudolph, and Alan Bussell was keeping his nose in front of Joe Campbell. Far away at the end Wolstenholme, playing with a majestic poise, was taking command of Hillman Robbins who was to become American champion a fortnight later, and Carr was still all square.

This was the position with only five or six holes to play in each of these matches, save Wolstenholme's, and he was plainly going to win. It did not matter that Thirlwell and Deighton were foundering. If these five could succeed then the match was won. Even though this may have been straining expectation too far, then at least there would be the satisfaction of hunting the Americans to a desperate finish, the like of which they had never known in their own land.

The outcome was most disappointing and again the villain was Billy Joe. On the thirtieth hole, with the game still all square, Jack played two beautiful shots to within three yards of the hole. Patton, after pushing his drive far out, somehow recovered but was still in rough near the green. However he got down in two and Jack missed his putt for a win. The next hole, an enormous downhill affair with a little lake in front of the green, was even worse for Britain. Jack played it straight in a conventional par five; Patton pulled from the tee then sliced a tremendous iron shot high on to a bank to the right of the green. He was left with a horribly difficult shot from an awkward lie but chipped it to the side of the hole and was one up. All this must have strained Jack's competitive endurance and patience to its very limits, but he is a man of steel and resource, and his glorious swing was there to sustain him.

The next two holes were exchanged but Patton was still one up as they came to the thirty-fourth. Yet again he missed the fairway and was deep in the rough with steep trees between him and the green. It really did seem that he was fixed but his incredible strength enabled him to cut the ball out of the heavy grass, carry the trees and finish a few feet from the hole. Then at last Jack had a break. Patton missed his putt, the ball stopping right on the lip of the hole and helping Jack, who bravely holed. All square again and we thought that the ends of justice, from the British viewpoint, would be served with a halved match at worst, but Jack's judgment for once failed him. A cross bunker guarded the green and the hole was cut only a few yards beyond. Playing first he had to be up but his pitch was overhit to the very back of the green. Patton, from the rough, of course, although just off the fairway's edge, played a masterly wedge shot, cut out with that fantastically swift hand action of his, which pitched and held within range for a certain four. This was good enough, for Jack, faced with a huge downhill putt at the end of an exhausting day, could not get it close. His next one rimmed the hole and a half at the last gave Patton a wonderful victory.

The man's courage and flair for the unexpected were astonishing and obviously he had loved every moment of it. A lively spirit, that shines at you through his glasses, and rings in the swift flow of his southern voice, belongs to no ordinary person. His is a rare character that thrives on challenge; the situations he faced time after time in that match with Jack were manna to him; the feel of the people expectant and wondering; the challenge to his strength and ingenuity, and the responsibility of his match in the whole scheme of the day, all these things brought forth the finest and the most fortunate that were within his powers. Had the match been in an early round of a championship, with few people watching, I have not the slightest doubt that Jack would have murdered him. Two years later at Muirfield he did beat him easily but then the American cause had been won the first day, with four points from the foursomes, and, although Patton would be trying his utmost to win, there was nothing to give him that deadly surge of inspiration.

from *Masters of Golf*, William Heinemann (UK)

PALMER v. ALLISS   Peter Alliss

Sure enough the many people who had visualized a Palmer *v* Alliss match got just that. We came out third in the list of each team, and so I was to go in against the British Open Champion.

If you can ever describe any man as 'the greatest golfer in the world', I suppose it was Palmer, the man who had picked up the mantle of Ben Hogan. It is difficult to put down clearly what my thoughts were at the time. I know I thought back to David Thomas, two years earlier at Palm Desert, waiting for the draw and saying 'I'm sure to get Snead, sure to get Snead.' David worshipped Snead, held him in such awe that he convinced himself that it would be impossible to beat him. David was beaten by 6 and 5. I did not imagine there was anyone alive who could beat me 6 and 5, and I told myself I would do my very best and play my very best and he will have to play damn well to beat me. I was probably nervous in a definite and positive way at the prospect of playing Palmer, but at the same time rather proud to be part of what was obviously going to be the 'big' match next day. Strangely, I am never afraid of playing the very good players. I always play well against the top men, and am more likely to play badly against an unknown player, or in what appear to be ordinary straightforward matches. I have been beaten by many lesser lights in match play championships!

The match was very interesting in many ways and for many reasons, and I think it is worth setting out in some detail. Lytham you could call a classic links course, but a lush links, a good half-mile from the sea—and more than a mile at low tide!—and therefore without the terribly tight, fast grass one can find at St Andrews or Troon or Hoylake. This was October in morning misty weather with a mild afternoon sun each day, so there was plenty of growth on the course and the greens were in fine, velvety condition. The plan of the course runs south-easterly, the first nine running more or less straight down the railway line, the second nine zig-zagging back inside them. The first half was more or less into the wind. At Lytham the first hole is just over 200 yards.

We both hit good 4-iron shots into the green, two-putted. At the 2nd, we both left our approach shots short. Palmer chipped and one-putted from about eight feet, I chipped and two-putted, he went one up. At the 3rd, 456 yards, playing long into the wind, I hit a fine 4-wood second just short of the green after hitting the fairway plumb centre with a good drive. Palmer hit a long drive with a bit of draw or even a slight hook on it that just took it into the rough on the left. He then smashed a long iron of some kind and cut it away to the right, between the bunkers towards the railway line. I chipped on about five feet away and holed for the four. He hit a wedge about twelve feet from the flag but missed the putt and we were square. I was surprised to find over these early holes that he was not really any longer than I was. Palmer's swing is tremendously intense, an action that bristles with explosive power, and he has a habit of looking so tense and intense that it becomes almost frightening. All this gives a watcher the feeling that nobody in history has ever hit a golf ball as far as Arnold Palmer does, but in fact at least on five occasions in the round I took less club than he did to hit the greens. At the 4th, again two fine drives were followed by a lovely wedge shot from me, two and a half feet from the hole, and one from Arnold six or seven yards away. I holed, he missed. One up. At the short 5th, 188 yards, we were both on with 6-iron shots, each made two putts. After we had reached our drives up the sixth fairway, I felt this might be a critical hole. Palmer again had drawn his drive just slightly into the rough on the left. I was well placed on the right side of the fairway, but probably further from the flag because of the dog-leg turn to the left. I hit a good 4-wood, going towards the right-hand front corner of the green and as the ball left the club I felt it had just a chance to make the green. The sixth hole features an undulating fairway, then some cross-bunkers and a largish hollow in front of a mound green. Palmer in the rough took his 4-wood and tried to hit a real big shot, forcing it up wind to try to pitch the green. Instead he hooked it way left, into the rough fifty yards from the hole, a good forty yards from the green. From there he played a very good pitch—it took a lot of time and he had to move a lot of people—and two-putted for his five. When I reached my ball, I had just slid into a bunker, right and short of the green. I got it out, about eight feet away, but could not quite make the putt. Halved hole; Alliss one up. One third of the round had gone. Palmer was a charming, open, free, unaffected opponent. The crowd was swelling and storming along with us. I felt my game was going well. Palmer was by no means out-gunning me.

The 7th, the longest hole on the course at 553 yards, was a very long hole into what had become quite a strong wind. We each hit two very good shots and were still well short. I took the more direct line, down the right side, but it left me with a tighter shot into the green. Left with quite a firm pitch, I didn't play it very well, but thought it would come down off a big bank on the right side of the green. It didn't. Arnold pitched a good one, but went about four feet over the green off the putting surface. I chipped down to about four feet from the hole. He took his putter from off the green—and holed it. This was the first of three times on the round when Palmer took no putts. He holed a chip shot at the 10th, and holed a bunker shot at the 15th. For me, a putt is only a putt when the ball is on the putting surface. In other words when you are in a position where you can clean your ball. If you can't clean the ball you can't say you're on the green and vice-versa. However, that squared the match. At the 8th, we both hit fair drives. I was a little left, but in a good position. I hit a good punch with a 5-iron into the wind and up to a high plateau green (the hole is 394 yards) finishing seven or eight yards short of the hole. Palmer about fifteen yards in front of me with the drive, tried to punch up a 4-iron and went over the green by some ten yards. He half-fluffed the chip back. I putted stone dead, six inches from the hole, he missed and Alliss was one up again.

The short 9th was halved in three, and on this hole Palmer had the edge. I hit a 7-iron into a bunker on the right, splashed out and somehow willed in the putt from five feet. He was in the middle of the green nicely, but took two putts. Alliss one up at the turn. At the 336-yard 10th, he hooked his pitch and went through some three or four yards, into rough about nine inches thick. I pitched a fine shot not much more than a yard from the flag, and marked my ball, whereupon this man chips out of the rough, on to a down-sloping green and straight into the hole. My yard putt suddenly seemed to stretch a long way from the hole, but I made it. Eleventh hole, 483 yards, good drives, good second shots with the 3-iron, two putts each, halved. Short 12th, both hit 8-iron shots on to green, two putts each. Thirteenth, Palmer down the fairway, Alliss bunkered on the right from the tee. From there, I played a super shot with an 8-iron right into the green. It was a shallow bunker, the ball was lying fairly well and the sand had been beaten down hard. I hit the ball right off the sand. In that situation I always make a conscious effort to keep my head down. The trick is to hit the ball as hard as you can, but look hard at it, try to see the club-head go through the ball. In bunker shots like this, especially long-range bunker shots, you can drive the ball underneath the lip of the bunker if you look up too quickly. Both on, two putts, another halved hole. At the 14th, we both rather under-clubbed our approaches, thinking the ball would run down farther in each case, but each chipped and missed the first putt from around ten feet. Another half, this time in five.

Now came the 15th, where Palmer halved the match. Two good drives. Palmer hooked the second into bunker left of green. Alliss good shot just short of green, five feet short of right front corner. I chipped the ball four feet from the hole. Palmer got himself well planted in the bunker, opened up the blade of his sand iron and hit hard right underneath his ball. It came flying out, took one bounce on the green, and pitched straight into the hole. If his ball had missed or clipped the side of the pin, it would have finished at least eight feet away. I must have looked very rueful. I felt very rueful. But then, in golf as in all other sports, these things happen. It occurs to me only now that this may well have been the true finish to our match. We both played the last three holes as though subconsciously we knew this. At the 16th, drives, pitches, each almost but not quite holed for birdies from a dozen feet. At 17th, good drives, 6-iron shots, Palmer twelve feet left, Alliss ten feet behind. He putted two inches to the right, I putted two inches short, bang in the centre of the hole. All square, one to play. Palmer hit a real corker of a drive far down the fairway. I hit mine left to drift it back but it did not come. It pitched over the bunkers but went into the semi-rough and was sitting about two inches off the ground. I told myself I must hit very hard at it with the wedge, but as I feared, I skidded under it a bit and left the ball six yards short of the green, with the pin set right at the back. Palmer pitches on, about half a dozen yards short of the hole and we started that final fateful trek to the green, with the red sandstone clubhouse looming above it, at the end of a tunnel of people lining the fairway and hooding the green.

Filling my mind as I walked to the green was the thought of 'here we go again, another one hole defeat'. If you care to dredge through the Ryder Cup records you will see that in all the matches I have played I have lost by something like twelve holes, twelve in ten matches. The possibility of another narrow defeat made me persuade myself furiously, 'Come on, come on, you can do it—something really good here. If he is to beat you make sure he has to do it with a birdie.' I had a chip of about forty yards to the flag. As I walked from the ball to the flag, I saw the windows of the clubhouse brimming with people, and sitting right there, in the centre window was my father. I took a 9-iron and hit the ball sweet as a nut. As it ran up the green I thought, 'That's going to be pretty good.' When I looked again, I thought, 'My God, it's going in the hole!' It certainly looked like doing just that, but it had just a little too much steam. It caught the side of the hole and broke twenty inches past the flag. There was a prodigious cheer from the crowd. I would have hated to have lost the last hole and the match to a four on the last green. I would have hated to have lost such a match in any way, but losing to a birdie on the last green is perhaps a little less tragic, especially to a fine opponent like Palmer. In goes Palmer for his birdie putt, and true to his character, he gave the ball a really big crash, and missed, and went thirty inches past the hole. He gave me my putt, and I took it thankfully. In my mind I was not savouring moving that ball over twenty inches of lawn. To this day, it has bothered me what I should have done in the little situation that followed. He had a quick look across at me, standing on one side. I didn't say anything. Palmer has a very fierce look sometimes and now he looked livid, perhaps because he had not won the match. I decided he was angry because he had missed the putt. Knowing him now, I would say that was the reason. I was thinking in a woolly way, 'Well, I have done reasonably well, he has not beaten me.' Palmer was lining up his short putt and I kept thinking, 'He might miss—I might still win.' He got right over the ball in the Palmer crouch when quite suddenly something inside me made me say, 'That's all right Arnold, pick it up.' And he did. He looked up, and picked the ball up and the crowd broke into a storm of applause. I said, 'That's all right, we have had a good match, let's leave it at that.' We shook hands and walked off. Very many people commented on this finish, coming up to me and saying, 'You have made a lot of friends today,' 'True sporting spirit,' and so on, but I wondered. I wondered what they would have said if I had been in Palmer's position, and had to make the putt, and failed. That would have been Wentworth all over again. It makes one think about this business of international sport. I had become wrapped up in the match. For a time I had probably forgotten that we were playing for the Ryder Cup and I was involved in the business of playing against this individual man without a thought of much else. I respected Palmer as a fine player trying to play his best, trying to beat me. And I think he respected me in the same way. We had a fine match and it ended square and there was satisfaction enough in that, at least for me.

But seeing Palmer crouched like a lion over that last putt made me think of international sport and the naïve things that are said of it, the ridiculous values that are put on it. Far too much importance is placed on winning or losing when in fact it is of no great importance. Sport is a legitimate part of the character of a nation and its cultural expression, and international sport grows inevitably and quite naturally and properly out of the simple fact of national sport, but whether or not the British win the Ryder Cup, or England wins the Ashes or Wimbledon, is scarcely going to affect the march of human progress. It will not have the slightest influence on the Berlin situation, for example, or the United Nations or outer space or the underprivileged nations of the world, or of the writing of books or plays or symphonies—all the truly great issues which confront the world. The Press, radio and television, the media that beat the drum and fly the flag and to a great extent condition the minds of the public to believe that international sport is important, would be doing a service if they got the thing in proportion.

In this case, when they wrote, 'Alliss halves with Palmer,' I felt they got that, too, slightly wrong. There is no doubt in my mind that it was Arnie who got the half. He had holed a chip shot. He had holed a bunker shot, first bounce. On three greens he had had no putt at all. It was Palmer who had halved with Alliss. I was a little hurt when I heard what Palmer said to some journalists at lunch. He was sitting at the next table to me, the American players table, and he rather implied that he had played badly that morning. He probably meant that he had not hit the ball quite as he wanted to. He had hooked two or three drives, over-clubbed twice, but I felt he might have been a little more graceful about it. I was sure that if I had been in his place, I would have been stupid enough to say, 'Well, I was rather fortunate to get a half because I did so and so.' For a moment I had the impression that Palmer was saying that if he had hit them straight he would have won 5 and 4, which I was convinced he never could have done. Then I got to thinking that all these top players are like this. They seldom *do* anything wrong—it is always something that happens *to them*.

from *Alliss Through the Looking Glass*, Cassell & Co (UK)

A SORT OF A GOLF MATCH   Michael Hobbs

Well now, not all golf matches are of epic quality. So for a change of mood let me tell you all about how I got through the first round of the world's largest golf competition. Yes the *largest*. *The Daily Mirror* 1975 North of England Amateur Golf Tournament had just a touch short of 6,000 entries. I was one of those in April hoping not to disgrace myself too utterly in the first round from one of the six qualifying areas. By around the end of October I might be the one to qualify for the 16-player final.

The start was not encouraging. It had rained steadily all day and insomniacs remarked that it had been doing much the same all through the previous night as well. When I got up to the venue—my own course, Beamish Park—it was awash. However, the course had not been closed for that affects bar takings very badly indeed. Instead, the beginning and the end sections were closed. This meant that the match would have to be staged from the 4th to the 13th and then round again, missing something or other out so that there should be 18 holes rather than 20.

My opponent and I had a brief discussion beforehand as to how we should adjust the open parts of the course to the requirements of playing 18 holes. A very sensible agreement was reached by which we would, on the second trip round, miss out the 5th and 6th. They meant walking 452 yards out and then 505 back again.

As we went to the 1st hole (I'd best stop talking about the 1st which was really the 4th and so on from this point) the loudest noises were caused by the gentle popping of bubbles in the subsoil and the squelch of our feet. No one else was playing. It was obvious that the course must be closed.

Most handicap golfers have a tendency to slice their wood shots and hook irons. For some reason, I do the reverse. My 4 iron to the 160 yard 1st, which I hit about one time in eight did its usual thing. Quite nicely struck, started off right of the green (I'm lefthanded) began to slice in nicely towards the flag and kept on slicing until it was pin high and 20 yards off to the left. With a bunker between me and the hole. My opponent was probably encouraged by this and hit his shot with an elegant follow-through. It shanked quickly 40 yards away to the right. A half in 4 it was after adequate pitches and two putts from each of us. The 2nd hole is stroke index 1 and with good cause. It is a par 4 measuring 450 yards and the tee shot has to be hit very firmly indeed if there is to be a vestige of hope of reaching the green with the second shot. The reason for this is that the green is at the top of a steep rise and, if your driver second does not pitch directly onto it, you will roll back down to the bottom of the slope and have a full wedge shot up, and hopefully over, the brow of the hill.

Both of us were reasonably near the hole in three shots but he was receiving a stroke from me here. After two putts each, he was one up.

At the next, he played a good chip to go two ahead and after three halved holes he holed a long putt to be three up. By now, the rain had returned. Soon putting was a matter of observing the casual water on every green, going through a performance of trying to move your ball to a line that was not blocked by puddles, and then giving up and thrusting the ball at the hole any old how.

The quality of the golf matched the weather and there is no need to dwell on it at length. Each had his chances: for me to pull back a hole here and there or for him to go even further ahead but the point of this story, as in most golf encounters, concerns the finish.

With five holes to go, disaster of disasters, he had just got back to three up again. We had both hit long drives at a short par 4 but he had put his short approach shot sufficiently near the hole to be able to surf through the water in two more. Mine pulled up as if it had run into a waterlogged blanket.

So, I thought, that really is just about it and, to prove my point, he hit his longest and straightest drive of the evening. It left him just a punchy half 9 iron from the flag. Mine was skied and I was left with a full 2 iron still to go.

Now it does occasionally happen that a handicap golfer, even when the cause is hopeless, manages—let's say once in every few weeks—a long-iron shot that encourages self-admiration. This one of mine bored straight at the flag. God, would it soar on for ever . . . and over the green? All was well. It pitched just past the pin, bit, and the surface water brought it quickly to a halt.

His crisp flick with a 9 iron must be looking a bit more difficult now, I thought. He took a nice swing at it. The ball flew low at the flag, and pitched past both the flag and the green. He'd thinned it.

It looked as if I was shortly to be a mere two down. For he now had to flip his ball blind up and over a steep 10 foot bank. He looked up as he struck; the ball skittered and hissed through the grass. He had more or less the same shot to play again. Would he concede me the hole?

But he did better the next time and left himself a 3 foot putt for a 5. By now it was some time since I had hit a shot. My opponent had been watching his full share of TV golf and had learned a great deal from the Great Ones. From Trevino he had acquired the technique of prowling around the green and examining the line of his putt from behind his ball, in front of it, from either side and occasionally diagonally as well. Once that ritual is over, Trevino then taps his ball with no more ado. This was not for my opponent. At this point Jack Nicklaus became the model. After the Trevino preliminaries came the Nicklaus age or so of frozen immobility.

But before all this he employed, for every shot into the green, their practice-round technique of pacing out the distance to the flag, sometimes half repeating the process—to reassure himself the putting surface hadn't gone away?

By now I was very wet indeed but I had only to get down in two from 12 foot to take the hole. My fight-back was about to begin, and none too soon at that.

I had been tapping my putts rather nicely so far. Just about all of them had taken a look at the hole but had then gone that nasty 2 foot past. Now, I didn't need a birdie. This time no Casper wristy tap. Just a prod up to the hole.

It stopped 4 foot short. Of course I missed the next and he holed his. So my delicious 2 iron had been wasted and he was still three up and only four holes to go. That appeared to be that.

Next he hit a quick hook up the wrong fairway but still had a possible wooden-club shot to the green. He began to pace out the distance with due ritual.

I had skied mine straight a bare 180 yards but had a good enough lie for a driver and sent it away through the encroaching dusk on about the right line for the green. When I got to my ball, I found I had just a chip left from the front edge. I went for a short stroll as my opponent resumed his preliminary pacings to and fro for his longer pitch to the green. Eventually, he struck it—again firmly through the back—and I chipped up dead. Two down now with three to go. The rain had stopped but it was growing darker, minute by minute.

Both of us hit good drives but I again had the advantage of hitting my second shot first. My 6 iron pitched on the front edge of the green and ran on to stop about 8 foot short of the hole. I dare say that the recent shots through the back of the last two greens were still in my opponent's mind. He underclubbed, struck it beautifully, and finished well short.

Only one down with two to go; the next hole a 150 yard par 3. With the wind against I took a 4 iron and as usual was pin high to the left. He was to the right but had left himself with a chip over a bunker from a bare patch of ground. He lifted his head on the shot but, alas, his ball ran through the bunker and nearly hit the flag. However, all's well that ends well. He was through the green and now had a similar chip at the flag to mine—but I had a shot in hand. I hit it nicely on line but a touch too strong. My ball skirted the edge of the hole and ran 3 yards past. Damn. He now needed only to get down in two for a half but chipped cautiously and was the same distance short. I struck my putt truly and it was in all the way. All square and all to play for on the last.

This was a 360 yard dogleg to the left. If you were too far to the left, you were in a pond. I got my drive away straight down the fairway and was then pleased to see his quick hook reappear. However, he hadn't struck it cleanly enough to reach the water and had a straightforward shot to the green—providing he didn't scrape it into the pond.

We both hit towards the green and went to look for our balls—it was now far too dark to follow the flight. We were both a few yards off the edge. He had a good lie but there was a downhill run to the hole. Fine judgement and touch were needed and I hoped he hadn't any of either after his lead had vanished so quickly. He played the chip well and left himself with a four-footer.

My ball lay half buried in rough, though only about 8 yards from the hole. No chance getting it close except by luck rather than precision. I decided to chop down at it. The ball came out cleanly but I was about double his distance from the hole.

My putt had a right to left borrow and I did not choose quite the right line and hit it a little too strongly. The ball hit the hole and spun round. He had his putt for the match.

Well, as I said at the beginning, I got through this round so it follows that he didn't sink it. Sudden death.

We went back to the 160 yard 1st hole and I hoped he would remember his first shot of the round there—the shank. He did.

I hit one that I felt was about the right length and we went off to look for our respective balls.

Fortunately the fairway had had its first cutting of the season a couple of days before or neither of us could have found his ball. By 9.15 pm in mid-April under low, dense clouds it's about as dark as it's ever going to be. He was well short on the right but pitched up about six yards short of the pin. I went to see if I had played my usual sliced 4 iron. There it was as usual, about 15 yards from the pin with a bunker in between. Mustn't scuffle it into that. My ball lobbed comfortably over and stopped about 3 foot away. As long as he three-putted, I was home. He putted up dead and I knocked his ball back to him. Pity, I now had to hole my putt. I didn't. As much as anything this may have been because I knew I had to: the next hole was stroke index 1. I am 11 handicap, he 12. Now he was due a shot and it was beginning to seem unfair.

'We've got no chance of finding a wood shot,' he said. 'Let's keep on playing this hole until one of us wins or we can't find the balls.' Well, I had already composed in my head a brief account for any friends polite enough to conceal their boredom of my dramatic comeback that had been foiled only by my having to concede a stroke at just the wrong time. I told him I thought this was a very sensible idea indeed and added a few more sensible ones of my own as we walked back, such as how we would be keeping near the bar and that the clubhouse lights just about picked out the white of the flag stick.

'That sounded like a good one,' he said as I hit. I grunted noncommittally. It had felt more like a half-topped push to me but I didn't want him to feel too lighthearted. His shot went off with a good swish and from the bounce in his strides I could sense he was eager to see how near the flag he was.

I went to see if mine had indeed been a half-topped push and I soon came upon it. A good firm putt would have taken me about as far. However, I gave myself a little talking to about the necessity of hitting through with the hands towards the flag, advice which seems to work for the short irons. I pitched onto the green, about 6 yards from the hole. Might be able to get it down in two more.

And where then was he? Well, we looked to the left and the right, short of the green, through the green and even in the hole. I was feeling a virtuous glow, having made an irrevocable decision to tell him where his ball was if I found it.

Eventually he found it himself . . . in a bunker.

'Never get it out of here,' he said, looking at sand as heavy and furrowed from the rain as if a tide had just gone out. At a guess, he took the ball cleanly and it didn't seem that his ball had pitched on the green. One of us would probably have heard it. Perhaps he's knocked it over the carpark wall, I thought.

Well perhaps. I was through to the second round.

DISBELIEF IN THE ENEMY'S PLAY　　　　Sir Walter Simpson

It is scarcely ever politic to count the enemy's chickens before they are hatched. Cases constantly occur of holes being lost because it seems absolutely necessary in order to save them to get home from a bad lie. Your forcing shot sends the ball from bad to worse, and what might have been won in five is lost in seven. A secret disbelief in the enemy's play is very useful for match play.

This contempt must, however, be largely seasoned with respect. It does not do lightly to lose the first two holes, or any hole. When one is down it is natural to hunger for holes, but even with five up play greedily for more—play a yard putt as if the match depended on it. Likely enough it will turn out that it did. With five up express, as is polite, regret at laying a stimy, but rejoice in your heart.

from *The Art of Golf*, David Douglas (UK) 1887

GAMESMANSHIP CAN GO TOO FAR　　　　Stephen Potter

G. Odoreida, I am glad to say, did not often play golf. By his sheer ruthlessness, of course, Odoreida could shock the most hardened gamesman. Woe to the man who asked him as a guest to his golf club.

He would start with some appalling and unexpected thrust. He would arrive perhaps in a motor-propelled invalid chair. Why? Or his hair would be cropped so close to the head that he seemed almost bald.

Worse still, he would approach some average player of dignified and gentle-manly aspect and, for no reason, *ask for his autograph*. Again, why? One was on tenterhooks, always.

I remember one occasion on which his behaviour was suspiciously orthodox. The club was Sunningdale. 'Thank heaven,' I thought, 'such ancient dignity pervades these precincts that even Odoreida is subdued.'

I introduced him to the secretary. It was a bold move, but it seemed to work. I was anxious when I saw, however, that on that particular afternoon the secretary was inspecting the course. As he came near us Odoreida was near the hole. Without any reason, he took an iron club from his bag and took a wild practice swing on the very edge, if not the actual surface, of the green. A huge piece of turf shot up. 'Odoreida!' I said, and put the turf back with an anxious care that was perfectly genuine.

Two holes later the secretary was edging near us again. Odoreida was about to putt. He took the peg from the hole and *plunged it into the green*. 'Odoreida!' I cried once more. Surely, this time, the secretary must have seen. But I remember very little of the rest of the afternoon's play. I know that Odoreida won by 7 and 5. I am glad to say that I refused to play the remaining holes.

In other words, gamesmanship can go too far. And the gamesman must never forget that his watchwords, frequently repeated to his friends, must be sportsmanship and consideration for others.

from *The Complete Golf Championship*, William Heinemann (UK),

McGraw-Hill Book Co (US)

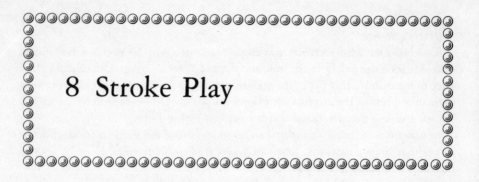

8 Stroke Play

MANY of the great golfers of the past have feared matchplay. They knew that anyone, especially over 18 holes, can be beaten by the sudden half hour of inspiration of an unknown. Today, however, the supreme test for the club golfer is to hold a round together over the last few holes in medal play; for the tournament golfer, it is to maintain a standard higher than anyone else over 72 holes. For both, the examination is far more severe than the universal four-ball in which that seven on the drive-and-a-pitch 4th hole is forgiven and forgotten—providing one's partner got the half.

The club golfer is often heard protesting that he 'can't do anything with a card in his hand'. In Britain, if not the US because everyone holes out in a four-ball and writes down a score, he may never do a medal round but play around the same course, the same days of the week with the same three companions. If he ventures to mention what he has gone round in 'If I hadn't picked up at the 12th when you were already on in two shots' no one will be much interested; the matchplay of two against two is what their game was about.

But in his heart each golfer knows that the most accurate measure of his ability is stroke play. Can he, over the full stretch maintain the rhythm of his swing for the longer shots and his nerve when chipping and putting? Does he ruin his card in the first few holes because of the fear of making a fool of himself or at the end, when fears of winning descend on both meek and mighty alike.

THE PRESSURE OF STROKE PLAY   Peter Alliss

I feel like an onion that has been put in vinegar and it's in the back of a pantry for fifty years and it's soaked up with vinegar so much that there is nothing left in it at all.

Most of the time it isn't putting at all, it is other departments of the game that fold up. It's difficult to overcome it . . . I've tried so many things, and thought of going to America and . . . But I hate it, you know, some days I feel I hate the whole business of playing golf . . . it's such a struggle to get any confidence in myself at all. Now yesterday I did 72 and quite honestly I played pretty well yesterday, and I look at that board and see people there with 70, 71, a stroke or two strokes better than me, when I really am about half a stroke a hole better than them . . . I ought to be nine strokes a round better than them every time out, yet they've beaten me. So then I think how has this happened and I start to analyse the round and how I three-putted the second, and deliberately went too short there because I was scared of going through, and how I was a bit nervous there and a bit conservative there and a bit defensive there, and when I piece it all together I find I have squandered shots wantonly. Then I am left with a tremendous effort at the last hole to make a four, because 147 will qualify, 148 will not. I had to gear myself right down and make sure I was thinking, now get it back here and make sure the hands and arms go through the ball and make sure I watch the ball as long as I can and don't grip too tightly and take the club three-quarters back and keep the body still and on and on and on. I got the drive away, got it on the green somehow, then putted into an imaginary circle three feet round the hole and got it a foot away and made the four. But it was such a tremendous effort.

There is something there, something blocks my brain.

from *Alliss Through the Looking Glass*, Cassell & Co (UK)

MORE STROKES, MORE FUN   Bernard Darwin

The tearing up of a card is generally regarded as a rather discreditable business, showing at once vanity and pusillanimity in the tearer; and I must say that I do feel something more of a man when I have gone on to the bitter end and handed in the horrid thing. Circumstances, however, alter cases; there are occasions when, if only for the sake of the players behind, we are almost justified in the cowardly act, and I am about to write of one.

As a rule, when a golfer tears up a card he does so not merely figuratively, but literally, and no one but his marker knows the exact facts. A card has now come into my hands which, I think, its owner must have intended to destroy. He did not, however, and his marker first secreted it and then passed it on to another who, thinking that it might be useful, gave it to me. The whole business is, as you will perceive, a shady, if not a positively dishonourable, one. I feel rather ashamed of it; but so poignant a 'human document' as this card cannot be allowed to lie hidden. So, with all due precautions of anonymity as to player and course, it shall be set out.

The score was compiled in a qualifying competition on a well-known seaside course, and here it is as far as it goes:

Out: 10, 12, 9, 9, 10, 7, 11, 9, 8.
Home: 12, 17, 12, 9, 20, 8.

That is to say, the player took 85 to go out and he had taken 78 for six holes on the way home when he gave up the unequal struggle. Statisticians will note that he took double figures at eight out of the fifteen holes played, and that his average score for a hole was 10 13/15. There appears to be some doubt whether the tally was duly kept. Both marker and player, though persons of the highest probity, may have grown a little tired, and one who played behind them declares that in the twenty recorded for the fourteenth hole 'air shots were not counted'. I entirely dissociate myself from any such slanderous statement, but there it is.

With nothing but the card and the length of the holes to help us, we must employ the methods of Sherlock Holmes if we are to discover anything about the round, and those methods, as Watson found, are easier to admire than to apply. We are probably justified in guessing that the wind rather favoured the player on the way out, but, on the other hand, his later falling off may only have been due to a natural and cumulative fatigue. In those first nine holes, I think, he must have played more or less his normal game, for there are no purple patches, and the two holes at which he took fewest strokes, the fifth and ninth, are both one-shot holes. He holed them in seven and eight respectively and, judged by that standard, his eleven at the seventh, which is 478 yards long, was a noteworthy achievement. On the way home, seventeen was superficially bad at the eleventh—a mere 352 yards long—but my recollection is that at this hole there is a deep and cavernous ditch running along the left of the fairway, and once the player is in it, anything might happen. Of course, the twenty at the fourteenth was a real tragedy, because this is only a one-shot hole of 162 yards. Heaven forbid that I should call it an easy three; it is not that, and especially not in a wind, but it is a little hard to understand where there is enough trouble to account for an 'approximated' twenty.

No praise can be too high for the way in which, after this calamity, the player pulled himself together and did his second eight of the round, and that not this time at a one-shotter. This makes it all the sadder that he never holed out the sixteenth. It is a long and severe hole (510 yards) in hilly country, and I am told that the getting there was a long business. He had almost reached the green when suddenly his courage forsook him. His marker urged him to go on, but he answered quietly that he had 'no chance *now*,' and picked up his ball. So his card only remains a noble fragment. Had he been able to hole the last three holes in thirty-six shots—an average of twelve—he would just have beaten 200. There was a one-shotter coming at the seventeenth, where another eight might have been hoped for. Could he have done it? That we shall never know. An inscrutable riddle, he mocks us to the end of time.

It chanced that this card was handed to me at the hour of the cocktail in a place where people congregate before luncheon. Several sniggered over it with me, but there was one who took a rather different and serious view. He said, possibly with some exaggeration, that his golf was of the same quality as that of the man who made the score, and that he and his like got much more pleasure out of the game than did superior persons. Would I, he asked, write an article to that effect, and then, in an inspired moment, he exclaimed: 'More strokes, more fun, there's your title ready-made for you!' So, having adopted his suggestion, I must do the best I can with his subject, but I am not convinced that he is right. His title might be true of cricket, where, roughly speaking, the more strokes the more runs, or, at any rate, the more prolonged the innings. It might be moderately true of lawn tennis. Give me an opponent of exactly my own futile calibre, and we can now and again have quite a long rally by means of our mild little lobs backwards and forwards over the net, which we find exhilarating and enjoyable. Our strokes are contemptible, but they do, during that rally, attain two primary objects of getting the ball over the net and into the court. Our ambitions are strictly limited and are satisfied. On the other hand, the man who takes twelve to a hole at golf is nearly all the time failing miserably to attain his object: a large proportion of those twelve shots must be tops or fluffs, unless, indeed, they are, most of them, accounted for by a rapid rain of blows in a bunker which leave the ball *in statu quo*. And surely nobody, except a man who is blind with fury and wants to hit something, can enjoy mere unsuccessful thumping.

Admittedly, my friend, taking him at his own valuation, is much more easily pleased than the superior person. One good, honest drive, if he hits one, will give him a greater thrill than a champion will get from a whole round of perfectly struck tee shots. Just to see the ball rise into the air is, for him, something, and when it flies over a tall bunker and disappears into the happy valley beyond he is doubtless ecstatic. Moreover, he is not unduly bothered about hooks and slices; as long as the ball soars, its direction is a secondary consideration. Granted all these things, I still think that his joys are few. 'I 'ate heights,' said a famous professional, who did very few of them. The lowliest must come to hate them when they are part of the regular routine. If an eight could represent perfect play, judged even by the humblest standards, it would be a different matter, but on no course of my acquaintance is there a hole which can be described as 'a good eight hole'.

This is not to say that the very best of golfers must enjoy the game more than the next best, and so on down the scale. I do not believe that for a moment, but I do say that beyond a certain pitch of badness golf cannot be very much fun. Probably the exceedingly steady and trustworthy golfer with a handicap of five or six gets as much pleasure as most people. Within his powers he makes a great many good shots, he gets a little the best of it in match making, he wins, by means of his steadiness, a large proportion of matches and half-crowns. He is not tortured by mad ambitions to be a champion: but stay! is he not? We do not know what is going on inside that old grey head of his, and it may be that he would give all his steadiness just to hit one drive like that young slasher in front. 'See how strangely we men are made!' said Prince Florizel.

from *Out of the Rough*, Chapman & Hall (UK), reprinted by permission of A. P. Watt & Son

HOPE   Sir Walter Simpson

. . . every moderately good golfer, on the morning of the medal day, may lie abed and count up a perfect score for himself. He easily recalls how at different times and often he has done each hole in par figures. Why not this day, and all the holes consecutively? It seems so easy. The more he thinks of it the easier it seems, even allowing for a few mistakes. Every competitor who is awake soon enough sees the necessity for preparing a speech against the contingency of the medal being presented to him in the evening. Nor is any one much crushed when all is over, and he has not won. If he does well, it was but that putt, that bad lie, that bunker. If his score is bad, what of it? Even the best are off their game occasionally. Next time it will be different. Meanwhile his score will be taken as a criterion of his game, and he is sure to win many half-crowns from unwary adversaries who underrate him.

The game of golf is full of consolation. The long driver who is beaten feels that he has a soul above putting. All those who cannot drive thirty yards suppose themselves to be good putters. Your hashy player piques himself on his power of recovery. The duffer is a duffer merely because every second shot is missed. Time or care will eliminate the misses, and then!

from *The Art of Golf*, David Douglas (UK) 1887

THE FEARS OF LEADING   Peter Thomson

Friday. All but 70s and ties were gone. The field strung out [in the 1968 British Open] like Brown's cows. The wind returned after its day of rest to torment the run home and holiday mothers with their tots huddled in the sand dunes. Few children braved the beach.

The third round is the one where championships are supposed to be won and lost. The leader usually succumbs to the pressure and the pursuers, with nothing to lose and only hope in their hearts, take the bull by the horns in an effort to catch him. Amongst the pack of them one at least finds his gambles paying off while the unlucky ones fall further behind.

From the ones who have lost all chance to win come record scores, for once the fear of winning or the unbearable strain of playing well is gone, the course takes on a simpler guise.

From anyone but Casper we might have seen signs of cracking but the Mormon preacher began with a birdie as though he was starting off the first round again.

He carried on more or less correctly until the ninth where he had rough trouble. This plus a mistake at the 5th earned him 37. Nobody else made much impression on him except Bob Charles with whom Casper was drawn to play. Charles has a slightly ungainly left-handed style which disguises a great deal of down to earth ability. Actually he is naturally righthanded and righteyed which might explain why the long shots of golf have never come easy to him.

Most of his shots have a bend one way or the other if ever so slight, but in the last few years he has come to know exactly his range and limit.

On the green he has no superior and it was in that department that he began to make his presence felt.

He holed a putt at the drive and pitch third, then, a monster up and round the big slope at five, and all of a sudden he became a threat.

Casper was not going to have it all his own way.

Barnes had dropped from the hunt, but Jacklin was going great guns; Player like a terrier was clinging on.

Carnoustie's real terrors come over the 9th, 10th and 12th. Here is where 5s come more easily than fours although the pars are each four.

Only Jacklin of all the pack got by these holes in par and they all headed home, Jacklin, Player, Charles and Nicklaus more or less equal with Casper's lead reduced to two strokes.

Then Player came into his own. Still dressed in black to match the weather he captured an eagle at the fourteenth with 2 big woods and a long putt.

Then he negotiated successfully the pitfalls at the next three and after playing safe with an iron from the eighteenth tee he powered a three wood into rough just short of the burn and made a stabbing pitch to two feet.

This all got him home in 34 and the best round of the day, 71. Charles meanwhile nibbled at Casper's heels, although it was Casper's own mistakes that squandered his leeway. He missed the short thirteenth and also dropped another at the seventeenth with a mistake approach.

Charles looking lean and hungry gathered up these crumbs and ended the day matching Player and sitting on the American's wheel! Britain's hopes deflated as Jacklin ended with a rash of bogies. For him it was actually the beginning of the end.

Nicklaus appeared about to join the heel-snapping bunch when he eagled 14 like Player. But the 16th crashed his hopes.

His tee-shot cut into the wind wide and short to the right, into a deep trap. From there he could not quite explode on to the 'deck' and he found himself in that uncut untidy gutter on the right of the green. He attempted to putt out of this but it turned out to be unwise for he left himself far short and missed his putt for four.

Double bogies are disasters of the first magnitude. Since he was to lose by only two strokes this hole in retrospect was very costly.

However he birdied the last as usual with the greatest of ease and trailed Casper by 4.

The situation was now pregnant with possibilities.

Casper now found himself in an unenviable position. He led by a mere stroke into the final round with Player, Charles and Nicklaus on his heels.

Brewer and Jacklin were still within long range striking distance. He had passed the ordeal of leading the third round, escaping with his lead of four cut to one—not an experience likely to build great confidence for his next and final round. It is accepted now that only the real champions win from in front. Unfortunately it seldom happens. Mostly tournaments follow a familiar pattern. The leader into the last round ties himself into a knot trying to keep his nose in front, and one of the bunch at his heels, with nothing to lose and everything to gain, gives his very best.

Casper, by this stage, was deserving of first place. He had posted the lowest score of 68 in the second round, led by four, and survived a chase by the pack, even if only by the skin of his teeth.

It might have been lucky for him had Charles or Player caught him and taken over as front runner.

As it was he had to saddle up again for the same treatment for the second day in a row.

The ones behind him had no such worries. Each was full of hope for two things—one that Casper would score another 74 or worse and that they might find the putts dropping and finish off in 68!*

The leader always fears he will lose. The pursuers in contrast hope they will catch him. Hope builds and fear destroys.

from This Wonderful World of Golf, Pelham Books (UK)

I SHALL RETURN   Walter Hagen

Dickie said, 'Just keep going and try for second or third, if you can't win.'

'I don't want a second. If I can't win I don't care where I finish,' I told him. 'I won't be any better tomorrow, maybe, but I'm going out to win. I figure I'll either be under 70 or I'll be up over 80.'

I was determined to beat the British pros and they were just as determined to beat the Americans. We all extended our efforts way beyond the stretching point. I tried to keep fighting. I suppose I should have picked up my ball, as most golfers would. I've never done that and I intended to show the British that I could take a beating and still smile. I took the beating all right. George Duncan won with a not too creditable score of 303. I trailed *fifty-third* in a field of *fifty-four*.

One of the British sports writers reported that finish this way, 'Duncan finished but not too triumphantly, and made his exit as if he had lost. Yet there was the American, Hagen, finishing with his head up as if he himself had won instead of finishing far down among the also-rans.'

---

* Player won with 289, followed by Nicklaus and Charles, 291. Casper had a final 78 to finish on 292.

But it took Deal's little Mr Secretary to polish me off. 'I'm sorry you didn't do better, 'Eye-gen,' he gloated, 'but golf over here is very difficult. I do hope you'll come back some future year and try again!'

'Don't worry about me,' I told him. 'You'll see my name on that cup.'

He did, too, no fewer than *four* times.

from *The Walter Hagen Story*, Simon & Schuster (US), William Heinemann (UK)

HOW SAM SNEAD NEVER WON THE US OPEN   Sam Snead

Going into the final eighteen holes, it looked like I just might win my first [1939] National Open. My 212 score tied me with Denny Shute, Clayton Heafner, and Craig Wood, 1 stroke behind Johnny Bulla's first-place 211.

I was loose as a goose, mentally. The night before the final day of play, I did some catsprings and some other calisthenics around the hotel-room floor. My roommate, Gene Sarazen, was already in bed and thought my exercises were tomfoolery.

'This stuff helps me to relax,' I told him.

'Yes, and you can sprain your back,' said Gene, snapping out the lights and practically ordering me to bed.

I finished my sit-ups in the dark and then slept like a possum in his mother's pouch. I felt another 68 or 69 coming on when I woke up. Couldn't wait to get out there and win me that $100,000 Open.

With seventy holes played, it looked like I'd make it. Two pars on the finishing holes would give me a 69 for the final round and a seventy-two-hole total of 281. A 281 seemed good enough, as it would tie the all-time Open record. I went for the first par on the par-4 seventy-first, where I hit a beautiful 300-yard drive. My second shot was over the green into thick clover grass. Chipping out short, I missed a 5-foot putt by an inch and took a bogey 5.

Right there is where my most famous 'blowup' began.

For some reason, nobody wanted to tell me the facts of the situation I was up against—which wasn't anything to worry about. As matters stood, I needed only a par on the last hole to beat the best score registered so far, Byron Nelson's 284, and win. A bogey would tie Nelson. No one else still playing the course was in shape to beat Nelson.

But I didn't know any of this, and my bogey on the seventy-first had made me nervous. Ed Dudley, my playing partner, and others around me knew what Nelson had done, yet not one of them spoke up. When you're in the dark, your fears close in on you. I felt I had to gamble on a birdie on the par-5, 558-yard closing hole.

People were swarming the fairways and I had a thirty-minute, nerve-racking wait while the marshals cleared the way to build up the decision to play that last hole wide open.

The tee shot was hit squarely, but my right hand turned a bit too quickly and the ball started to hook. I said, 'Whoa, ball, whoa'—but it hooked into trampled rough anyway. The lie was in sandy soil. Up ahead were traps, short of the green and around it. Normally you'd use an iron to make sure of getting out and up. It was still 275 yards to the pin, however, and I still had the idea that the only way to win was to gamble.

Taking a custom-made 2-wood, with several degrees more loft than a driver, one of my favorite sticks, I went for the pin instead of playing safely out. Hit badly, the ball had no height. It was a low liner pushed down the fairway, and I said, 'Giddyap, giddyap,' when I saw it failing near a trap 160 yards away.

It fell into the trap. It was partly buried.

Every expert I've read claims that I played the trap shot before I thought it out. That's not true. With 2 shots used up, I had to reach the green with the next (or believed I did) and the green was still 110 yards away. My bunker lie wasn't too bad. Half the ball was visible. Above me the collar of the trap had been resodded with squares of soil topped by rough grass. This lip had to be cleared at a height of about 5 feet. A heavy sand wedge would get me up but wouldn't give me the needed distance. I asked the caddie for a shallower-faced club. 'Give me the 8-iron,' I said.

Even in 1939, when I was only a two-year touring pro, I knew how risky it can be to use a semilofted iron from a semiburied lie. The danger is that you'll catch the ball too clean. If you don't take enough sand, you don't get it up. Weighing that against the need to reach the green in 3, I gambled.

The ball went 4 feet, slammed into the collar, and stuck in a crack left by the resodding. The moans and groans that went up were nothing to my feeling when I caught it too clean and saw it plug in there. In hitting too clean, you don't get under the ball; you hit too high on it and lose the lofted effect of the club. Now I had to chop sod, grass, ball, and all, while standing on sand below the ball.

To cut it out required a sideswiping blow, and she slashed out to the left 40 yards into another bunker. I was sick ail over. Still thinking I needed a birdie on No 72 to win, all my hopes were gone. In landing in that second trap, I'd used up my birdie shot. And now I was shooting 5 from another tough lie in sand.

Just then somebody stepped out of the gallery and said, 'Nelson finished at 284. You've got to get down in two more to tie him.'

I thought I'd explode at this news. All those gambling shots had been needless. 'Why didn't somebody tell me that back on the tee,' I snarled, 'so I could play it safe?' I was mad enough to plow through that crowd, swinging a club right and left. People will give you nine million miles of advice when you don't need it, but here in the clutch, they had dummied up on me.

If there's anything in this story I'm not ashamed of, it was the 9-iron recovery I made then. I was shaking all over. But I was still thinking. My ball rested 4 or 5 inches below my feet at the bunker's edge. In any situation where you must stand in the trapside grass with the ball below you, the danger is 'falling into' the shot and slicing it. Unless you're careful, because your body is tilted forward, you tend to shift weight too soon from your right leg, on the backswing, to the left leg, on the downswing. Which gives you a push or slice. A photo I have of this Spring Mill explosion shows how I avoided that. I bent my knees more than usual, 'sitting down' to the ball. My weight was back on my heels to prevent overshifting. I choked down on the club, to make sure I stayed down to the ball throughout the swing. If you rise up even a little bit on a lie like this, you're ruined. The clubface was closed slightly to counteract any slice. And I scraped the ball onto the green, 40 feet from the cup.

To tie Nelson, I needed the putt, and again I'm not ashamed—the 40-footer came close. It lipped the cup and twisted 3 feet away.

After that, I was an awful sight. I didn't give a damn anymore. The collapse was complete when I missed the 3-footer. One more putt gave me an 8—the most talked-about 8 ever taken in golf, I guess. Some women were crying and men were patting me on the back as I walked to the locker room. It was worse in there. There was dead silence. The other pros avoided looking at me, to spare me embarrassment. The sportswriters stayed far away, too. All except one, George Trevor of New York, who walked up with a pencil and notebook in hand and asked, 'Sam, what happened on that last hole?'

The boys led Trevor away before I did something I'd regret.

from *The Education of a Golfer*, Simon & Schuster (US), Cassell & Co (UK)

THE FIRST WIN   Frank Beard

I can't help thinking . . . about the first tournament I ever played in Palm Springs, the first tournament I ever had a good shot at winning, the Frank Sinatra Invitational in 1963.

It was my first year on the tour, and the week before, at San Jose, I missed the cut and since I didn't have an exemption, I had to qualify at Palm Springs on Monday. I just made it. I shot a 77 and, as I recall, the highest qualifying score was 78.

In the first round of the Sinatra Invitational, I shot a 68 and tied for first place with Bob Rosburg. I didn't feel much pressure. I didn't expect to stay up that high. The next day, I shot a 72 and fell back into a tie for fourth place with Rossy and several other guys. Dow Finsterwald and Ray Floyd, who was a rookie like me, were tied for the lead at 138, and Casper was only a stroke behind.

In the third round, Tommy Bolt shot a 67 and I shot a 69, and we were tied for first place at 209. The next morning, I went to Mass and, for the first time in my life—and the last—I asked God to let me win. Most times, I just ask Him to let me do the best I can, but that morning, I asked Him to let me win. I felt it could be a real turning point in my career. It could establish me as a professional. It would give me an exemption for the following year. I was more nervous than I've ever been since. I wanted to win so bad.

I played in the next-to-last threesome with Bob Rosburg and Jerry Steelsmith, who'd been playing the tour a few years. The final threesome consisted of Bolt, the former U.S. Open champion; Mason Rudolph, one of the top ten money-winners that year; and Howie Johnson. Mason and Jerry Steelsmith were tied for second, just a stroke behind Bolt and me.

On the first four holes, I struggled for pars. Then I birdied five and eight, which put me six-under for the tournament and moved me into first place. But I bogeyed nine and then eleven, an easy par-five, and I felt like I'd blown my chance. All I could think about then was trying to hold on and get second or third or fourth money.

I scrambled for desperate pars the next four holes, and when we got to the sixteenth tee, with three holes to play, we saw an up-to-date scoreboard for the first time. Gardner Dickinson was in first place at five-under, and Steelie, Mason, and I were at four under. 'Wait a minute now,' I said to myself. 'I've faltered, and I'm still only a shot out. I can still win this.'

The sixteenth hole was a dogleg to the left about 250 yards out, then another 220 yards to the green. I tried to cut the corner and hit some palm trees and just managed to trickle out into the rough, past the dogleg. I was still some two hundred yards from the green, and I had to hit out of the rough over a lake to reach the green.

Something possessed me, I don't know what. I had just a fair lie, and I should've played safe, out to the left and maybe bounce on the green for a two-putt, but I remember thinking, 'You're never gonna have a better chance to win a tournament than right here.'

I took out a four-iron and went right for the hole. My shot barely cleared the lake protecting the green, then rolled up within six feet of the pin. Steelie got on in two and two-putted, and I sank my birdie putt; suddenly I was tied for the lead. My head just about blew off from the heat and the excitement.

Gardner Dickinson was playing right in front of us, and we watched him on the seventeenth, a par-five bending to the right. He tried to reach the green on his second shot with a three-wood and hooked the ball out of bounds. He dropped a new ball and hooked another shot out of bounds. Gardner finally took a nine. About the same time, we heard that Bolt and Rudolph had played themselves out of contention behind us. There were only two holes left to play, and it was just me and Steelie, and I had a one-stroke lead.

I hit a big drive on seventeen, some 250, 260 yards, but in the rough. Steelie drove down the middle of the fairway. I must've been 220 yards from the green, but I knew from my lie that the ball was going to fly, going to take off. I had to get over some palm trees to reach the green.

I took an eight-iron—an *eight-iron*—one of the smartest moves I ever made. I really pumped it. I hit it almost two hundred yards, over the palms, right up in front of the green. Steelsmith hit his second shot to the edge of the green. I was away and I was shaking like crazy. I had visions of shanking the shot or topping it or just missing it completely. I hooded the club a little, to give me better control, and I chipped up to about eight feet from the pin. Steelie chipped up inside me, maybe five or six feet from the pin.

Again, I was away. I lined up my putt, sweating, shaking. If I missed and then he made his putt, we'd be all even. 'Now, c'mon,' I told myself. 'If you make your putt, he won't be able to handle the pressure. He'll miss his, and you'll have a two-stroke lead.'

I hit my putt a little too hard. If it'd been off-line, it would have gone way past the hole. But the ball went right into the center of the hole and stayed there. I just watched it and shook. I don't remember ever taking the ball out of the cup. I don't know how I could've, my hand was shaking so much.

Steelie missed.

Steelie and I have talked about that hole several times since, and he's convinced, and I am, too, that if he'd picked up a stroke on me then, he probably would have gone ahead to win the tournament and launch a great career. But that tournament, that hole, just broke his back. Steelie has never won a tournament, has never become the golfer he might've been.

We still had to play the eighteenth hole, even though I had a two-stroke lead. When I walked up to the eighteenth tee, I was still shaking. I looked down the fairway, and saw out of bounds on the left and bunkers on the right, and the fairway didn't look any wider than a pool table. Bob Rosburg walked over to me. 'Frank,' he said, 'don't do anything stupid. You got this thing locked up. Take an iron and knock it down the middle and then knock it on the green and two-putt and win the tournament and forget it.'

If Rossy hadn't said anything, I might've taken a driver and hit the ball out of bounds. But I just stroked a two-iron down the middle of the fairway, then watched Steelie drive his ball a mile, maybe fifty yards past me.

I was still about two hundred yards from the middle of the green, and something popped into my mind, that good rule I still follow: when you're pumped up, always take less iron than you think you need because you'll hit it farther than you normally would. For two hundred yards, I'd normally take about a three-iron. I took a five-iron. On a normal lie, under normal conditions, I couldn't hit a five-iron two hundred yards if my life depended on it. But I busted this ball right in the middle of the green, maybe twenty feet past the pin. If I'd hit a three-iron, I probably would've gone over the clubhouse.

Steelsmith hit a nine-iron and landed about three inches inside me. I had to putt first, and I was shaking, but I could still add. 'If I can two-putt,' I said to myself, 'I win—even if he sinks his.'

I lined up over the ball and I couldn't draw the putter back. My mind was telling my hands to bring the putter back, but my hands wouldn't listen. I must've tried three or four times until, finally, I brought the putter back and stroked the ball. It stopped a foot from the hole, twelve inches away. I walked up to putt out—I wasn't in anybody's line—and I couldn't even see my ball. My vision was all clouded up, sweat or tears or imagination or something. I still don't know how, but I tapped the ball in the hole, and I had my first tour championship.

from *Pro: Frank Beard on the Golf Tour*, Thomas Y. Crowell Co (us)

AN AMAZING GOLF OCCURRENCE   Henry Cotton

It was the last week of August, 1936, and a small band of professionals, including Auguste Boyer, Marcel Dallemagne, Joe Ezar, and myself, arrived at Sestrières in Italy to play in the Italian Open Championship. We stayed in one of the famous tower-shaped hotels, better known to winter sports holiday-makers than to summer tourists, as Sestrières is primarily a winter resort, some 6,000 ft. up in the mountains, not far from Turin. This is not the story of the result and play in this championship (I cannot imagine any golfing event of less interest to the golfing public in general), but the story of some events that even to this day puzzle me. The story revolves around Joe Ezar, a colourful figure in two senses of the word, known to most golfers in England as he has made several visits to these shores, and not altogether unknown in USA, his home country.

Joe was a much better player on this visit to Europe in 1936 than ever before; he even beat Alfred Padgham in a 36-hole match during the latter's very successful year when he collected all the prize-money and the Open Championship.

Joe arrived at Sestrières complete with a magnificent camel-hair coat, bound on its edges in leather, and bought in Berlin with the marks he had won as his prize in the German Open the previous week, for no money could be exported. Besides the superb coat, he had bought a red enamel wrist-watch with the few odd marks he had left, after, of course, buying his rail ticket. This has nothing to do with the story, except that Joe insisted on wearing this coat thrown over his shoulders like a cape when playing, despite the fact that the weather was fine and very warm.

The course at Sestrières is quite a good one, 18 holes of just about 6,000 yards, and although only used for less than three months each year, the summer holiday season being short in the mountains, it was kept in very good condition. The record for the course was 67. I went round in this score twice on the first day and had a lead at half-way. I cannot remember who was next, but it doesn't matter, anyway. That evening Joe Ezar had been given a fee to give his trick-shot exhibition by the 9th hole green, situated just below the hotel. All the Italian golfers and the visitors were anxious to see what he could do.

Well, Joe ran through the usual trick-shot repertoire, a hook, a slice, a straight one (the hardest shot of the lot to do), a high ball, hit two balls at once, hit two balls at once and catch one, hit a further two balls at once, one to the left, the other to the right, tee up three balls one on top of the other and hit the centre one, hit a ball left-handed with a right-handed club, hit a ball and catch it, etc., then pitch the ball on to a green (a holding one) and make it come back, a ribbed club being used to this shot. These are a few of the ordinary trick shots which Joe did very well, but his patter, copied from the other famous Joe (Kirkwood) was not quite as good as that of the 'original Joe.'

Then Joe went on to the putting-green, put down three balls at least 20 ft away from the hole, and said: 'To hole one ball in three shots.' Well, we all knew this green and this particular putt down the hillside, so we nudged one another and said, 'What a hope!' Well, the third ball went in. 'What a fluke!' said we. Joe went to the front of the green, put the balls down again, and announced, 'To hole the third ball.'

The first ball struck was short, the second ball was wide and the third ball, *was in*! This looked almost too deliberate to be a fluke, but there is was, two nominated performances, always difficult feats to attempt, particularly at golf, a game I know too well. Other spectators were equally amazed.

We were impressed 'more than somewhat', as Damon Runyan would say, and the president of the club, a non-golfer, was even more impressed and said something on these lines when congratulating Joe and handing him his fee. 'It is a wonder with your skill you do not break the record.'

Joe said, 'How much would you give me if I do break the record?'

'One thousand lira,' said the president, 'for a 66.'

'How much for a 65?' said Joe.

'Two thousand lira,' said the president.

'And for a 64?' said Joe.

'Four thousand lira,' laughingly said the president.

'Right,' said Joe, 'I'll do a 64.'

Joe wrote down on the edge of a cigarette packet borrowed from the president's pocket the score he could do hole by hole to make up his 64. It was on, but it meant perfect golf with some birdies in it to do it.

I saw very little of the round as I was playing myself, but Joe was left with a three at the 9th for a 32 out and he was at least 50 yards from the pin in two shots, but he announced to the president that he must hole this shot to keep to schedule and he pitched it on to the green and it trickled into the hole. He came back in 32; hole by hole he scored as he had written down on the edge of the cigarette box, and there was his round of 64.

The president of the club saw the whole round, and his partner and several other spectators testify to the score, which was a remarkable one. We all knew of the four thousand lira prize for a 64, but treated the matter as a joke, not even as a boast. Anyway, there it was on the score board: Joe Ezar, 64—*and nominated hole by hole*.

This is one of the most amazing occurrences I have ever known in the game of golf. With this round Joe picked up many strokes on the player running for second place, as I had a big lead on him and added a 68 to my two 67s. I won the event and Joe was second. I do not remember his score, but he was delighted to beat Boyer and Dallemagne, those two very fine French professionals.

Knowing golf as I do, and its uncertainty in particular, I count these feats as some of the most extraordinary I have ever heard about. Whether they were just colossal flukes, like the two nominated putts, or whether they were combinations of skill and luck, was debated that night at a dinner given in the hotel. But there the fact remains—they did happen, and Joe collected his 4,000 lira from the president, who must have considered his offers, made spontaneously and laughingly, as a bad business. But who would not offer even more money for a nominated score at golf? I must add that I did a 66 in the last round, and this and my two 67s were the three other lowest by any other player in the championship, which makes Joe's round all the more extraordinary.

Joe, with his dark skin and curious slouching walk, did well on his trips over here and was able to pay his way home usually on the boat, but he has worked his passage to and fro on several occasions. He was quite a character and somehow seems to have disappeared from competitive golf, but this story remains. What do you make of it?

Trevor Wignall, the famous sporting journalist, told me the story of Joe Ezar's trip on the maiden voyage of the 'Queen Mary'.

Trevor went to his cabin on arrival at the boat, and was amazed to see an enormous bag of golf clubs with Joe Ezar painted on the pocket. Thinking it must be a mistake on someone's part, as being connected with sport such a mistake could happen, and possibly there was a reasonable explanation, he forgot about it, and went on deck to watch the historic sailing of the, then, largest ship afloat.

When the boat was well under way and heading for the Channel, he went down to his cabin to see about unpacking and was quite startled to see the wardrobe door open and Joe Ezar's smiling face peep out.

Joe was 'stowing away'. Trevor was very embarrassed about the compromising position he was in, and insisted that Joe should report immediately to the purser. This Joe promised to do, and apparently as the purser was very busy getting his affairs in order and with the expectance of more passengers joining the ship at Cherbourg, every time Joe approached him to have a heart to heart talk he was told to come back later after Cherbourg.

When the ship was heading for New York, Joe stated his case and got into the expected trouble. However, with the aid of friends and well-wishers he finished up in Tourist class and gave demonstrations and exhibitions to collect money to pay his fare and incidentals for the trip.

I met Joe Ezar in Florida in 1947; he was much heavier and wore a little grey moustache, and so did not seem the same person. But he still does his trick shots, and is good for a low score any time.

from *This Game of Golf*, Country Life Publications (UK)

NOW NO GOOD, SAME LIKE YOU   Patrick Campbell

Sooner or later, as the player advances along the narrow fairways leading to Scratchdom, he will probably find himself assisting professional golfers to win serious money in pro-amateur tournaments, the most socially glittering of which is the Bowmaker Tournament at Sunningdale.

Here, the professional plays 36 holes medal, so that he puts in three scores— one off his own bat, one his best ball with Amateur A, and one his best ball with Amateur B.

It often takes Amateurs A and B several hours of patient listening and questioning to understand the system, but an example usually makes all clear.

If the pro takes five at the first, which he usually does, and Amateurs A and B take four and six respectively, the three cards will read:

Pro: 5.
Pro plus A: 4.
Pro plus B: 5.

From this it will be seen that while the amateur can improve the pro's score, he cannot make it any worse, a comfort to the amateur when quick hooking breaks out, if not to the pro.

Last year at Sunningdale, on his own card, the pro stood to win £350, and with one of the other amateurs, £250, so that the pro has a sympathetic interest in his partner's progress. One year, playing with Ugo Grappasoni, from the Villa d'Este, I discovered how sympathetic this interest could be.

We played the first nine holes in complete silence owing, as I thought, to Ugo's failure to come to grips with the English language. I wanted to speak to him, as I wasn't playing very well. When I got one off the tee that finished on the fairway I put the next one into the woods. When I got one off the tee that finished in the woods I picked it up.

Ugo watched these enervating activities with a cold black eye that put me in mind of vendettas and the Mafia's revenge.

Held up briefly on the ninth, I decided to take a chance on speech. I asked him if, perhaps, I was doing something fractionally wrong. The right hand creeping a shade too far underneath? A minute fault in the stance—the ball, perhaps, half an inch too far back—?

Ugo made his first and last observation of the day. 'Isa ponch, ponch,' he said. 'Isa noh swing. Isa a whole t'ing isa noh good.'

That's the kind of discovery the budding Scratchman is liable to make when he moves up into the big time. Isa whole t'ing isa noh good. And the professionals do not hesitate to tell him so, with £250 slipping out of their hands into the bushes.

I played a year later with Leopoldo Ruiz, the Thin Crust of Bread from the Argentine ...

In the first round Leopoldo, taking a 2-iron off the tee and hitting all of them 270-yards, notched a spirited 65, unassisted in any way whatever by myself.

In the second round, however, he got a bad kick with his pitch to the seventh and found an unplayable lie in a small bush at the back of the green. He prowled round it for some time with cries of, 'Carramba!' and 'Mamma mia!', had a hack at it, knocked it into the deep bunker on the left and finished with a seven. Things began to go wrong from then on until, after failing to get anything like a three at the short fifteenth, Leopoldo abandoned hope. He turned to me with charming Latin-American courtesy. 'Now,' he growled, 'I play no blahdy good, same like you.'

from *How to Become a Scratch Golfer*, Blond & Briggs (UK)

THE THIRD MAN   Herbert Warren Wind

There is no question at all in my mind but that the 1964 United States Open Championship, which Ken Venturi won ... at the Congressional Country Club, in Washington, will be remembered as one of the greatest Opens. Such an assertion takes in a good deal of territory, I know, because over the years since 1895, when ten professionals and one amateur teed off in the inaugural US Open, the national championship has, far more often than not, produced climaxes that have outfictioned fiction ...

The 1964 Open was notable for much more than a powerful third act. From the morning of the first round, when Sam Snead, the ablest golfer who has never won our national championship, insured his twenty-fourth failure in the event by four-putting the fourth green and then three-putting the sixth (after which he flung his ball in disgust into a convenient water hazard), the tournament was charged with exceptional golf and exceptional human interest, and both kept building until we were presented with the improbable spectacle of a winner emerging from golf's deepest limbo to stagger ashen-faced down the long incline to the final green after beating off not only his last challengers but the threat of heat prostration. To my knowledge, there has never been anything like this in golf history.

A hundred and fifty qualifiers started the Open this year, as usual, but the championship is really the story of three players—Venturi, Palmer, and Tommy Jacobs. Thursday, the day of the first round, belonged almost completely to Palmer. He was a comparatively late starter, going off at twelve-twenty-five, when two thirds of the field were out on the course or already back at the clubhouse. One of the first men out, Bill Collins, who had the advantage of shooting to greens that hadn't yet been baked hard by the fierce sun, had succeeded in matching par—70—but in general the scores were running high, and so was the feeling among the golfers that once again an Open course had been made a bit too severe. For a change, the chief complaint was not that the United States Golf Association, which conducts the Open, had narrowed the fairways too drastically and allowed the rough to grow impossibly high and lush; in fact, it was agreed that the fairways were wide almost to the point of generosity, and that the rough, emaciated by a prolonged dry spell, was eminently playable. Since there was also a minimum of fairway bunkering, Congressional undoubtedly constituted the easiest examination in driving of any Open course in at least a decade. What, then, was giving everyone so much trouble? Well, a number of things. To begin with, Congressional, at 7,053 yards, was the longest course in Open history, and some of the Brobdingnagian par 4s—particularly two holes that are ordinarily played by the club members as par 5s had been converted into par 4s for the championship—were breeding all kinds of bogeys. On these holes, some of the shorter hitters were unable to reach the greens with two woods, and the longer hitters, who could get home with an iron, found that their low-trajectory approaches were bounding off the greens. Another complaint—and again a legitimate one—was that the greens, a blend of grasses known as Arlington Bent and Congressional Bent, were exceedingly grainy. On long approach putts against the grain, it took a real rap to get the ball up to the hole, and on sidehill putts it was hard to judge how much to allow for the break—sometimes the ball didn't break at all.

Just when the conviction was setting in that, under the existing conditions, no one would be able to score below 70, Palmer went out and brought in a 68. He was not in his most impressive form either—especially on the first nine, where he hooked several drives badly. Palmer is a resourceful scrambler when he has to be, though, and he bailed himself out of trouble with deft chipping and putting until he got his driving under control. He paced himself shrewdly, picking up his birdies on the short drive-and-pitch par 4s, and coming through with his best tee shots on the long par 4s, where his tremendous power enabled him to play his approaches to the hard greens with lofted medium irons. (For example, on the thirteenth, 448 yards long and with the green lying at the top of a fairly steep rise, he got home with a 5-iron on his second.) Still, his most conspicuous assets were, as usual, his huge confidence and poise. Whereas the awareness of participating in an important championship like the Open rattles most players, even the seasoned ones, Palmer thrives on the pressure, the crowds, the noise—the whole charged-up atmosphere. As he put together his 68, to take a two-shot lead, he seemed more relaxed than a man strolling around his own back yard, and one got the feeling that he might very well be on his way to repeating his classic performance in the Masters last April, when he jumped into a tie for the lead on the first day and then pulled farther and farther away.

Friday, the day of the second round, was humid and breezeless, with the temperature hovering around ninety, but the course played a shade more easily, because, for one thing, a rainstorm shortly after daybreak had taken some of the starch out of the greens. For another thing, a threat of more rain during the day had prompted the officials to place the pins in high spots that would drain well and were less exacting targets. Palmer, one of the earlier starters, reached the turn in 34, one under par. He was playing very well. When he rolled in a curving 35-footer for a birdie 3 on the tough thirteenth, to go two strokes under par for the round and four strokes under par for the tournament, it looked as if he would be holding such a comfortable lead at the end of the first thirty-six holes that on Saturday, when both the third and the fourth rounds would be played, a pair of steady, unfancy 72s would be all he would need to wrap up his second victory in the Open.

Only one other player was making any substantial headway against par. This was Tommy Jacobs, a twenty-nine-year-old Californian who was appearing in his seventh Open. One of the most mature young men on the professional circuit, Jacobs is quite an interesting golfer. Essentially more of a swinger than a hitter, he has a tendency to become a little erratic when the tempo of his swing goes awry, but he can get awfully hot, particularly on long, punishing courses. He plays a much bolder game than most of his all-too-odds-conscious colleagues, and, in addition, he has streaks when he holes putts from all over the greens. On his first round at Congressional, Jacobs had been two strokes under par after the first eleven holes, only to finish weakly with four bogeys on the remaining seven holes, for a 72. On his second round, playing two threesomes in front of Palmer, he was once again two under par after eleven holes, but this time, instead of faltering, he started to take Congressional apart as if it were a hotel course in Switzerland. Having birdied the thirteenth just before Palmer did, he proceeded to birdie the fourteenth, by planting a 6-iron approach 5 feet from the cup, and then birdied the par-5 fifteenth with a 14-foot putt. This burst put him five shots under par for the first fifteen holes, and spectators from all over the course, including a few Palmer men on detached service from what is known as Arnold's Army, raced to the sixteenth hole to see if Jacobs could hold on the rest of the way. Jacobs occasionally becomes a bit nervous under the strain of competition, but there was not the slightest suggestion of tension about him as he parred the next two holes and then confronted the eighteenth, a par 4 an intimidating 465 yards long, on which the last four hundred yards of the fairway sweep down to a thumb-shaped green that juts well out into a sizable pond. After driving down the left side of the fairway, Jacobs, rejecting a more cautious shot, fired a 5-iron right at the pin. The ball had perfect line, but after plummeting down onto the front edge of the green it stopped dead, a full 60 feet from the cup. Jacobs stepped up and coolly holed that monstrous putt. His 64 did several things. It gave him a halfway-mark total of 136 and catapulted him into the lead, a stroke in front of Palmer, who added a splendid 69 to his opening 68. It equalled the record low score* for an Open round, set by Lee Mackey, Jr., at Merion in 1950. (Mackey, incidentally, had an 81 on his next round.) It demonstrated that Congressional, like the first-class course everyone was beginning to realize it was, required excellent golf but would yield to brilliance. Furthermore, as all the facts of Jacobs' round became known—that he had missed the fairway only twice with his tee shots, for example, and that in hitting all but two of the greens on the regulation stroke he had eleven times put his approach 20 feet or less from the pin—there was much speculation as to whether his 64 might not be the finest round ever played by a man in serious contention in a major championship. For my part, I would place it ahead of Palmer's 65 in 1960 at Cherry Hills, Gene Sarazen's 66 in 1932 at Fresh Meadow, on Long Island, and Henry Cotton's 65 in the 1934 British Open at the Royal St George's, in Sandwich, for all three of those courses were far less demanding than Congressional. Indeed, Hogan's 67 in 1951 at Oakland Hills, near Detroit, is the only round that seems to me to be in a class with Jacobs' 64. (It should, however, be noted that Palmer's 65, Sarazen's 66, and Hogan's 67 all came on the fourth round and carried all three to victory.)

Ever since 1898, when our Open, taking its cue from the older British Open, was extended to seventy-two holes, the final thirty-six have been played in one day. Once, most seventy-two-hole tournaments were set up this way, but in the years after the Second World War there was a trend to a less demanding (and more lucrative) arrangement—one that called for four days of play, with a single round each day. Today, the Open is the only tournament of any consequence in this country that still adheres to the climactic double round. It does so because the United States Golf Association remains convinced that endurance as well as skill should be a requisite of a national champion. Certainly only the soundest swings can stand up under the attrition of thirty-six holes in one day, and that is what the USGA has in mind when it speaks of endurance. On Saturday morning at Congressional however, with the temperature climbing into the nineties, it was apparent that sheer physical endurance would also be necessary. For this reason, most veteran observers felt that Palmer, who is probably the strongest man in golf, would outlast and outplay Jacobs. Another point in Palmer's favor was that the two leaders were paired, as is customary on Open Saturday, and it was thought that Jacobs would find the stress of a head-to-head duel harder to take

---

* The record is now held by Johnny Miller. He had a 63 in the final round to win the 1973 US Open.

than Palmer. No other golfer was given more than an outside chance of catching the front-runners. The nearest man, Collins, stood at 141, four shots behind Palmer and five behind Jacobs. Venturi and Charlie Sifford, the outstanding Negro professional were next, at 142.

The first surprise of the long, scorching day was Palmer's rocky start. Obviously impatient, he went aggressively for the pin on his approaches from the very first hole. Despite the fact that the greens had been soaked by a heavy rain during the night and were holding well, these were questionable tactics—or at least they seemed so after Palmer missed the first five greens. He hit the sixth, but when he then three-putted it, he fell four shots behind Jacobs, who was playing placidly and well. At this point, a third man most unexpectedly entered the picture—Venturi. Paired with Ray Floyd two twosomes in front of Palmer and Jacobs, Venturi had birdied the eighth at about the time Palmer was three-putting the sixth. It was his fourth birdie of the day. He had begun his rush on the first green, when his 10-foot putt for a birdie had hung on the lip of the cup for almost a minute and then toppled in. After that happy augury, he had gone on to birdie the fourth, the sixth, and the eighth and to par the other holes, and so, as he moved with his habitual splay-footed stride down the ninth fairway, wearing his habitual white cap and frown of concentration, he was no longer on the periphery of contention, he was in the thick of it. He had actually overtaken and passed Palmer.   .

The ninth hole, a par 5 measuring 599 yards, is the longest hole at Congressional. It is called the Ravine Hole, because, about 110 yards from the green, the fairway, after ascending a gentle hillside, plunges abruptly down some 40 feet and then rises as sharply to a relatively small, well-trapped green. It is doubtful if any player in the field could have reached the ninth green in two shots, and, in any event, no one was of a mind to try it; on both banks of the ravine, the fairway had been allowed to grow up into rough, so there was nothing to be gained by taking the gamble. The sensible way to play the ninth, and the way every man in the field attempted to play it, was to lay up short of the ravine on the second shot (usually with a long iron) and hope to put the third shot close enough to the pin to have a crack at a birdie. On his third round, Venturi did precisely this, punching his third, a firm wedge shot, 8 feet from the pin. He got the putt down to reach the turn in 30, five shots under par. (His irons to the green had been so accurate that his score could have been even lower; he had missed holeable birdie putts on both the third and the seventh greens.) Venturi kept on going. After getting his pars on the tenth and eleventh holes, he hit what was possibly his best iron shot of the morning on the 188-yard par-3 twelfth—a fullblooded 4-iron, which stopped hole-high about 16 feet to the left of the pin. He played the sidehill putt to break down some 3 inches, and it fell into the middle of the cup. That birdie put Venturi six under par for the round and four under par for the tournament. A glance at a nearby scoreboard brought the news that Jacobs had meanwhile

WHERE'S THE FLAG?

16   Gary Player and caddie (Alfie Fyles), 1972, Muirfield

IN TROUBLE

17 Arnold Palmer, 1961, Royal Birkdale
18 Peter Oosterhuis, 1973, Wentworth

19 Tom Watson, 1975, Wentworth
20 Gary Player (*left*), lost on the 71st hole of the 1974 Open

THAT ONE MISSED ...

21 Peter Alliss, 1966, Stoneham
22 Sam Snead, 1967, Wallasley

23 Johnny Miller, 1976, Royal
Birkdale
24 Well first of all I'll light up.
Then see if this piece of driftwood
with its billiard cue shaft has lost its
magic ... Max Faulkner

PERFECT BALANCE AT THE FINISH

25 Gene Sarazen, 1952, Royal Lytham and St Annes
26 Ben Hogan, 1956 Canada Cup, Wentworth, with Sam Snead watching
27 Lee Trevino, 1972, Wentworth

28 Severiano Ballesteros, 1976 Open, Royal Birkdale

bogeyed both the eighth and the ninth and was now only three under par for the distance. It was hard to believe, but it was a fact: Venturi was leading the Open.

If any golfer in the field had swept to the front on Saturday in such a fantastic fashion, his surge would naturally have excited the galleries at Congressional, but the fact that it was Ken Venturi who was working this miracle made the air incalculably more electric. Venturi's rapid rise to fame and subsequent tumble back into obscurity are familiar to all who follow golf. The son of the manager of the pro shop at the Harding Park public course, in San Francisco, he first achieved national recognition in 1953, when, a slim, handsome twenty-two-year-old amateur, he was selected for our Walker Cup team. In 1956, still an amateur after completing a tour of duty in the Army, he confounded the golf world by decisively outplaying the whole field in the first three rounds of the Masters at Augusta and entering the final round with an authoritative four-stroke lead. Then he shot a jittery 80, and lost the tournament by a stroke. It should be remarked, I think, that his play on that last round was not the utter collapse it has since been called, for he hit no really bad shots; rather, he kept missing the greens on his approaches by small margins, and he failed to hole any of the 5- and 6-foot putts that his chips left him. In two subsequent years, he came very close to winning at Augusta. In 1958, when Palmer first broke through in the Masters, Venturi was paired with him on the final round, was only a shot behind as they entered the stretch, but Palmer shook off his challenge by making a memorable eagle on the thirteenth. In the 1960 Masters, Venturi fought his way back into the battle after a spotty first round, and had the tournament apparently won when Palmer, the only man he still had to worry about, caught him by birdieing the seventy-first hole and beat him by birdieing the seventy-second.

After this third disappointment in the Masters, something went out of Venturi's game, and in a relatively short time it was apparent that he was no longer the superb golfer he had been between 1956, when he turned professional, and 1960. In those days, he had been not only one of the leading money-winners on the professional tour but probably the most proficient shotmaker in the country. I believe that the Venturi of that period was the finest iron-player I have ever seen—not excepting Byron Nelson, Venturi's teacher. Venturi's style with the irons was not particularly graceful. He took the club back in an upright arc with three rather distinct segments to it, but he arrived at the top of his backswing with his hands in an ideal position and his body perfectly balanced, and it seemed that all he had to do then in order to come into the ball just as he wanted to was to move his hips a notch to the left at the start of the downswing. Moreover, he possessed a rare instinct for iron play; he adapted his shots not only to the wind and the weather but also to the terrain he was playing from and playing to. For example, he would feather one approach in to the flag with a little left-to-right drift and burn his next approach in low and hard and dead on the target. By 1961, though, as I say, he was no longer playing golf of this caliber, and in the succeeding years his game continued to disintegrate. A succession of physical ailments, ranging from a back injury to walking pneumonia, contributed to this decline, but even when Venturi was feeling fit he played unimpressively. His confidence seemed completely shot. He failed to qualify for the Open in 1961, 1962, and 1963, and last year [1963] his total winnings on the professional tour came to less than four thousand dollars. This spring he suffered the crowning humiliation of having to watch the Masters at home on television, because he had not qualified for an invitation to the 1964 tournament.

Venturi's behavior during his protracted ordeal was exemplary, and it won him the admiration of his fellow professionals. He never bellyached about his lot, he was not envious of his friends' successes, and he quietly kept trying to put his game together again. This display of character came as a surprise to a number of people around golf. As a young man and one of Hogan's heirs presumptive, he had shown himself to be pleasant and very likable, but, perhaps because his honors had come to him so quickly and easily, there seemed to be large areas in which he lacked perception and tact. After a low round at Augusta, for example, he would come sweeping up the stairs of the clubhouse, the reporters and photographers at his heels, and, sailing by the likes of Hogan and Snead, he would scale his cap halfway across the players' lounge as if he owned the world. He was not arrogant, though; he was simply very young. In adversity, he grew up, and revealed himself as a man of fiber. Late this spring he suddenly began to play quite well again. In June, in the two weeks preceding the Open, he tied for third in the Thunderbird Open and then tied for sixth in the Buick Open. Though his putting stroke remained somewhat unsound, which it always had been, and though he hit a few wild shots in each round, he was setting himself up far more comfortably before the ball than he had done in years, he was playing with a new vigor, and he was concentrating well.

At Congressional, I watched a good part of Venturi's first two rounds, for, like everyone else, I wanted very much to see him do well. His opening 72 could easily have been several shots higher, for he played a number of holes very loosely. He topped one bunker shot cold, fluffed another bunker shot completely, and, on a hole where his heeled drive wound up deep in the rough, did not even reach the fairway with his recovery. On his second round, he played much more surely, en route to a 70. Early in the round, he sank a few bothersome putts, which did his morale a great deal of good, and he was rifling his irons like the Venturi of old. At the same time, not even his warmest supporters would ever have dreamed that on Saturday he would have the shots, the fire, and the emotional composure to birdie six of the first twelve holes and go out in front.

Venturi did not stay out in front very long. Jacobs, summoning up some fine attacking shots, played the second nine in 34—one under par—to post a 70 and a fifty-four-hole total of 206. Venturi, after taking a 36 in for a 66, stood at 208. Near the end of the morning round, he had wavered discernibly. On the seventeenth green, he had missed a putt of just 18 inches, and on the last green he had missed one of 30 inches, in both cases also missing his par. We could only give him all credit for his gallant dash and conclude that apparently he had just run out of gas. Perhaps, after all, that was inevitable for Venturi. Strangely, everyone at Congressional, I think, felt a bit better about things when, shortly after he returned to the clubhouse at the luncheon interval, it was announced that he had been near collapse from the heat on the last five holes. His seemingly imminent failure could at least be attributed to forces beyond his control. On the advice of a doctor, he spent the bulk of the fifty-minute interval resting. He drank some tea but ate no solid food. Then he took some salt tablets and headed for the first tee, accompanied by the doctor, who walked the final round with him.

The leaders had hardly begun the final round when, for the first time in hours, Palmer got back into the picture. In the morning, harried by his wretched putting, he had never really recovered from his poor start and had ended up with a 75, giving him a total of 212 at the three-quarters mark and putting him six shots behind Jacobs and four behind Venturi. All morning long, Palmer had not made a single birdie, but he started his afternoon with a flamboyant one. Jacobs then double-bogeyed the par-3 second, after pulling his tee shot into deep trouble, and Palmer closed to within three shots of him. It now looked very much as if we might be seeing one of Palmer's patented whirlwind finishes. However, when he failed to make even his pars on two of the next four holes it became clear, tardily, that the significant thing about Jacobs' double bogey was that it had thrust Venturi back into a tie for first. Playing two holes ahead of Palmer and Jacobs, Venturi looked drawn and pale, and he was walking slowly on stiff, old man's legs, but he was executing his shots with poise and hitting the ball with an astonishing sharpness. He came to the ninth, the 599-yard Ravine Hole, after parring seven of the first eight, still tied for the lead with Jacobs.

I arrived at the ninth too late to see Venturi play his drive or his second shot. His drive must not have been very long, for, I was told, he played a full 1-iron on his second. What a shot that must have been! There was his ball sitting up in the middle of the fairway a mere 5 yards from the edge of the ravine. Only an extremely confident golfer would have attempted to lay up so daringly close to the brink, and as I gazed at the ball it occurred to me for the first time that Venturi could win the Open. In any event, that audacious 1-iron put him in position to birdie the hole. The flag was set far to the back of the green, so that there was a menacing trap only about 20 feet directly behind it, but Venturi went for the pin and stopped his wedge 9 feet past it. Faced with a delicate downhill putt that broke to the left, he played it exactly right; his ball caught the high corner of the cup and spun in. When it dropped, I felt for the first time that Venturi *would* win the Open. With his beautifully engineered birdie 4, he had regained the undisputed lead, and, as it turned out, he not only held on to it the rest of the way but widened it—eventually to four strokes—for he played par golf in, and both Jacobs and Palmer, forced to gamble at this stage of the game, ran into a succession of bogeys.

Indeed, after the ninth it became increasingly evident that only the possibility of physical collapse stood between Venturi and victory. The sun was still beating down furiously, and on the fourteenth hole, where he had started to wobble in the morning, his slow walk decelerated into a painful trudge and his head began to droop. Into my mind's eye, as I watched him, came a photograph from old sports books showing Dorando Pietri, the little Italian marathon runner, being helped by his countrymen across the finish line in the 1908 Olympic Games after he had crumpled in exhaustion only a few yards from his goal. Venturi hung on tenaciously, however, and while he hit at least one very tired shot on each hole after that, some fortunate bounces and his own tidy work around the greens saw him safely through to the eighteenth hole, the long par 4 sloping gradually down to the peninsula green. He needed only a 7 there to win. His tee shot was weak but straight. He blocked out his 5-iron approach to the right, away from the water, and went into a bunker about 40 yards from the pin. He played a much braver recovery than he had to—a beautiful, floating wedge shot that sat down 10 feet from the cup. He holed the putt. He had done it.

While I think that the thousands encamped the length of the eighteenth fairway will always treasure that moment when Venturi walked triumphantly off the final green, a champion at last, I am sure they would agree with me that the Open reached its dramatic peak a few moments earlier, when, after hitting his second shot, he came walking shakily down the long slope. He was going to make it now, he knew, and in response to the tumultuous ovation he received as he descended the hill he removed his cap, for the first time that day. A little sun would not hurt now. I shall never forget the expression on his face as he came down the hill. It was taut with fatigue and strain, and yet curiously radiant with pride and happiness. It reminded me of another unforgettable, if entirely differ-ent, face—the famous close-up of Charlie Chaplin at the end of *City Lights*, all anguish beneath the attempted smile. Venturi then put his cap back on and hit those two wonderful final shots.

Few things repair a man as quickly as victory. At his press conference back in the air-conditioned clubhouse, Venturi, who has a bright wit, made a number of trenchant remarks. Since we live in an age when every golf hero's band of supporters bears a catchy alliterative name, such as Arnold's Army, Nicklaus's Navy, and Lema's Legions, the new champion got perhaps his biggest laugh when, as he was commenting on how much the cheering of the crowds had helped him all day long, he interrupted himself to say, 'For years, all I ever had was Venturi's Vultures.' Perhaps he had said this before, but if he had no one was listening.*

from *Herbert Warren Wind's Golf Book*, Simon & Schuster (US), originally in *The New Yorker*

RULE 38, PARAGRAPH 3   Herbert Warren Wind

They say that if a man builds anything really well, whether it is an empire or a business or a golf tournament, it will continue to function almost as efficiently in his absence. My guess would be that in 1990, when Jones and his gifted associate Clifford Roberts, the perennial chairman of the tournament, will both have long since ceased to make it to Augusta in the spring, the Masters will still be the most flavorful, evocative golf event in the world. We had a sort of glimpse of this prospect this year [1968]. Not only was Jones confined to the sidelines and Hogan absent but on the eve of the first round Gene Sarazen, who has always added so much to the occasion, had to withdraw because of a torn leg muscle, and at the halfway mark the tournament was deprived of its most idolized contemporary champion, Arnold Palmer, who failed to survive the thirty-six-hole cut after a second round of 79. Yet, for all these losses, it turned out to be one of the best Masters tournaments ever—indeed, one of the most genuinely thrilling championships of modern times. For one thing, it is hard to remember a championship in which so many golfers were in a position to win throughout the full seventy-two holes. On Friday, the day of the second round, six different players held the lead at one time or another, and at the close of the day only four strokes separated the top nineteen players. On the third round, there was a chaotic log-jam all afternoon long, and it looked as though we would end up with six co-leaders at 211—Don January, Bob Goalby, Bruce Devlin, Ray Floyd, Frank Beard, and Gary Player—until Player, the last of them to come in, holed a sinuous 30-foot birdie putt on the last green to stand at 210, six under par. We had a leader, finally, but no fewer than sixteen golfers were bunched within four strokes of his fifty-four-hole total. What with this unprecedented congestion, Sunday, the day of the final round, promised to be a day to remember. It was, but not in the way that had been anticipated.

The first thing that aroused the immense, expectant crowd on Sunday afternoon was an amazing opening charge by Roberto de Vicenzo. In the Masters, as in most stroke-play events these days, the players with the lowest scores go out at the end of the field. De Vicenzo, a veteran from the Argentine, standing at 212, two strokes off Player's pace, and Tommy Aaron, a young Georgian, three strokes off the pace, teed off at one o'clock, in the fifth-from-the-last twosome. On the first hole, a 400-yard par 4, the pin was positioned on the extreme left, about 20 feet

---

* Venturi's resurgence was brief. He put in a few good performances over the next two or three years and once again faded from sight—mainly the result of trouble with his hands. But this Open win and the two losing Masters performances will not be forgotten.

from the front edge and directly behind the green's solitary bunker. De Vicenzo, after a long right-to-left drive (he plays everything with draw), had only a 9-iron left. He hit a gorgeous shot. The ball cleared the bunker by about 3 yards, hopped for the cup, and rolled in—an eagle 2. As quickly as that, de Vicenzo had jumped into a tie for the lead. He went out in front by a stroke when he birdied the second hole, then in front by two when he birdied the third. (Actually, he came within a foot of holing his approach for a second eagle.) By this time, de Vicenzo had collected a fervid gallery of rooters, which continued to swell as he made his way to the turn in 31, adding a birdie on the eighth to go five under par for the round. He is an easy man to root for, Roberto de Vicenzo, the ex-caddie from Buenos Aires.* By far the most accomplished golfer ever developed in South America, this strong, handsome, baldish man, who has a droll sense of humor and a congenial nature, has travelled the world the last thirty years like the golfing equivalent of a Guiomar Novaes or a Claudio Arrau. One week he is in Nairobi for a television golf match, the next week in Le Zoute for the Belgian Open, the next in Bogotá winning his umpteenth Colombian title. All told, he has won 140 tournaments, but until last July, when he captured the British Open at Hoylake after twenty years of trying and half a dozen near-misses, he had never won a major championship. The British adore him, and if even an English or a Scottish golfer had presumed to overtake de Vicenzo at Hoylake with an eleventh-hour rally the spectators would probably have chased the upstart off the course. In our country, he has won a fair number of tournaments—his first the Palm Beach Round-Robin in 1951—but he had never been a force in our big events. His best finish in our Open was a tie for eighth in 1957, and his best at Augusta a tie for tenth last year. On this latest Sunday at Augusta, the old campaigner was celebrating his forty-fifth birthday. I should have said it was at least his forty-fifth; de Vicenzo is not the kind of fellow who aspires to be a senior golf champion.†

That great burst on the front nine placed de Vicenzo nine under par for the tournament. This is the language in which one always converses at the Masters, for on the scoreboards around the course the progress of the ten leaders is posted hole by hole not in terms of that day's round but in terms of a player's composite score in relation to par; green numerals denote the number of strokes a player is over par, red numerals the number of strokes he is under par. De Vicenzo's red 9, however, gave him only a one-shot lead over Devlin, who was playing four twosomes behind him and had gone eight under after birdieing the first three holes, and it gave him only a two-shot lead over Goalby, two twosomes behind him, who stood seven under after birdieing the fifth and the sixth. Nine holes are a long, long way to go in golf, and especially at the Augusta National, where on

---

* If ever you are down that way amongst golfers past the first flush of youth you'll find that Roberto caddied for all of them—say about 200,000.

† He has been since.

no fewer than five of the last nine the green is protected by a water hazard, and disaster can be instant and final. There was nothing defensive about de Vicenzo's golf as he started home, however. He saved his par on the tenth with a beautiful explosion shot that ended up 4 feet from the hole. On the 445-yard eleventh, he took the bold line over the water and fired a 4-iron 9 feet from the flag, only to miss the putt. On the short twelfth, with the flag tucked dangerously close to Rae's Creek, he put his tee shot, a 6-iron, 11 feet from the flag, and this time he made his birdie putt. Six under par now for the round, ten under for the tournament. Ordinarily, that kind of scoring would have shaken off the rest of the field, and the concluding holes would have been a comfortable, triumphant march, but not this day. Goalby was still coming. After a birdie on the eighth and pars on the ninth and tenth, he was still only two strokes behind. As the steamed-up spectators began to realize, the outcome of the tournament could very well hinge on how the two men fared on the two par-5 holes on the second nine—the thirteenth and the fifteenth. The thirteenth, 475 yards to a green guarded by a creek, and the fifteenth, 520 yards to a green guarded by a pond, are the logical birdie holes down the stretch; they are, you might say, par-4½ holes, since each can be reached with two long, accurate shots. On the thirteenth, de Vicenzo, after finding a greenside bunker with his second, had to be satisfied with a 5. On the fifteenth, he bunkered his second again, but this time he got his 4, with a nice sand shot and a 10-foot putt. He wanted that putt so badly that when the ball fell he did something—quite unconsciously, I'm sure—that I had never seen him do before: he punched the air forcefully with his right hand, the way younger and showier players do. Eleven under. That could do it.

Not at all. At about this same moment, Goalby, on the thirteenth green, holed for a birdie 4. Ten minutes or so later, he rammed in a 20-footer from just off the back edge of the fourteenth for yet another birdie. He was ten under par now, with the eminently birdieable fifteenth coming up. He could catch de Vicenzo there. Goalby's stirring countercharge, it must be said, came as rather a surprise. It is not that Goalby isn't capable of very hot golf. During his eleven years as a touring professional, he has put together a lot of brilliant passages—including a run of eight consecutive birdies in the 1961 St Petersburg Open—but most of these have come in comparatively minor tournaments. In seven previous starts in the Masters, he had never placed among the first twenty-four finishers. The main reason he has had to be content with second-echelon status among the pros has been his chronic wildness off the tee. Like de Vicenzo, he has long had to battle a hook, and often the correction is an overcorrection—a lavish slice. He is a good iron player, however, very adept with the wedge, and he is also a sound putter, but perhaps his most valuable asset is his flair for competiton. A husky six-footer, now thirty-seven, he was the best all-round athlete that Belleville (Illinois) High had ever produced, and, after that, a quarterback for the University of Illinois, and although his temper has given him trouble at times, the drive and resourcefulness that made him a star in team sports have been a great help to him in professional golf. He had certainly shown his stuff in his pursuit of de Vicenzo, and he showed it again on the long fifteenth—*the* critical hole. After a fine drive far down the fairway, he settled on a 3-iron. He played an almost perfect shot. On the flag all the way, the ball carried the pond with plenty to spare, pitched softly on the front part of the green, and finished 8 feet from the hole. This 'career shot' of Goalby's prefaced what must surely stand as five of the most dramatic minutes in the history of tournament golf. Playing the seventeenth, a 400-yard par 4, which parallels the fifteenth, de Vicenzo answered Goalby's challenge almost immediately by planting his approach—a pitching wedge—3 feet from the hole. Moments later, 300 yards apart, de Vicenzo bent over the putt for his birdie as Goalby simultaneously bent over the putt for his eagle. If either missed, the other would be in the lead. Both putts were struck at almost the same instant. Goalby's went in. De Vicenzo's went in. Two tremendous roars cut the air, and two red 12s went up on the scoreboard.

After that, both men wavered slightly, for the first time. On the eighteenth, a 420-yard 4 that climbs uphill all the way, de Vicenzo, after pulling his 4-iron approach to the bottom of the bank at the left of the green, eventually missed the 8-footer he needed for his 4. Goalby, with two pars to win, three-putted the seventeenth from 45 feet. Now he needed a 4 on the eighteenth to tie. He sliced his tee shot badly into the trees on the right but got an enormous break when the ball ricocheted back onto the fairway; he reached the back of the green with a superb 2-iron, and got down in two putts from 50 feet. Two red 11s on the scoreboard. A mood of happy exhaustion among the spectators. A playoff on the morrow.

I have gone into this detail about the de Vicenzo-Goalby duel for two reasons. First, golf of this surpassing quality—a 65 and a 66 under the harshest strain— deserves to be described, for, as far as I know, never before have two men, thrusting and parrying on the last round of a major championship, both scored so low. (The pace they set was so fast that a closing 69 by Devlin, a 67 by Nicklaus, and a 65 by Bert Yancey, which might normally have won for any one of them, were rendered irrelevant.) Second, I think it is important to record the golf that Goalby and de Vicenzo played, because it is almost bound to be forgotten in the cruel, depressing aftermath of that memorable afternoon. It was discovered soon after de Vicenzo had completed his round that he had signed an incorrect scorecard. Aaron, his playing partner and 'marker', had put down a 4 for de Vicenzo on the seventeenth, instead of the 3 he had made. De Vicenzo had not detected the error. Under Rule 38, Paragraph 3, of the Rules of Golf, 'A score higher than actually played must stand as returned.' This changed de Vicenzo's score for the last round from a 65 to a 66 and made his four-round total a stroke higher than Goalby's. The tournament was over. There was no need for a playoff. The 1968 Masters champion was Bob Goalby.

from *Herbert Warren Wind's Golf Book*, Simon & Schuster (US).
Originally in *The New Yorker*

PLAYER—MASTER FROM START TO FINISH   Donald Steel

Card of course: Royal Lytham and St Anne's

Hole	Yds.	Par	Hole	Yds.	Par
1	206	3	10	334	4
2	206	4	11	542	5
3	458	4	12	201	3
4	393	4	13	339	4
5	212	3	14	445	4
6	486	5	15	468	4
7	551	5	16	356	4
8	394	4	17	453	4
9	162	3	18	386	4
Out:	3,298	35	**In:**	3,524	36

Total: 6,822 yds. Par: 71

Back in 1955 when Gary Player made his first appearance in the British Open at St Andrews, they said he would never make it. It was thought his physique was against him and his method unsound, but they reckoned without an indomitable spirit, an unparalleled determination, competitive instinct and capacity for practice—plus the simple desire to be the best in the world.

Whether he has achieved the latter is a delicate point, although only Jack Nicklaus can dispute the claim, but not even Nicklaus could deny Player his supremacy in the 103rd [1974 British] Open, and Player's victory was perhaps the greatest example of his quite remarkable powers.

Like Tom Weiskopf last year [1973] he led from start to finish. And on a last afternoon, blessed with sunshine and another enormous crowd which comfortably broke the aggregate attendance record, he won like an exceptional champion.

Having left the door open on Friday, he banked it off its hinges at the first two holes of the final round, eventually adding a 70 for a total of 282.

His winning margin has only been exceeded three times since the war and he and Harry Vardon are the only two players to have won in three different decades.

It was Player's third and best victory in the British Open and his eighth in the world's four major championships, a number which compares most impressively with Nicklaus's 12* (excluding his two US Amateur titles), particularly when one marvels at the hundreds of thousands of miles he has travelled in the last twenty years. At 37, it is a tribute to his fitness that perhaps the best years lie ahead.

So Player continues to amaze with his exuberance and skill in characteristically British conditions which he seems to like more and more and play better and better.

I don't think I have ever seen him display more complete mastery or control in a wind and on hard ground but Oosterhuis, whose previous best was equal sixth in 1970, also showed a control both of himself and his game which must have delighted him. Let us hope that he is soon able to make the same impact in American tournaments and championships.

If this will always be known as Player's Open, the contribution of Peter Oosterhuis and Nicklaus should not be forgotten.

Oosterhuis, with his best performance so far, showed that he must have an Open in him, and Nicklaus playing somewhere near his best, maintained a sequence in the championship which may never be bettered.

In 13 appearances he has finished in the first three no fewer than eight times. In addition he has been 4th, equal 5th and equal 6th. Golf is fortunate in having Nicklaus and Player at its head.

So many possibilities existed at the start of the day that the morning saw a steady build-up of expectations. The first cheer went up long before they had finished serving breakfast in the clubhouse, and for a moment or two there was the charming sight of a small boy, scarcely more than 11, sitting alone high up in the huge stand on the right of the 18th green, surveying the action on the first green through binoculars and putting them down only to applaud.

Maybe he was dreaming of the time when he is the star of the show, but at least he will be able to recall in years to come a memorable week in which the big ball was used for the first time in the Open. For this experiment, the weather co-operated fully and there is no doubt that it proved a merciless exposer of frail nerves and unsound techniques.

To my mind, this is its greatest strength because too many, amateurs and professionals, have got away with too much with the small ball for too long, a situation which has led some players to believe that they are better than is the case.

Certainly, in the winds that blew for most of the week, they were scholarship questions which the players had to answer, and many former players with whom I spoke were glad to be firmly behind the ropes.

It was mighty hard work for past champions like Locke and Daly, who came principally to see their friends, but any climax involving Nicklaus and Player,

---

* He has since added a few.

Peter Oosterhuis, the best British player for the past three years, Weiskopf, the defending champion, and Hubert Green, currently lying second in the money winner's list in the States, is a great recommendation for the decision to adopt the large ball.

Player's form on the first two days was simply terrific and more impressive than anything I have seen from him before. His control in keeping the ball down was an object lesson to those who see golf merely as an exercise in hitting the same, standard shot time after time.

For a while, in fact, it looked as if the championship was going to be monopolised entirely by him, and it was relief that his third round was human enough to let others back in on the act.

Nicklaus's advance on Friday was most important, because there is absolutely no doubt that any championship lacks something if he is not having his say; and the record crowds, which showed emphatically that it is no longer just the Scots who appreciate their golf, owed more this week to Jack than any one man.

Having a bedroom immediately above the room where all the money was counted, I can testify that the tellers were busier than anyone, but the Open is now so big that hardly anything is forgotten, or unusual.

The medical centre, set up two years ago at Muirfield, where the hot weather kept the sun tan oil flowing reported a brisker trade than at Troon, although nothing worse on Friday night than a broken leg. An official, however, revealed later that the leg in question was a wooden one and that the only help they could give was to put him in touch with the local carpenter.

Although the early starters could look on the final round as little more than an exercise to improve self-respect battered on the first three days, there was a marvellous opportunity for the crowd, numbered at over 12,000 by ten o'clock, to watch several of the players who may hitherto have been only names to them.

The younger school of Americans such as Crenshaw and Mahaffey; a sight of Graham Marsh who, despite great success in the Far East, had only one birdie on the first three days; or of the old favourites, Littler, de Vicenzo and Trevino who, in his last round, became the only player to have threes at the 14th and 15th.

The practice ground, too, made a fine study where players looking for an escape from tension as the anxious minutes before tee-off ticked away. The putting green, where even the greatest clutch at straws, was the last port of call before the walk through to perhaps the most secluded first tee in championship golf. Then, with the waiting over, talk finally became fact.

Not surprisingly, Nicklaus was the man to whom everyone looked as the main challenger to Player, partly on account of a reputation that all things are possible and partly because, in the last two years, his parting shots have taken the form of a 66 at Muirfield and a 65 at Troon.

His golf at the start was immaculately solid but, as he said on the third evening: 'I thought I was playing my Saturday round on Friday!' Yesterday the putts he needed to keep in touch kept getting away.

Nor, after a 2 at the first, could Green, with his old-fashioned putter and old-fashioned method, make any impression.

Mr Lu, in fact, went off as well as anyone with three birdies and four pars in the first seven holes, but nothing beat the start of Player, who thus made his intentions abundantly clear.

A five iron, breaking in off the bank, brought him an opening 2 and, from the left-hand side of the second, where he used an iron from the tee, he hit his second to four feet and holed for a 3.

His fount of inspiration was flowing well, and as Oosterhuis left the first green after taking three putts, the road he faced must have seemed alarmingly steep. Just as Tony Jacklin did in 1969 on the same course, he knew that he carried British hopes and it was good to see another British player making such an impression.

Looking down the course from the third, one could see the stands rising into the sky, with Blackpool Tower beyond and everywhere a blaze of colour in the sun. Although he had other things on his mind, it must have made Oosterhuis feel good—but nothing like as good as the ten-yard putt for a 3 which rolled on and on, an indication of the gathering pace of the green and the course since play began on Wednesday.

More encouragement came at the fourth, where Player bunkered his second and was prevented from exerting his usual magic on the recovery.

But though both Oosterhuis and Player took 4 at the short fifth, Player approached the prospect of possible birdies at the 6th and 7th four shots ahead of Oosterhuis and Nicklaus, and five ahead of Lu, Green and Weiskopf, who was not finding the greens quite as receptive to his second shots as he did at Troon.

If the fourth and fifth seemed at the time to represent a minor crisis, it was the only one. Player, as he has always done, came bouncing back, a long iron to seven feet at the sixth giving him an eagle and a well-judged pitch a birdie at the long seventh.

This gave him a five-stroke lead over Oosterhuis who, on turning for home out by Ansdell station, promptly took 5 at the tenth and lost second place to Nicklaus's 4 at the 11th.

All week the wind has drummed it into everyone that no chances could be taken with the back nine but nobody was more aware of this than Player and, if need be, he could have dispensed with half the clubs in the bag which his colourful caddie 'Rabbit' Dyer humped round . . .

Nicklaus and Oosterhuis did their best to whip up the pace and Nicklaus, despite taking two putts on the first nine greens, still felt he had an outside chance. Breaking point, however, came with the missing of a five-foot putt for a 3 at the 13th.

The error was, no doubt, responsible for a pushed drive at the 14th and, with the knowledge that all was now lost, he took 5 at the 15th and 16th as well before finishing typically with a 3. This left the way clear for Oosterhuis to reclaim second place and four 4s over the notorious finish did the trick.

His driving here has looked far more convincing and equally important he had the confidence to play his game in company with Player, who matched Oosterhuis's 3 at the 13th. This left Player with the opportunity of equalling the eight-stroke record margin for the Open but he was twice in the rough at the 15th and the 17th and 18th produced second shots which ran through both greens, errors which might have been disastrous in different circumstances.

At the 17th, in fact, a dozen or so in attendance scrabbled in search of Player's ball as though quelling a fire but all went well and in the traditional triumphal march up the packed 18th hole, everybody meant every cheer.

Meanwhile, Lu, Weiskopf and Cole had fallen away leaving Green in fourth place on his first trip to Britain but equally creditable were the 69s of Swaelens, Townsend, Graham and Garner, who managed the hottest spell of the week with 3, 4, 2, 3, 4, 3, from the turn; and Morgan and Dawson completed the best golfing week of their lives with the promise that they may now make their mark in British professional events.

*How they finished**

282
G. Player (S. Africa) 69, 68, 75, 70 (£5,500)

286
P. A. Oosterhuis (Fiji) 71, 71, 73, 71 (£4,000).

287
J. Nicklaus (U.S.) 74, 72, 70, 71 (£3,250).

288
H. Green (U.S.) 71, 74, 72, 71 (£2,750).

292
D. Edwards (U.S.) 70, 73, 76, 73
Lu Lang-Huan (Taiwan) 72, 72, 75, 73 (£2,300 each)

293
R. Cole (S. Africa) 70, 72, 76, 75
D. Swaelens (Belgium) 77, 73, 74, 69
T. Weiskopf (U.S.) 72, 72, 74, 75 (£1,716.66 each).

294
J. Miller (U.S.) 72, 75, 73, 74 (£1,500).

295
J. Garner (Hartsbourne) 75, 78, 73, 69
D. Graham (Aust.) 76, 74, 76, 69 (£1,350 each).

296
N. C. Coles (Holiday Inns) 72, 75, 75, 74
A. Geiberger (U.S.) 76, 70, 76, 74
J. Morgan (Stoneham) 69, 75, 76, 76
A. Tapie (U.S.) 73, 77, 73, 73
P. Townsend (Portmarnock) 79, 76, 72, 69 (£1,000 each).

297
P. Dawson (Filey) 74, 74, 73, 76
A. Jacklin (Potters Bar) 74, 77, 71, 75
G. Littler (U.S.) 77, 76, 70, 74
D. Weaver (U.S.) 73, 80, 70, 74 (£550 each)

298

R. D. Shade (Duddingston) 78, 75, 73, 72

L. Wadkins (U.S.) 78, 71, 75, 74

299

C. O'Connor, Jnr. (Carlow) 78, 76, 72, 73

B. Gallacher (Wentworth) 76, 72, 76, 75

A. Gallardo (Spain) 74, 77, 75, 73,

H. Irwin (U.S.) 76, 73, 79, 71

300

B. Crenshaw (U.S.) 74, 80, 76, 70

D. Jagger (Tobago) 80, 71, 76, 73

D. McClelland (Hartsbourne) 75, 79, 73, 73

301

P. J. Butler (Golf Domes) 75, 77, 77, 72

A. O. Cerda (Mexico) 80, 74, 77, 70

D. Chillas (Turnberry H.) 72, 78, 77, 74

T. Horton (Ham Manor) 78, 76, 76, 71

H. Jackson (Holme Hall) 78, 76, 73, 74

L. Trevino (U.S.) 79, 70, 78, 74

302

G. Brewer (U.S.) 78, 77, 74, 73

V. Fernandez (Arg.) 78, 73, 78, 73

from *The Sunday Telegraph* (London), 14 July 1974

* Note how well down the pack some leading names came — the then new US Open Champion Irwin, for instance, or Trevino and Brewer.

ALMOST ANYONE'S OPEN   Michael Hobbs

The scorching summer of 1975 in Britain ought to have put a few golfers straight about what really leads to low scoring. At your local course about the only thing you wouldn't have heard over the midday Sunday drinks is that deafening silence that comes when not a single golfer is bewailing all the putts that got away. In the final analysis then, is it the putts or the long game that makyth the round? The answer, of course, is both simple and equivocal—both. But let's take the thing a stage further.

By mid-summer you could top a drive or hit that ball a gentle little slice and it still bounced and skidded along for 200 yards or so. Similarly a half-hit approach with a long iron still clawed its way along to within a chip of the flag. In such conditions the better players are in trouble. Although the real measure of superiority at all levels of golf is how well a man can hit his average fairway wood, long iron or even 8- and 9-irons into the green, once the ground encourages a ball to hop, skip and bounce onwards any event is wide open to the people who are playing that 'game within a game' well (chipping and putting). However perfectionist and purist we all may be, it's more encouraging to see a mediocre shot finish somewhere near the green than observe it hiss a few yards along sodden turf—and know you may be about to do the same thing all over again.

The famed terrors of the 1975 Carnoustie were laid to rest by drought and lack of wind, so that the crush on the final day was predictable: hardly anyone, if he had the nerve *not* to be overwhelmed by doing quite well in the British Open Championship, ought to have been able to dart through on the flanks of the great ones if he could, for an hour or so, get his putts lancing or curling into the hole.

Yet how different opinions about Carnoustie were until the last couple of weeks before the tournament began. Nicklaus, for example, thought it the hardest championship test of all. A glance at the records for Opens held there does nothing to discredit that opinion. The first occasion, 1931, Tommy Armour won with 296 (no misprint) and when Henry Cotton won six years later with 290 he said he had played the greatest golf of his life. Part of the Hogan legend is that he won the British Open on his first—and only—attempt. A measure of the achievement was that he had completed his four rounds in 282 and in doing so had left the rest of the field a considerable way behind him. The extent of his superiority in 1953 was underlined in 1968 when Gary Player won at Carnoustie in similar conditions—with a score seven strokes worse than Hogan's. In the 1975 Open you could perhaps say that a worthy winner ought first to better Hogan's score by four strokes (to allow for the fact that the 18th had been shortened some 70 yards to make it a par 4) and ought to do a great deal better than that if the championship were fought out in fair weather.

In the practice days all the talk was of Nicklaus. He had won the 1975 US Masters in a struggle with Weiskopf and Miller that is already golfing legend and had then come very close in the US Open only a few weeks previously. If he had felt that the course could not be attacked, his play in practice did not betray the fact: 67, 65, 67, 65. Fearful that he would use up all the good golf before the championship began and that the course he had described as 'the toughest in the world' would turn and rend him, Nicklaus did not keep score in his last warm-up round and claimed he had gone round in 96. When the chips were down he would have to attack; it was evident that Carnoustie was about to yield good scores to golfers other than Nicklaus. If he could maintain the scoring of his practice rounds, he would win; otherwise the new ease of the course meant that any very good golfer might pull it off. But Nicklaus, despite the splendour of power that deceives, is a defensive player. Peter Dobereiner, writing in *The Observer*, put it succinctly: 'Most of the time he plays with the timidity of a middle aged spinster walking home through a town full of drunken sailors, always choosing the safe side of the street. Sometimes he gets home safely. But more often he gets grabbed.' It had happened recently, said Dobereiner, when Nicklaus faltered on the last three holes in the US Open.

Indeed, there were plenty of other very good golfers to watch out for. Some had shown good recent form. Watson had led the US Open after two rounds and then, as in the Masters, had disappeared from sight. Bobby Cole had just discovered the 'secret' of golf which had to do with shortening the left thumb—a somewhat obscure dictum but one that worked for him. Oosterhuis was getting the putts in; Weiskopf and Miller freely confessed to hitting the ball well. What, however, of Gary Player? He had swept up a hatful of tournaments the previous year, held the British Open and had also won it the last time it had been played at Carnoustie. He was complaining of the worst hook on the world golf circuit, but when Player bemoans his golf, it's a good time to wager £5 on his chances.

Nicklaus began as if he'd used up all his good golf in practice. He found the first green with his second shot but then pulled his birdie putt badly. At the 2nd he thinned a chip and threeputted. At the 3rd he left himself a nasty 3ft putt but managed to get it down for his par. At the 379-yard 4th he missed the green entirely and sank a long, long putt of at least 20 yards for a birdie. (The 4th at Carnoustie shares a double green with another hole—hence the fact that Nicklaus was able to take a putter.) No doubt encouraged by such undeserved good fortune the great one was again himself. From this hole to the 12th he was four under par and then holed another huge putt for an eagle on the 488 yard 14th, before having a birdie at the next. He had now reached the three finishing holes. They were to prove the key to the championship. The 16th varied between 210 yards and 235 yards—depending on where the tee markers were set—and the narrow green was a difficult target. The difficulty of playing the hole is doubled by the fact that any shot that fails to strike the centre of the green, or which has insufficient bite, is thrown off by the domed surface either into the bunkers which flank the green or down a bank into light rough. Nicklaus took a long iron and his ball hit the green but toppled off to the left and down. He pondered the problem and elected to putt through the rough and up the bank, hoping that his ball would then dribble over the few yards of green up to the hole. The putt was not quite firm enough and his ball curled away, leaving him with a 7 foot putt. He missed it. The 17th, under the conditions that the Open was played, was arguably the most difficult hole on the course—certainly few complained that they had failed to birdie it and anyone was glad to get away with a par. From the tee, two winds of the Barry Burn confront the player. If his name is Nicklaus he may hope to clear both and set up a short iron to the green. As far as I know, no one, Nicklaus included, attempted the carry. All took a long iron, aiming to clear the first meander but stop short of the second. Even then, the shot had to be well struck. A long iron with draw on it tended to reach the second line of the hole's defences, and many sad figures were to be seen picking out under penalty after their balls had rolled too many extra yards; others were in the same predicament at the first wind of the burn after hitting entirely unenigmatic bad shots.

Nicklaus placed the tee shot exactly but failed to solve the problem set by the approach shot to the 17th green. There were two routes. You either played left, pitched short and counted on a swing round with the slope and onto the green—perhaps off the bank at the left side of the green—or you played a high-flying shot over the humps directly at the flag. If you didn't fly that one quite long enough there followed a test of your technique in the pot bunkers that lay concealed below a crest. Nicklaus came in from the left, stopped short, and followed with a pitch and run to 2 yards. He was a little too far right with his putt but the ball decided to drop in nevertheless.

The 18th was the hole they had altered and the consensus was that it had become a testing par-4 rather than a tedious par-5. From the tee, the Barry Burn again had to be crossed twice before the green was reached: first with the drive and then as it curved across the front of the green. Nicklaus found a bunker to the right of the green, came out to 3 yards and missed the putt. Two over par then for the last three holes and a pattern frequently repeated. Nevertheless, he had a 69 in his pocket and that must have looked an unlikely prospect when he had lined up that huge putt on the 4th a couple of hours before.

The rest of the first day was left to the funny names: Oosterhuis, Oosthuizen and Huish. Throughout the championship British eyes were focused mainly on the first of these, a name that the Press will insist, for the purposes of headlines and general matiness, of compressing into the distinctly unattractive form 'Oosty'. Now there was another of them and no one knew how to say the 'huizen' bit. In the end it came out as Peter 'Oosterhouse' and Andries 'Oosthazen'. Oosterhuis, who had finished as runner-up at Royal Lytham and St Anne's the previous year, led the field at the end of the first day. No one had quite been able to believe how easy the sleeping giant of Carnoustie had been playing the first day, it seemed, but Oosterhuis was home early with a 68. He faltered a little at the last hole but then nearly everyone else coped far less well with the 16th and 17th as well. Oosterhuis was out in 33. He dropped a shot at the 5th, where he pushed a 5-iron to the right into one of the few areas of rough that had survived the drought, but otherwise had three birdies in the last four holes of the outward half. The lack of rough was, at least in part, the story of this Carnoustie championship. A player could carve his shots from the tee in all kinds of improbable directions but, as long as he didn't come to rest in a gorse bush, he came to little harm. Oosterhuis missed birdie putts on three of the next four greens but picked up one at the par-5 478 yard 12th.

Oosterhuis is two quite distinct players. Once he is near enough the green to rely on touch it looks as if he can scuffle the ball up dead to the flag from the middle of any tuft of grass, bush or cedar of Lebanon that there happens to be around. He is perhaps a touch less sure as a putter but still the man to bet on to get the short ones in. But watch him take a tee shot. Only Doug Sanders is his close rival in making the preliminaries convince an observer from Mars that the business of swinging at a golf ball with admittedly peculiar-looking tools is a highly unnatural and foredoomed activity. As such observers from Mars, let's have a look at him.

For a start, Oosterhuis is obviously too tall for the whole project. The little white ball is an impossible distance away from the eye, 6½ ft above it, striving to keep the object in focus. But the player seems to have no particular difficulty in *seeing* it; his problem is transparently concerned with where he is going to plant his feet. He edges them this way and that and in the due course of time arrives at a final position that seems remarkably similar to where he began the shuffle. He is doing the handicap golfer's thing of taking aim negatively, concerned not so much with where he wants to hit the ball to but where he *doesn't* want to put the thing. With a fine expanse of dense undergrowth to his right, the handicap golfer edges around with equal perseverance until he has achieved a set of the feet that makes a curving slice into the middle of it inevitable: it is a natural law of golf that if you need desperately *not* to slice that's just what you will do. Likewise for the hook.

By the 14th Oosterhuis may have been wondering when his particular bogey was going to appear. That bogey is a push or slice—sometimes a combination of the two—of grand proportions. At the 14th he took rather a short quick swing at the ball and got it in the heel of the club and was relieved not to reach wooded territory. Nevertheless it was a par-5 on a 488 yard hole where such as Miller were taking a 5-iron into the green. Worse was to follow. From the 15th tee he carved one away to the right and onto the adjoining 4th fairway. It was a fortunate escape but he was unable to reach the green at this 461 yard hole with his next and again took 5. On then to the 16th, where his 1-iron hit the green and then ran down the bank and away. But unlike Nicklaus Oosterhuis chipped it into the hole and advanced on the 17th much refreshed. No push this time and he was 12 feet or so from the hole in two and down went the putt. Suddenly five under par and no one yet out on the course was matching those figures. There came another prodigious slice at the last hole and he was left with a full 1-iron to the green from an angle at which the Barry Burn was more of a threat. Furthermore, if he hit the shot too well, it could skip through the green and out of bounds. Oosterhuis looked up a little too briskly to see what the result was to be. His ball hit a mound directly in front of him and bobbled along for only about 40 yards. His third shot then ran off the green, leaving a chip up the bank that had to be judged to a nicety. It was, and Oosterhuis holed the short putt for a 68. It was a championship record for Carnoustie—matching Hogan's winning final round in 1953—and good enough to give him the lead at the end of the day.

Oosthuizen's name was prominent through that first day even though few could pronounce it and many others, who had not before heard of the blond 21-year-old South African, put down his achievements to the credit of Peter Oosterhuis. Oosthuizen came to the last tee needing a 4 to share the lead. If he had done it, two of the most unlikely sounding names in world golf would have given headline writers something to think about: 'Oosty and Oost Slam Field'? Hardly. Fortunately for them he put his second into a bunker and had to be content with a 69. With five others, he shared second place.

David Huish, a club professional at North Berwick in Scotland was one of them. He reckons to play only a handful of tournaments during the year but was in good form and had recently won the Scottish professional championship. Despite this, he had been required to prequalify and had done so with nothing at all to spare. At one hole he had lost a ball in a bush and had taken a four-over-par 8. Not content with that disaster, he drove out of bounds a few holes later. On the last green he holed a 12ft putt for a birdie and found that he had a sudden-death play-off with seven others to qualify. Huish drove the first green and was in.

The spell was still there when he began at Carnoustie. He birdied the 1st, hit a 4-iron a couple of inches from the hole at the 464 yard 2nd and then birdied the 3rd as well. Three holes played, three under par. A little shocked perhaps by so superb a start he played the next three holes in 5 apiece to drop back to only one under par. But he parred the 174 yard 8th and birdied the 421 yard 9th to be out in 34. His worst moment came at the 11th, where he drove down the middle and then shanked his approach. His next attempt from the rough finished on the green, however. He pitched well at the 12th and 14th holes for birdies and held his game together over the finishing holes to be back in 35. Perhaps because David Huish is a Scotsman, there was no problem over the pronunciation of his name—Hush, of course. Of course?

The others on 69 were Jack Newton and Bob Shearer of Australia and Hale Irwin. Two over par after five holes, Irwin had birdied seven of the next ten and at one of them, the 488 yard 14th, he had hit the flag-stick with his wood into the green (a blind shot for everyone) and had then missed the eagle putt of rather less than a yard. Newton went to the turn in the lowest of the day—32—but came back less surely in 37. Shearer attracted little notice as he was playing right at the end of the field but his 33 for the second half was as good as anyone managed. A holed bunker shot on the 17th had done him no harm at all.

On 70 there were: Hobday, Edwards, Leonard and Tapie; and on 71: Miller, de Vicenzo, Burns, Barnes, Cahill, Watson, Floyd and Mahaffey.

Only a few of the big names seemed out of it already: Trevino with 76, Player, Lanny Wadkins and Gene Littler with 75 and, perhaps, Palmer and Charles with 74s. It certainly looked fatal to have dropped behind while conditions were so easy. The Carnoustie rough was not going to jump out of the ground again as soon as it rained but everyone knows that it blows just about every day of the year at Carnoustie. *Where was that wind?*

It rained that night, making the greens medium paced, while they were very receptive to incoming shots. There was hardly a breath of wind all day. The target golfers that liked to fly their shots in high at the flag and see them bite and stop ought to have a field day in these conditions. They did. The previous record of 68 was beaten time and again.

One man who didn't beat it was Peter Oosterhuis. He went out in 31 and followed that thrust with a par and then his sixth birdie of the day. Alas, he didn't get another genuine* par until the 18th and it all added up to a second half of 39. Against strict par he had dropped six shots between the 12th and the 17th. After the 11th, he was looking for something like a 64; his 70 by the end of the day put him two strokes behind the leader but still joint second. There was plenty for Oosterhuis to play for still but what does a golfer feel when he has been grabbed on the point of triumph by the self-same fault—the push to the right—that is always lying in wait for him?

The man who was two strokes in the lead was David Huish, and engagingly delighted about it. It is by no means rare for a 'minor' golfer to lead a major championship after one round but we know he won't be there a day later. Lightning, even the benevolent kind, does not often strike twice. Scotsmen were just as pleased. They had produced no winner of the British Open since 1931, when Tommy Armour won it at Carnoustie—and he was by then a sufficiently naturalised American to be playing in the US Ryder Cup team. Otherwise, Eric Brown had led at the halfway stage in 1953 and 1957. These apart, the ghosts of Young and Old Tom Morris and James Braid have had no inheritors to look down upon.

Huish began with a 5. 'Oh dear', they said. But it was not 'oh dear' at all. He holed a putt of 20 feet at the 2nd for a birdie, did much the same thing at the 5th, though from a little further away, after a birdie at the 4th. He dropped a stroke to par at the 9th but the rest were all pars and he was out in 34. Could he keep it up? On the return he holed some medium-length putts and got his regulation birdies at the par-5s and saved his final gem for the 16th. For this 235 yard hole he took out a driver, put his ball on the green and holed a putt of about 7 yards. He was round in 67, one of those who broke the old record.

The only golfer to better his round was Bobby Cole, who had finished well up in the previous year's British Open. That shortened left thumb, however, was going to make all the difference this year. Cole claimed it made his swing firmer at the top of the backswing and that this minor alteration of grip prevented the club going back past the horizontal. There were, however, those to say that more important was the fact that Cole had come near to the perfect putting round. He had birdied each of the par 5s, two of the three par 3s on the card and two par 4s. After an opening 72 he had pushed up into joint-second place together with Oosterhuis, Oosthuizen and Tom Watson. Quite a few were liking what they saw of this 25-year-old and he would probably be happier lying in second place than exposed at the top at the halfway stage. He had followed a sound 71 with a 67. He too had birdied all the 5s on the card and had picked up four others.

Undoubtedly it was the ease with which the long holes could be played in four shots that was taming Carnoustie, making strict par no more than 69. A howl had gone up at Hazeltine National at the 1970 US Open when no one could reach

---

* The 12th measures 478 yards and the 14th is 488 yards. Unless there is a headwind no professional in the conditions prevailing would see these holes as anything more than par 4s. Oosterhuis took 5 at each.

the long holes in two shots and certainly all golfers should pay less attention than they often do to the numbers on a scoreboard that tell what the par is. Muirfield has the answer perhaps. There, the Honourable Company of Edinburgh Golfers stipulate no par figure for any hole, neither are lengths stated at the tees.

Others besides Huish were causing surprise by having produced two good rounds in a row and therefore being in contention. One was the Irishman Leonard, if anything more of an unknown than Huish, but his performance of 70, 69 was virtually ignored by the Press. Yet there was a feature of his style sufficiently individualistic to be worth a few words: the basis of his putting method was to separate the hands, putting the right far down the shaft and only a few inches above the head of the club. The result—for some—is the feeling that the right hand is bowling the ball at the hole. However, most of us, champions or not, are afraid of looking ridiculous, let alone grotesque. I cannot conceive, for instance, of Hogan or Nicklaus risking titters from the galleries as a result of putting with any technique more original than elegant. Consider the fate this writer met with when he made himself a putter out of 2in-by-2in pine, with a shaft of ¾in dowelling. If I left a putt a couple of yards short or sent it confidently well past the hole even my best friends rejoiced and said, 'You'll never putt with a thing like that.' On my good days the comment followed a different pattern altogether but one no easier to bear. 'That thing you've got there isn't legal, you know.'

The several people who followed Leonard around saw him hole out very steadily indeed with this split-hands method. If he'd won the Open perhaps even Nicklaus would have turned his thoughts upon the techniques required and then we'd all have been doing it. However, Leonard did not win the 1975 Open though he did keep going commendably over the full four rounds with his scoring subsiding only a little. He added a 73 and a 74 to his first two rounds and finished on 286. That was worth £1,750—a lot more at that than the likes of Weiskopf, Player, Trevino and Palmer took back home with them.

And, alas, David Huish. A lot of Scotland came along for the final two days, more in hope than confidence, to see how the local boy made out against the great ones. Surely he couldn't keep it up? Perhaps content with the thought that he'd be able to tell his grandchildren all about 'How I led the Open after 36 holes' he no longer got the important putts in and subsided to a 76. Worse followed on the final day when he took 80—only two players who had got that far scored higher. Never mind, to have kept it up over two days is a memorable achievement. I hope the members at North Berwick have clubbed together and put up a suitable plaque somewhere.

The third day usually sorts them out: at the end of it you often have a couple who seem to have almost escaped the field, followed by a few more who still have a chance if they can pull off something special in the final round. Not so at Carnoustie in 1975. The boys were getting used to the idea that strict par really was no more than 69: anyone who didn't beat the rated par of 72 this day put himself finally out of contention and eight scored below 69. One equalled the best score ever returned in a British Open: Jack Newton with 65. He had taken some advice from Jack Nicklaus about his putting and was setting his hands higher up the club and trying more to get the feel of having his forearms in the stroke. Well, the only fixed rules of putting technique are that if it doesn't work it's no good and if it does, believe in it. Newton did. He holed from several yards at the 1st and then from not much less at the 3rd and picked up one more birdie while going out in 32. At that point he faltered, putting his next shot to the green into a bunker. He came out well but his putt to save a par was weak and short. Taking an iron from the tee at the 372 yard 11th he was headed for trouble but ended in a good lie and eventually birdied the hole. Three more followed in succession and he passed the difficult 461 yard 15th in par. Now for that final stretch of three. At the 235 yard 16th he pushed his drive and his little pitch shot failed quite to get to the putting surface. From the fringe, Newton put his next one into the hole and was visibly delighted. Nor less so after the 17th, where he was safely on in two and then holed out from about 7 yards. As he stood on the last tee a birdie would have beaten the Open Championship record round of 65, set by Henry Cotton in Sandwich in 1934. That round, coupled with a first round of 67, had left the rest looking about pessimistically to see who they would have to beat for second prize. Newton's did not give him the lead.

For instance, Cole's short left thumb* was still working very well indeed thank you and one of the most natural-looking and fluid swings in golf had taken him round in another 66. His round had a certain numerical perfection: both halves in 33, four birdies on each and a shot dropped. Cole no doubt preferred the simple golfing perfection of his play at the last when, with all to play for at this 448 yard hole, he fired in a 6-iron to within 3 or 4 yards and holed the putt to a roar of applause.

At one point Tom Watson had been in the lead. He had begun par, birdie, birdie, birdie, par, birdie (this last one very nearly an eagle after he had struck a superb 3-wood into the 524 yard 6th). All this meant that he stood ten under par for the championship. Two more pars followed and he came to the 9th tee—and sent his drive out of bounds to the left. Watson had been pleased with the way he had changed his natural game and, like Nicklaus, was hitting the long shots with a right to left drift. But even Nicklaus hooks sometimes and so did Watson. However, he seemed undisconcerted, got a par with his second ball and went on to pick up three more birdies by the time he had reached the 16th tee. On this long par 3 he missed the green for the third time running and took a 4 and then

---

* I am still trying to work this one out. Cole had apparently withdrawn his left thumb up the shaft so that it *no longer showed between his right thumb and forefinger*. 'Ah yes,' I said to myself, picking up a golf club to investigate this particular secret. My thumb, however, refused to show at all until I Vardoned no less than three fingers. Perhaps you have to have a long thumb to be able to shorten it?

dropped another shot on the last to finish on 69 for a three-round total of 207.

But the golfer attracting more attention than anyone else was Johnny Miller. There was the feeling that he must soon win the British Open; memories were fresh of his brilliant two closing rounds in the US Masters. After those, and the earlier drama of his last-round 63 in the 1973 US Open, everyone tends to be waiting for Miller to do it again and his unparalleled scoring in the early-season US tournaments of 1975 had done nothing to lessen expectations. At Carnoustie the conditions were also ideal for Miller's pattern of shot: both the greens and—more important than it might seem—the fairways were holding. His high-flying woods and irons would pitch and grip and there was no need to play the manufactured, thought-out, running shots that Miller has yet to learn. He began by holing from about 5 yards and then 6 yards on the first two greens and already here was a good round in the making. On the 397 yard 5th he floated in an 8-iron from what rough there was on the left and it came to rest a yard from the hole. At the long 6th he did not reach the green in two but chipped and putted for a birdie and then missed the green at the 7th. No matter. He got it into the hole from 4 yards off the green. That made it three successive birdies and five in the seven holes played. He was in the lead for the first time and maintained his position by continuing to the turn in par. Out in 31, a total for the first half equalled only by Oosterhuis on the second day.

On the 10th Miller encountered trouble for the first time. There *were* little patches of rough amongst the scorched earth of Carnoustie that you could find if you searched long enough. Miller found one when he pulled his drive. The Barry Burn winds across in front of the green at this long par-4 of 453 yards and Miller sensibly played short of it. But it was a shot dropped. He was back to par at the next and now there came the two holes that in retrospect Miller may well feel cost him the 1975 Open. The 12th was one of those short-playing par-4s that everyone was gobbling up. In two shots Miller was a touch short but still had a putt for an eagle. He went at the hole with the aggressive putting he had displayed throughout the round, shaved the hole and stopped about 5 feet past. He missed the return. An opportunity gone; another went as he missed for a 2 at the 166 yard 13th.

So, though he had parred both holes, perhaps the edge of inspiration was dulled just a little. There was no mistake at the 488 yard 14th: his 5-iron second found the green and his putt was but a hair's breadth short of an eagle. He completed the testing last four holes in level par, though he had to get down in two from a bunker at the 17th. That was a 66 and a three-round total of 207—two shots behind Cole, one behind Newton.

The betting at the end of the day now made Miller favourite at 11/4; Cole and Nicklaus (he had a 68 for 208) were at 5/1; Newton 6/1; Watson 7/1; Irwin 9/1.

As the final day began, this is how they stood:

204 Cole
205 Newton
206 Miller
207 Watson
208 Irwin, Nicklaus, Coles, Mahaffey and Oosthuizen

The latter young man had impetuously gone for the green when bunkered on the last but had found only the Barry Burn short of it. In the end, a 6. That kind of finish leaves a sour taste in the mouth. Oosthuizen faded from sight the next day—but everyone now knew how to pronounce his name, and a few could also spell it.

Betting apart, it was still anybody's championship and there were a host of questions waiting an answer before the day's play began. Miller had been made favourite because only he of the four leaders had won an open championship and, of course, Nicklaus was highly favoured because of his unsurpassed record. A new factor on the morning of the final day seemed likely to work for him and those with extensive experience of golf in British conditions. At last there was a wind; pin positions were more severe—closer to protecting bunkers, on trickier areas of greens.

The principal effect of the wind was to make the outward half play longer and players would have to be using a couple of clubs more for their shots into the greens. The wind would help on the inward half but the critical last three holes were not made substantially easier even if the wind became a following one. Nicklaus's price came down to 3/1.

Perhaps most of the players had become just a little too accustomed to the conditions of both the practice days and the three tournament rounds played. True, the breeze did make the first nine holes play longer but it was only a matter of degree: the course had not overnight become really difficult. Nevertheless only Watson got to the turn under par and at that by only a single shot. He threw that one and a couple of others away when he three-putted each green between the 10th and the 12th. It looked as if he could safely be forgotten.

Miller gave himself a jolt at the 1st hole. He went boldly at a very long putt, spun off the hole and finished a few feet away. He didn't get the next one in and made up no ground with birdies going out, though he dropped no more strokes. He was putting bravely, finishing past the hole most of the time. None dropped.

Nicklaus also did not prosper to the turn. He missed a rather short putt at the 524 yard 6th (this hole was no longer yielding routine birdies playing into the wind), put a poor tee shot into a bunker on the next and made another mistake on the 9th. It all meant that he was 38 to the turn and had a lot of ground to make up.

Newton started more steadily than anyone, having four pars and a birdie on the first five holes. Then he took 6 on the 6th and immediately dropped a further stroke on the 7th. Completing his outward half with no more alarms, he stood one over par. On the next five holes he was not over par and birdied the two long holes. At this point, he looked to be the winner by about two strokes—if he could play the last four in par.

And what of the overnight leader, Bobby Cole of South Africa? As far back as 1966 he had won the Amateur Championship at Carnoustie but for year on year thereafter had not achieved the glittering prospects forecast for him. But at last, in 1974, he had become a truly major golfer. He had still to take a major championship but he had threatened to do so in the 1974 British Open and the US PGA, had come close to winning his first US tour event and had won the South African Open after a last round of 64. Towards the end of the year he had won something that perhaps *ought* to rank as a major championship—the individual title in the World Cup. There seemed no particular reason why the 1975 British Open should not make up the pair with the 1966 British Amateur. Cole went out steadily, though he was bunkered at the 2nd.

As they came into the finishing stretch from the 14th, there were really five in it: Newton, Cole, Nicklaus, Miller and Watson. Even to pick out just these five is to simplify matters too much. There were others—Graham Marsh, Neil Coles, Oosterhuis, John Mahaffey and Hale Irwin—who could all have conceivably taken the championship if they had come through with a late surge. The likelihoods, however, suggested that the winner would come from these five. Nicklaus, and Miller had to pick up the odd stroke on par while for Cole and Newton, following the rest of the field, the task was not to weaken rather than die risking stirring deeds.

Let us examine how the various players dealt with Carnoustie's final challenge. Nicklaus got one in from a couple of yards for a birdie at the 14th and thus gained ground; Cole on the other hand missed the green with a 5-iron from a perfect fairway position and finished in a bunker; Newton got his 4 and so did Watson.

At the 15th Nicklaus had a second putt of all of 2½ yards to get in for his par but did so; Watson put his second shot about 2 yards from the hole but failed to get the putt in; Miller just missed the green on the right but got safely down with a chip and a putt. Cole was a little wilder than this: he pushed an 8-iron way to the right and hit someone in the crowd. That was another shot gone. Newton pitched short of the green, his ball kicked on and continued to run until he was off the back. He then pulled his chip a little and needed two putts.

Nobody played the 16th well and it was indeed a hole that was offering more difficulty than ever. Cole did best. He had a putt of only 2 yards or so for a birdie and that might well have given him the lift to surmount the difficulties and tensions of the last two holes. But the putt did not go in. Newton put his tee shot into a bunker and came out too short of the hole to have much chance of holing his putt. Watson played the worst tee shot of the lot (this cannot be his favourite hole at Carnoustie: never once did he master the problem of hitting a straight shot over

200 yards at this hole). This time he squirted or thinned a shot away to the right and into the crowd. He was at least 30 yards from the green—a real long-handicapper's shot in fact. He followed with a good enough pitch but did not hole the putt.

Miller and Nicklaus both parred the 17th as did Watson, though in his case there was first a sliced iron shot to the green to be retrieved with a chip and putt. Neither Newton nor Cole had anything to be proud of in their tee shots at this hole, which was playing into the wind. Cole mishit and was almost in the Barry Burn. When he got to his ball he found he had a wood shot to play from a lie with the ball very much above his feet. He hit it out of the heel and had dropped another shot. Newton hit a good shot with the wrong club. Did he not realise that the carry over the first meander of the Barry Burn was made much longer by the stiff breeze or had he temporarily lost trust in his woods? It was a 2-iron he selected. He cleared the burn but by a matter of inches only. His ball came to rest on the far bank and from there he could hope for no better than the result of his next shot: it got him to within 100 yards of the green at this 454 yard hole. His pitch came to rest about 4 yards from the hole but he missed the putt. Cole's next was even better but he pushed the resultant 2 yard putt well wide.

As they each faced the last hole Newton and Miller needed a par for 279 whereas the three others needed a birdie to make this total.

Nicklaus and Miller played it first, into a fresh crosswind. Nicklaus was safely down the fairway and Miller too hit what looked like a superb drive—a little too much towards the bunkers on the right but he had allowed for that: the wind would bring his ball back. It didn't. His ball caught the edge and swung around before dropping in. Few relish their chances of hitting a long bunker shot, so there had gone the 1975 British Open as far as Miller was concerned. Nevertheless, he decided to give it a go, believing that he needed a birdie—no news that Cole and Newton were having their own problems on the 17th. Miller selected a 6-iron and hit his ball into the face of the bunker. He tried again and this time it came off; he finished a little to the left of the green but no great distance from the hole. His chip did not go in and he tapped in for a 5 and a total of 280. Nicklaus's approach was strong and went through the back of the green. His chip looked dangerous all the way but it was a par for him and the same total as Miller's.

Behind them, Watson had been observing the dramas ahead as he waited to play his approach. He put it safely on and had a putt of about 5 yards for a birdie. There is very little to say about a putt of this length. It's good (ie goes into the hole; quite good (finishes near); or poor (does not finish near). Tom Watson will therefore remember his as very good indeed and suddenly he had sprung into a position where Cole and Newton had to shoot at him, whereas before they had probably directed most of their attention to watching each other.

Cole had now to equal Watson's birdie to tie with him; Newton would get the same result if he parred the hole. Both drove well and safely. Newton had the shot to the green first and forced his approach about 5 yards from the hole. Cole studied his shot, the last of any length for the Saturday gallery. Perhaps savouring the drama, he took his time about it, striding out to the green and back and, even after this examination, consulting with his caddie about choice of club. The decision at last made, he played an 8-iron quickly and decisively to finish about a yard nearer than Newton.

Newton now had a putting problem that many of us would not mind having: shall I go for it and, if it goes in, be open champion or shall I prod it somewhere near the hole and make sure of the tie? Quite obviously he decided to settle for possible future glory tomorrow rather than joy today: his approach putt was just what the adjective implies. It could not have worried the attentive Watson as it made its way towards the hole to stop a couple of feet away. Cole's turn now. For him no mental conflict. It had to go in. It didn't and he had to settle for £3,866 but no mantle of championship. Newton carefully pushed his in.

So the real battle ended in a tie between Tom Watson and Jack Newton, two golfers only but in this 1975 British Open there seemed no reason why the Sunday's play-off shouldn't have been among another half dozen or so. If we now look at how they finished, we can see that of the top fourteen only Graham Marsh and Bob Charles had needed a really low-scoring round to finish top of the heap:

279	Watson (71, 67, 69, 72)
	Newton (69, 71, 65, 74)
280	Cole (72, 66, 66, 76)
	Miller (71, 69, 66, 74)
	Nicklaus (69, 71, 68, 72)
281	Marsh (72, 67, 71, 71)
282	Oosterhuis (68, 70, 71, 73)
	Coles (72, 69, 67, 74)
283	Irwin (69, 70, 69, 75)
284	Burns (71, 73, 69, 71)
	Mahaffey (71, 68, 69, 76)
286	Charles (74, 73, 70, 69)
	Leonard (70, 69, 73, 74)
	Oosthuizen (69, 69, 70, 78)

You could extend this list even further. Both Bernard Gallacher and Alan Tapie of the US would also have won had they respectively shot a 67 and a 69 though it must be admitted that, in the changed conditions on the final day, only Burns, Marsh, Foster and Charles bettered par.

Of course, as it happened, that Saturday was not the final day. Watson and Newton had still to fight it out, but I think the main story of the 1975 Open ends with that Saturday afternoon's scramble when more players could have won than in any Open Championship, British or American that has yet been played.

For the record, Watson beat Newton eventually by parring the final hole comfortably, while Newton bunkered his approach shot and didn't.

from *Great Opens*, David & Charles (UK), A. S. Barnes & Co (US)

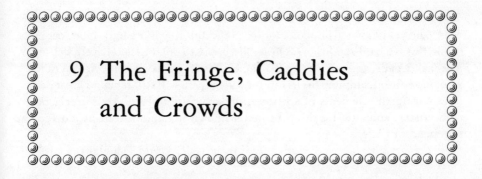

9 The Fringe, Caddies and Crowds

FOR me, the trouble with caddies is that they feel they have to earn their salt by giving advice. True, the advice is often good but I do not want to be told the line of a putt or what iron to take to the green. Such judgments are not the problem. That comes with trying to tap the ball along the right line and hitting the iron straight and true—and always with an accusing figure near.

However, cars and trolleys mean today that we can do without caddies and commit our follies under the eyes of an opponent or partner only—both of whom will have plenty of problems of their own.

Against crowds, I have a different kind of prejudice: I am not happy with the idea of anyone watching someone else do something when he could be doing it himself. However, the golf-watcher does have an excuse. He is there to see how the expert does it; something may rub off in time for the next Sunday four-ball. He will step onto the tee with an image of Nicklaus's massively deliberate backswing or of the elegant power of Weiskopf in the hitting area. Alas, for him there will soon be the old reality of the quick heave back, followed by a cutty little one curling right. The nearest he will come to emulation is in the time he will take pondering a putt—before leaving it 6 feet short.

FAMED BEYOND STATESMEN
Sir Walter Simpson

From men who have adopted carrying as a trade, the golfer is entitled to expect the highest standard of efficiency. If he carries for you regularly, the professional* ought to know what club you intend to take, and to give it without being asked. When you are in doubt about how to play your shot, he ought to confirm you in the opinion you have formed regarding it. He must never show the just contempt he has for your game.

Carrying clubs is one of the most agreeable trades open to the lower orders. In it an amount of drunkenness is tolerated which in any other would land the men in the workhouse. A very low standard of efficiency and very little work will secure a man a decent livelihood. If he is civil, willing to carry for three or four hours a

---

* At this time there was little distinction amongst the trades of playing golf, carrying clubs, or greenkeeping. Like the first pro I knew in the 1950s, you might well do all three—and then serve in the club bar!

day, and not apt to drink to excess before his work is done, he will earn a fair wage, and yet be able to lie abed till nine in the morning like a lord. If he does not drink (this is a hard condition, as he has little else to do), he is positively well-off; if he makes balls, and can play a good game himself, he may become rich. A caddy who, in addition, employs his leisure (of which there will still remain a great deal) in acquiring the elements of an education, may rise to be a green-keeper or a club-master, and after his death be better known to fame than many a defunct statesman or orator.

from *The Art of Golf*, David Douglas (UK) 1887

SHREWD BUT LIMITED   Horace G. Hutchinson

Once upon a time there was a caddie whose master's besetting sin was a snatching back of the club on the back swing. It had grown chronic, and chronic treatment was the only remedy. His caddie, therefore, was instructed, on each occasion of his master's addressing himself to the ball, to solemnly ejaculate, 'Slow back!' In course of time the master died, and the caddie was left survivor; but not without a heritage, for that inveterate habit of ejaculating 'Slow back!' refused to be eradicated. To the exasperation of many subsequent masters, by each of whom, in succession, he was forthwith incontinently dismissed, and to his own great mortification, he could not break himself of that croak of 'Slow back!' which prefaced, without respect of persons, each drive of each master. He lost all employment, and soon sank beneath the golfing horizon.

It is your caddie's business to find out how far you drive with each club; and since a life-long experience will have taught him the exact relative position to the hole of each blade of grass on the links, he ought to be always able to put into your hand the right club, almost without your asking for it. He will also know the idiosyncrasies of your play—to what extent he may allow you to 'greatly dare,' out of what lie you may be permitted to play with a brassy,* and all such little niceties. Up to a certain point the best of them show very shrewd judgment; but their horizon is strictly limited. Exceptional instances, which have not come within their previous experience, are quite outside the scope of any but the very best. They work in a groove, but a groove that, so far as it goes, is very accurate; just as some men of very limited brainpower are very shrewd within their own narrow sphere of business. Their three great principles, on which they ring the changes, are, 'Don't press,' 'Keep your eye on the ball,' and, in approaching, 'Be up.' And these contain volumes of wisdom, always with the very large proviso that one be wise enough to interpret them aright.

But though it is legitimate and proper that a caddie thus highly paid, as we are

* A 2-wood nowadays.

supposing, should supply upon these points his master's lack of experience, it is nevertheless pitiable to see the extent to which masters, many of whom really know better than the caddie, subordinate their volition to the latter's dictation. They do not seem to credit themselves with the intelligence of a tame rabbit; they do not even try to get away from the enervating influence; they are so much the creatures of their own paid servants, that if they lose their particular familiar they are helpless; they have lost all initiative; they do not know what club to take; they do not know how they ought to stand; they dare not trust their own judgment about 'the line' of an eighteen-inch putt; they are lost on the links like babes in a wood. Such subservience as this is lamentable; nevertheless, it is very common. Surely it is better to play one's own game, with reference to the subordinate only in a case of real difficulty, rather than to reverse the proper order of things, and transfer all the responsibility from the actual player to the paid assistant. There can scarcely, one would imagine, be any great satisfaction in holing a difficult putt when one of the chief points—the judgment of the line—has been referred to another. It seems almost like taking an unfair advantage over an opponent who may not be followed by an equally skilful adviser. This, however, is a point of etiquette, and custom, the queen of etiquette, has accorded it her august sanction.

Some of the very best players make their caddies indicate for them the line to the hole; but, apart from all other considerations, we would ask the golfer if he would not derive very greatly increased satisfaction from accepting upon his own broad back all the responsibilities which he should feel himself to have assumed when he struck from the tee the first ball of the match? It is scarcely conceivable that he could give any but an affirmative answer.

from *Golf*, The Badminton Library (UK)

MY FAVOURITE CADDY   Gene Sarazen and Herbert Warren Wind

After a few days in London, I went down to Prince's to practice. The first person I met, right at the gate, was Daniels. He was overjoyed to see me. While we were exchanging news about each other, I could see that the last four years had taken a severe toll of him. He had become a very old man. His speech was slower. That shaggy mustache of his was much grayer, his limp was much more obvious. And his eyes, they didn't look good.

'Where's your bag, sir?' Daniels asked, hopping as spryly as he could toward the back seat of my auto.

'Dan,' I said—I couldn't put it off any longer though I almost didn't have the heart to say it, 'Dan, this bag is too heavy for you. I know you've been in bad health, and I wouldn't want you to try and go seventy-two holes with it.'

Dan straightened up. 'Righto, sir, if you feel that way about it.' There was great dignity in the way he spoke, but you couldn't miss the threads of emotion in his voice.

'I'm sorry, Dan,' I said, and walked away. I had dreaded the thought of having to turn old Dan down, but I had never imagined that the scene would leave me reproaching myself as the biggest heel in the world. I attempted to justify what I had done by reminding myself that business was business and I couldn't afford to let personal feelings interfere with my determination to win the British Open. It didn't help much.

I was a hot favorite to win. The American golf writers thought that I had a much better chance than Armour, the defending champion, and the veteran Mac Smith, the other name entry from the States. George Trevor of the *New York Sun*, for example, expressed the belief that 'Prince's course, a 7,000-yard colossus, will suit Sarazen to a tee, if you will pardon the pun. It flatters his strong points— powerful driving and long iron second shots.' The English experts were likewise strong for me until, during the week of practice, they saw my game decline and fall apart. The young caddy from Stoke Poges did not suit me at all. I was training for this championship like a prizefighter, swinging the heavy club, doing roadwork in the morning, practicing in weather that drove the other contenders indoors. My nerves were taut and I was in no mood to be condescended to by my caddy. He would never talk a shot over with me, just pull a club out of the bag as if he were above making a mistake. When I'd find myself ten yards short of the green after playing the club he had selected, he'd counter my criticism that he had underclubbed me by declaring dogmatically, 'I don't think you hit that shot well.' I began getting panicky as the tournament drew closer and my slump grew deeper. I stayed on the practice fairway until my hands hurt.

Something was also hurting inside. I saw Daniels in the galleries during the tune-up week. He had refused to caddy for any other golfer. He'd switch his eyes away from mine whenever our glances met, and shuffle off to watch Mac Smith or some other challenger. I continued, for my part, to play with increasing looseness and petulance. The qualifying round was only two days off when Lord Innis-Kerr came to my hotel room in the evening on a surprise visit. 'Sarazen, I have a message for you,' Innis-Kerr said, with a certain nervous formality. 'I was talking with Skip Daniels today. He's heartbroken, you know. It's clear to him, as it's clear to all your friends, that you're not getting along with your caddy. Daniels thinks he can straighten you out before the bell rings'.

I told his Lordship that I'd been thinking along the same lines myself. Daniels could very well be the solution.

'If it's all right with you, Sarazen,' Lord Innis-Kerr said as he walked to the door, 'I'll call Sam the caddymaster and instruct him to have Daniels meet you here at the hotel tomorrow morning. What time do you want him?'

'Have him here at seven o'clock . . . And thanks, very much.'

Dan was on the steps of the hotel waiting for me the next morning. We shook hands and smiled at each other. 'I am so glad we're going to be together,' old Dan said. 'I've been watching you ever since you arrived and I know you've been having a difficult time with that boy.' We walked to the course, a mile away. Sam the caddymaster greeted me heartily and told me how pleased everybody was that I had taken Daniels back. 'We were really worried about him, Mr Sarazen,' Sam said. 'He's been mooning around for days. This morning he looks ten years younger.'

Dan and I went to work. It was miraculous how my game responded to his handling. On our first round I began to hit the ball again, just like that. I broke par as Dan nursed me through our afternoon round. We spent the hour before dinner practicing. 'My, but you've improved a lot since 1928!' Dan told me as he replaced my clubs in the bag. 'You're much straighter, sir. You're always on line now. And I noticed this afternoon that you're much more confident than you used to be recovering from bunkers.* You have that shot conquered now.' After dinner I met Dan by the first tee and we went out for some putting practice.

The next day, the final day of preparation, we followed the same pattern of practice. I listened closely to Dan as he showed me how I should play certain holes. 'You see this hole, sir,' he said when we came to the 8th, 'it can be the most tragic hole on the course.' I could understand that. It was only 453 yards long, short as par 5's go, but the fairway sloped downhill out by the 200-yard mark, and eighty yards before the green, rising twenty-five to thirty-five feet high, straddling the fairway and hiding the green, loomed a massive chain of bunkers. 'But you won't have any trouble on this hole,' Dan resumed. 'You won't have to worry about the downhill lie on your second shot. You have shallow-face woods. You'll get the ball up quick with them. I should warn you, however, that those bunkers have been the graveyard of many great players. If we're playing against the wind and you can't carry them, you must play safe. You cannot recover onto the green from those bunkers.' Yes, I thought as Dan spoke, the 8th could be another Suez.†

That evening when the gathering darkness forced us off the greens and we strolled back to my hotel, Dan and I held a final powwow. 'We can win this championship, you and I,' I said to Dan, 'if we do just one thing.'

'Oh, there's no doubt we can win it, sir.'

'I know, but there's one thing in particular we must concentrate on. Do you remember that 7 at the Suez Canal?' I asked.

'Do I!' Dan put his hand over his eyes. 'Why, it's haunted me.'

'In this tournament we've got to make sure that if we go over par on a hole, we go no more than one over par. If we can avoid taking another disastrous 7, Dan, I

---

* Sarazen claims to be the inventor of the modern sand-wedge.
† The hole at Royal St George's, Sandwich, which cost Sarazen the 1928 British Open. He took a wood from the rough, and then another ...

don't see how we can lose. You won't find me going against your advice this time. You'll be calling them and I'll be playing them.'

Mac Smith and Tommy Armour were sitting on the front porch when we arrived at the hotel. 'Hey, Skip,' Armour shouted. 'How's Eugene playing?'

'Mr. Sarazen is right on the stick,' Dan answered, 'right on the stick.'

The qualifying field played one round on Royal St George's and one on Prince's. There isn't much to say about my play on the first day at Prince's. I had a 73, one under par. However, I shall never forget the morning of the second qualifying round. A terrific gale was blowing off the North Sea. As I was shaving, I looked out of the window at the Royal St George's links where I'd be playing that day. The wind was whipping the sand out of the bunkers and bending the flags. Then I saw this figure in black crouched over against the wind, pushing his way from green to green. It was Daniels. He was out diagramming the positions of the pins so that I would know exactly how to play my approaches. I qualified among the leaders. You have to play well when you're partnered with a champion.

The night before the Open, the odds on my winning, which had soared to 25–1 during my slump, dropped to 6–1, and Bernard Darwin, the critic I respected most, had dispatched the following lines to *The Times*: 'I watched Sarazen play eight or nine holes and he was mightily impressive. To see him in the wind, and there was a good fresh wind blowing, is to realize how strong he is. He just tears that ball through the wind as if it did not exist.'

On the day the championship rounds began, the wind had died down to an agreeable breeze, and Daniels and I attacked from the very first hole. We were out in 35, one under par, with only one 5 on that nine. We played home in 35 against a par of 38, birdieing the 17th and the 18th. My 70 put me a shot in front of Percy Alliss, Mac Smith, and Charlie Whitcombe. On the second day, I tied the course record with a 69. I don't know how much Dan's old eyes could perceive at a distance, but he called the shots flawlessly by instinct. I went one stroke over on the 9th when I missed a curling 5-footer, but that was the only hole on which we took a 'buzzard.' We made the turn in 35, then came sprinting home par, par, birdie, par, par, birdie, birdie, birdie, par. My halfway total, 139, gave me a three-shot margin over the nearest man, Alliss, four over Whitcombe, and five over Compston, who had come back with a 70 after opening with a 74. Armour had played a 70 for 145, but Tommy's tee-shots were giving him a lot of trouble—he had been forced to switch to his brassie—and I didn't figure on too much trouble from him. Mac Smith had started his second round with a 7 and finished it in 76. That was too much ground for even a golfer of Mac's skill and tenacity to make up.

The last day now, and the last two rounds. I teed off in the morning at nine o'clock. Three orthodox pars. A grand drive on the 4th, and then my first moment of anguish: I hit my approach on the socket. Daniels did not give me a second to brood. 'I don't think we'll need that club again, sir,' he said matter-of-factly. I was forced to settle for a 5, one over par, but with Daniels holding me down, I made my pars easily on the 5th and the 6th and birdied the 7th.

Now for the 8th, 453 yards of trouble. So far I had handled it well, parring it on both my first and second rounds. Daniels had given me the go-ahead on both my blind second shots over the ridge of bunkers, and each time I had carried the hazard with my brassie. On this third round, I cracked my drive down the middle of the billowy fairway. Daniels handed me my spoon, after he had looked the shot over and tested the wind, and pointed out the direction to the pin hidden behind the bunkers. I hit just the shot we wanted—high over the ridge and onto the green, about thirty feet from the cup. I stroked the putt up to the hole, it caught a corner and dropped. My momentum from that eagle 3 carried me to a birdie 3 on the 9th. Out in 33. Okay. Now to stay in there. After a nice start home, I wobbled on the 411-yard 13th, pulling my long iron to the left of the green and taking a 5. I slipped over par again on the 335-yard 15th, three-putting from 14 feet when I went too boldly for my birdie putt and missed the short one coming back. I atoned for these lapses by birdieing the 16th and the 18th to complete that long second nine in 37, one under par, and the round in 70, four under. With eighteen more to go, the only man who had a chance to catch me was Arthur Havers. Havers, with 74—71—68, stood five strokes behind. Mac Smith, fighting back with a 71, was in third place, but eight shots away. Alliss had taken a 78 and was out of the hunt.

If the pressure and the pace of the tournament was telling on Dan, he didn't show it. I found him at the tee after lunch, raring to get back on the course and wrap up the championship. We got off to an auspicious start on that final round—par, birdie, par, par. On the 5th I went one over, shook it off with a par on the 6th, but when I missed my 4 on the 7th I began to worry about the possible errors I might make. This is the sure sign that a golfer is tiring. The 8th loomed ahead and I was wondering if that penalizing hole would catch up with me this time. I drove well, my ball finishing a few feet short of the spot from which I had played my spoon in the morning. Daniels took his time in weighing the situation, and then drew the spoon from the bag. I rode into the ball compactly and breathed a sigh of relief as I saw it get up quickly and clear the bunkers with yards to spare. 'That's how to play golf, sir,' Daniels said, winking an eye approvingly. 'That's the finest shot you've played on this hole.' He was correct, of course. We found out, after climbing up and over the ridge, that my ball lay only 8 feet from the cup. I holed the putt for my second eagle in a row on the hole, and turned in 35, after a standard par on the 9th.

Only nine more now and I had it. One over on the 10th. Nothing to fret about. Par. Par. Par. A birdie on the 14th. Almost home now. One over on the 15th, three putts. One over on the 16th, a fluffed chip. Daniels slowed me down on the 17th tee. 'We're going to win this championship, sir. I have no worries on that

score. But let's make our pars on these last two holes. You always play them well.'
A par on the 17th. On the 18th, a good drive into the wind, a brassie right onto
the green, down in two for a birdie. 35–39—74, even par. There was no
challenge to my total of 283. Mac Smith, the runner-up, was five shots higher,
and Havers, who had needed a 76 on his last round, was a stroke behind Mac.

Feeling like a million pounds and a million dollars respectively, Daniels and I
sat down on a bank near the first tee and congratulated each other on a job well
done. Our score of 283—70, 69, 70, 74—was 13 under par on a truly championship course, and it clipped two strokes off the old record in the British Open, Bob
Jones' 285 at St Andrews in 1927. (Incidentally, 283 has never been bettered in
the British Open, though Cotton equaled that mark at Sandwich in 1934, Perry
at Muirfield in 1935, and Locke at Sandwich in 1949.*) Much as I was thrilled by
setting a new record for a tournament that had been my nemesis for a decade, I
was even more elated over the method by which I had finally reached my goal. I
had led all the way. I had encountered no really rocky passages because I had had
the excellent sense to listen to Daniels at every puzzling juncture. Through his
brilliant selection of clubs and his understanding of my volatile temperament, I
had been able to keep my resolution to go no more than one over par on any hole.
The 8th, which I had feared might be a second Suez, had turned out to be my best
friend. I had two 3's and two 5's on a hole on which I would not have been
unwilling, before the tournament, to settle for four 6's . . . .

After a shower, I changed into my brown gabardine jacket and was going over
the acceptance speech I had prepared four years earlier, when the officials told me
they were ready to begin their presentation ceremonies on the porch of the
clubhouse. I asked them if it would be all right if Daniels came up and stood
beside me as I received the trophy, since it had really been a team victory. They
regretted to have to turn down a request they could sympathize with, but it was
against tradition. I scanned the crowd gathering before the clubhouse, looking
for Dan so that I could at least take him down front. I couldn't find him. Then,
just as the officials were getting impatient about delaying the ceremony any
longer, I spotted Dan coming down the drive on his bicycle, carrying a grandson
on each handlebar. On with the show.

After the ceremony the team of Daniels and Sarazen got together for a rather
tearful good-bye. I gave Dan my polo coat, and told him I'd be looking for him
the next year at St. Andrews. I waved to him as he pedaled happily down the
drive, the coat flapping in the breeze, and there was a good-sized lump in my
throat as I thought of how the old fellow had never flagged for a moment during
the arduous grind of the tournament and how, pushing himself all the way, he
had made good his vow to win a championship for me before he died.

It was the last time I saw Dan. A few months later some English friends, who

---

* No longer true, 268 is the record now, achieved by Tom Watson, harried to the last pulse beat by
Nicklaus in 1977.

kept me posted on Dan, wrote me that he had passed away after a short illness. They said that after the Open he had worn the polo coat continually, even inside the pubs, as he told the golf fans of three generations the story of how 'Sarazen and I did it at Prince's.' When old Dan died the world was the poorer by one champion.

from *Thirty Years of Championship Golf*, Prentice-Hall (US)

POSTSCRIPT   Sam Snead

The purse of $600 [for winning the 1946 British Open] was such a joke that I decided then and there not to defend the title. My traveling expenses alone were over $1,000, and nobody but me picked up that tab. On top of that, all my hitting muscles 'froze' in the icy wind at St Andrews. For days I ached in every joint.

Then there was my caddie friend, 'Scotty,' who got himself sprung from jail and begged me to give him the winning ball. 'Maun,' he promised, tearfully, 'I'll treasure it all my days.'

That ball was worth some cash, and Scotty proved it. An hour later he sold it for fifty quid. So he made more off the Open than I did.

For years afterward, British and American writers panned me for passing up the British Open, but like I've always said—as far as I'm concerned, any time you leave the U.S.A. you're just camping out.

from *The Education of a Golfer*, Simon & Schuster (US), Cassell & Co (UK)

ALL THIS—AND PINK ICING TOO!   Henry Longhurst

Whatever else the Halford Hewitt tournament may have done, it solved, for me, the pound-a-day caddie problem. The answer, in a word, is—boys. The golfer arriving at Deal was made to feel no end of a fellow. He was at once surrounded by hordes of clamouring boys—those, that is, who were not standing on their heads, swinging upside down on the ornamental chain in front of the clubhouse, or enjoying a rough-and-tumble between the feet of the players hitting shots on the practice ground.

When I asked Bernard Drew, the secretary, whether it would be in order to engage one of these imps, it appeared that he did not share my views upon them.

'Boys!' he said. 'Don't speak to me of these boys. I'll murder one of them before this tournament is over!'

This was uncharitable. Boys as golf caddies have much to recommend them, quite apart from the fact that they are pleased enough—and so they ought to be—with five shillings.

I have reached the stage where I am embarrassed by the expert adult caddie. He says I can 'do it easy with a three'. I do not like to tell him that, until the warm weather comes, I have no shot between the spoon and the No. 4.

Furthermore I have a light webbing-equipment bag—which I promise myself shall be blancoed if ever it appears again in a championship—and some twenty-year-old wooden clubs which have never worn any of these ridiculous modern 'hats'. Just the load for a boy. No trouble at all.

Then again, boys are easily impressed. They argue not, neither do they sneer. And they never tell you where Mr Tolley* drove to, when he was here.

For the Halford Hewitt I had a series of twelve-year-old assistants. One, it being his maiden voyage, was appropriately at sea. Another was an experienced hand. He had been out six times.

Boys have an engaging frankness. Thus the first, before we reached the tee, with the clubs already trailing from the bag, told me of his new football and how he was saving up for a pair of shorts. He earned the price of the first leg.

On the third fairway he looked up with a bland smile. 'Good game, isn't it!' he said. And a moment later, 'Scotch game, isn't it?' (incidentally, what would *you* have replied?)

The more expert of my assistants, having learnt the value of silence in golf, waited until the fourth before informing me of his home in Middle Street, his sister who works for the doctor, and the impending celebrations for her twenty-first birthday.

Next morning, hauling it from the bosom of his miniature battledress, he handed me a brown paper parcel. In it was a large slice of the birthday cake—raisins, plums, pink icing and all.

'Didn't go to bed till half past ten,' he said. 'Tst, tst,' I replied, not revealing the hour at which the last Old Carthusian had turned in.

Boys are the golfer's perfect alibi. They snivel, fidget, hiccup, wander off looking for larks' nests, rattle the clubs, or, as at one critical moment at Deal, drop the flagstick with a resounding thump. You can always blame 'that wretched boy'. And how gratifying once again to be shouting 'Stand still there!' in one's best barrack-square voice, and not be answered back!

All this, and pink icing too!

© Henry Longhurst

A GENTLEMAN'S VALET   Peter Alliss

Caddies are a race apart. Some people see in them the last of the romantic fringe, the anti-socials, the men who have opted out, the only 'characters' left in sport. I

* Perhaps the best and longest driving British amateur through the 1920s and 1930s until the arrival of James Bruen.

am never quite sure what a 'character' in sport means, but the truth about caddies is a long way short of this glamorous abstract vision when you consider that when the rain rains caddies get very wet indeed. They live very rough betimes, hitch-hike up and down and across the country, vanish as from the face of the earth in winter, emerge like mountain bears in the spring. Some of them live rough and are rough. Some are smooth. Many of them are overpaid, under-worked. Some are good lads, some are bad lads. Caddies, in short, are just people.

The earliest caddies were probably fishermen, estate workers, ghillies, farm labourers, servants from the 'big hoose' around Musselburgh, North Berwick, St Andrews and such places. The tradition probably emerges from the master's service, or the plain opportunity to earn a direct cash payment from the gentry for direct physical work. Now I often consider that caddies are paid too much. Almost anywhere they will ask for and get £1 for a round, and most professional tournament caddies will have £2 a day plus a share of the winnings. This compares quite favourably with regular trade wages, and your workman will be much more skilled at his craft than the average caddie is at his. The modern golf bag is heavy, but the professional these days expects little more of the caddie than to carry the thing round and keep himself and the clubs and equipment reason-ably tidy. The professional usually wants confirmation rather than direct advice during a round, such as whether the shot needs a 4-iron or a 5-iron. The caddie's opinion might confirm what the player had in mind, or make him change his mind. Caddies are not very good watchers of the golf ball. They believe that top players should hit the ball up the middle of the fairway with every shot, and if they miss one, well there are always a thousand people around with two thousand eyes to spot it for him.

In six months, one could learn to be a fairly good caddie. Jacky, the big blond boy you will see carrying for Peter Thomson, is a case in point. He used to work with his father, a builder in Southport, but he teamed up with Thomson, without knowing too much about it, and has turned out to be a very good caddie in the sense that he is always on the spot when Thomson wants him. Thomson's clubs are always spotlessly clean, there is a clean towel for every round, and there is always chocolate or an apple or something in the bag if Thomson feels hungry. Jacky always keeps up with his lord and master, and has the waterproofs and umbrella out in a flash if it rains. These are the things the professional looks for, rather more than golfing advice. I have been referring to the travelling caddies here; local caddies who work only one or two courses get to know them so closely that they can give you a line not on a house but on a particular window of the house. They tell the story of Wallace Gillespie, the St Andrews man who caddied for Thomson before Jacky came along. Wallace gave Thomson a line at St Andrews one day and Peter hit a perfect shot, precisely where Gillespie had told him. When he got up to the ball, it was lying between two pot bunkers which had only five yards of fairway between them. 'Hell,' said Thomson, 'you don't give a fellow much margin of error, do you?' 'Well,' says Gillespie, 'you're the Open Champion, aren't you?'

from *Alliss Through the Looking Glass*, Cassell & Co (UK)

THEY COST TOO MUCH   Frank Beard

Some of the pros have regular caddies they use most of the time, but I don't. I prefer to use a local boy, especially a high-school or college student, if they're available. I like to stay away from the traveling caddies, the few dozen who follow the tour, moving from tournament to tournament the same way the golfers do. Of course, some of them are good, hard workers, but I feel they're the exceptions. I just don't want to get involved with the touring caddies. It's not that they're bad caddies. They're good. But they think they're too good. They want too much money.

They want to get paid at a minimum what they call 'ten-and-three.' That's ten dollars a day and three percent of your winnings. I feel that's just too much money. Last year I averaged about three thousand dollars a tournament in prize money. In a normal tournament, you'll use a caddy for six days, Tuesday through Sunday, and that means he wants $150 for working about thirty hours. That also means if you win a tournament and collect an average first prize of twenty-five thousand dollars, the caddy expects $810, more than twenty-five dollars an hour. It's not worth it to me. It's the easiest possible work. I don't expect the caddy to tell me what club to hit; if I don't know my own game better than he does, I ought to be in a different business. I don't expect him to read the greens for me; I trust myself first. Once in a great while, you find a caddy who really helps you, but the majority are just bag-toters. The better ones carry your bag and clean your clubs after each shot and clean your ball on the green and obey the rules, and that's it. I don't want to pay as much as twenty-five dollars an hour for that.

from *Pro: Frank Beard on the Golf Tour*, Thomas Y. Crowell Co (US)

BRITISH CADDIES/AMERICAN OPINIONS   George Plimpton

Gay Brewer, the 1967 Masters champion, . . . felt a caddy's value was overrated. It was fine to have his reassurance on club selection, but a professional would be foolish to rely on anything but judgment based on knowledge of his own game. Brewer had a different caddy every week on the tour, never really trying to keep one on a regular basis, and indeed he had won tournaments with boys who had never been on that particular course before. He took the Masters in 1967 but he couldn't remember the name of the caddy with whom he won.

'But I'll tell you when the caddy *is* important,' he told me. 'in England. The caddy seems more devoted there, and God knows he *has* to be. The weather is such a factor—weird stuff—that the courses can change overnight. You'll have a hole which one day requires a drive and an easy wedge, and the next day it takes a drive and a *three wood* to reach the green. So yardage doesn't mean a thing—I mean, unless the conditions are absolutely perfect and static, which in that country is rare, hell, *unknown*. So you rely more on your caddy. They not only know the course but also how your ball is going to act in the air currents above, and how it's going to bounce and move on the turf. I think I was clubbed on nearly every hole in the tournaments I played there. Those caddies are incredible.'

Certainly the English* caddies were self-assured. Bobby Cruickshank told me that on his first practice round at Muirfield in 1929 he had a seventy-five-year-old caddy, Willie Black. Cruickshank hit a good drive on the first hole. 'Willie,' he said, 'give me the two iron.' 'Look here, sir,' Willie said. *'I'll* give you the club, *you* play the bloody shot.' I've always liked the story about the caddy at St Andrews who interrupted his 'boss' (which was the current term) at the top of his backswing, and shouted, 'Stop! We've changed our mind. We'll play the shot with an iron!' Frank Stranahan had a terrible problem with such caddies in one of the British Amateur championships at Muirfield. He fired a number of them, mostly because pride on both sides got the best of the situation. The caddies were furious and sulking because their advice was ignored, and Stranahan was upset and oversensitive because he could not, under the circumstances, keep his mind on his golf game. The climactic moment in their strained relationship came on a hole with the green hidden behind a high ridge. Stranahan sent his caddy up on the ridge to point out the direction of the green, indeed to place himself so that a shot soared over his head would be on the correct line. The caddy went up there with the golf bag, moving around on the ridge, sighting between Stranahan and the green, his head turning back and forth, and finally he waved Stranahan on. Stranahan hit directly over the caddy and then toiled up the hill to discover that the caddy had lined him up with a thick patch of bracken, waist-high, where it would be a miracle if he found the ball, much less knocked it out; the caddy looked at him and very carefully, like a dog laying down a bone, he dropped Stranahan's golf bag at his feet and set out for the golf house, saying over his shoulder, 'Now, sir, if you think you know so much about it, let's see you get yourself out of *there*.'

from *The Bogey Man*, Harper & Row (US), André Deutsch (UK)

THE SCOTTISH   Peter Alliss

Crowds vary to some extent. The most difficult in many ways are the Scottish crowds, because they think they know their golf when in fact they do not know of

---

* As Muirfield is a Scottish course, the caddy would probably not be English.

the real subtleties of the professional game. They play golf themselves, almost everyone up there, but they play the game in a rather one-track way, and some shots they simply cannot appreciate. They look at your ball and the green and decide '6-iron here'. You may have a good reason for deciding 'I'll give it a little push with a 4-iron'. They will never know the reason and if the shot does not quite come off, they immediately decide you have played the wrong club, or under-clubbed or over-clubbed or something. And they take good care that you hear their opinion! Scottish crowds are critical for the sake of being critical. Up in the far north, everyone is a golf expert. Most of the time they are critical without really knowing what they are criticizing. They complain if the ball doesn't go from A to B, which is what they have decided should happen. They are not really such great connoisseurs of the thing. Scottish crowds are usually fairly well-behaved if they are held in check. Give them an inch and they will take more than a mile, and flood all over the course. Irish crowds, alas, are Irish. They take a mile as a matter of right, and are a little hurt if you fail to offer them a mile in the first place.

from *Alliss Through the Looking Glass*, Cassell & Co (UK)

ARNIE'S ARMY   Frank Beard

I hustled away from the course and back to the motel and began thinking ahead to the opening round tomorrow, the first official round of competition of the 1969 professional tour. I'm absolutely dreading it, for one reason and one reason only: I'm playing with Arnold Palmer.

I dread every round I play with Palmer, Nicklaus, Casper, and possibly Gary Player, but playing with Palmer is far and away the worst. It's got nothing to do with Arnie personally. Arnie's easy to play with—he concentrates, he doesn't say much, he's fast, he always knows whose shot it is—but Arnie's Army is imposs-ible. They run and stampede to see Arnie. They knock you down. They know nothing about golf etiquette. They have no regard for anyone who's playing with Palmer. They're not real golf fans. They're what I call the center-field-bleacher types. They're just looking for some place to go. They look at the paper and they say, 'Hey, Arnie's in town, let's go see him, let's go see Arnie.' They don't understand the game at all. They wouldn't appreciate it if he did the greatest thing in the world. They don't even care if Arnie hits one good shot all day. If he pees in the fairway, they're happy.

from *Pro: Frank Beard on the Golf Tour*, Thomas Y. Crowell Co (US)

PALMER AND THE PORT–O–LET   George Plimpton

He cleared his throat. He said that well, nothing could compare with an experience *he* had had with Palmer and his Army. I've forgotten what tournament he said it was, possibly the Masters or the PGA, one of the great championships, for sure. He was a spectator on the golf course at a position where the big-name players were coming through. While waiting, on the side of the fairway, he had stepped into one of those sentry-box structures called Port-O-Let, chemical toilets that are set about courses during tournament week. After a while he opened the door, which made a shrill squeal, and he stepped out into the bright sunlight. When he had stepped into the Port-O-Let there had been quite a few people trudging by, the advance guard of Arnie's Army. Now, he said, with himself and the Port-O-Let at its apex, an enormous fan of people had materialized that stretched away toward the distant green, a double line of faces—thousands, it appeared—all straining to see. And there, not ten yards away, standing over a golf ball that he had hit nearly out of bounds, and getting ready to swing, was Arnold Palmer. At the creak of the hinges Palmer looked back, and he saw my friend standing in the door of the Port-O-Let.

'What did you do?' I asked.

'Well, my gosh,' my friend said. 'I stepped right back inside and pulled the door shut. It was the typical reaction, I mean, stepping out and seeing all those people. It was like slipping through a door and finding oneself alone on the stage of a fully occupied opera house. What happens is that your eyes pop and you back up right through the door you came out of.'

'Of course,' I said.

'I really slammed that door.'

'What happened then?'

'Well, after a second or two, there was this knock on the door of the Port-O-Let, and it was Palmer. "Listen," I heard him say, "come on out, there's no hurry." Well, I thought about that great mob of people out there, all looking and maybe getting ready to laugh and all if I stepped out of the Port-O-Let. So I said through the door, "No. You go right ahead, Mr Palmer. I'm in no hurry either. I don't want to disturb you." Well, I heard his footsteps in the grass, moving away, and the increasing quiet of the crowd, which had been murmuring, and I knew he was standing over his ball and they were settling down for his shot. But the murmur started up again, and I was surprised, because I hadn't heard the click of his club going through the shot. Then I heard footsteps and there was this knock on the door. "Listen," he said. He sounded very apologetic through the door. "I find it's hard to concentrate on my shot thinking about you shut up in that box. I'd appreciate it if you would come out." Well, I did, of course. I pushed the door open with that big screech, those damn rusty hinges, and I stepped out. It was very bright in the sunlight after the Port-O-Let, and there was Palmer looking worried and serious, and he said he was sorry to have inconvenienced me. I said, "Oh no, not at all." There was quite a lot of laughter, and I sidled off and tried to get lost in the crowd. But people kept grinning at me, heads turning, you know, "There's the Port-O-Let guy," so finally I hurried across a fairway and watched someone else, Kermit Zarley, I think, someone like that, where there weren't too many people around.'

'That's something!' I said.

'Yes, I think so,' he said.

'Some terrible things can happen out there in tournament golf,' I said.

'You're right,' he said. 'Terrible things.'

from *The Bogey Man*, Harper & Row (US), André Deutsch (UK)

10 The Outsiders: Women and Left-handers

I THINK just a touch of editor's prejudice has dictated both the inclusion and content of this chapter. As a left-hander I have a collection of grudges against the 'theys' of the rest of golfing humanity. Some of them will not bear the lower profit margins of making clubs for left-handers; others are professionals that advise one to stand the other way round; still more design courses to punish the right-hander's slice—fair enough—but the resultant layouts mean that the left-hander who succeeds in cultivating an elegant right-to-left draw on his shots will find only trouble; and then there are the teeing grounds: uniformly they are aligned so that the right-hander is confronted with the whole expanse of fairway as he sets himself up for his shot, while the left-hander always has the feeling that he has to jerk the ball around his body to reach safe pastures. 'But, of course,' you may justifiably object, 'we are all in the same boat. All of us are putting our feet down on one patch of ground and aiming at another.'

Agreed, but why is it then that so few golfers, right- or left-handed, can, in fact, disregard the pre-ordained aim of the teeing area? I am half convinced that this *must* be a trivial point yet this is the only advantage for a right- over a left-hander.

Obviously, there can be no glib answer to what it is that makes a left-hander an outsider. Perhaps something in the mystique of golf is more antipathetic to those who strike from the left than from the right. In other games and sports such antipathy obviously does not apply.

Who, for instance, is or was a better pitcher than Sandy Koufax? Has there been a definitely better slow bowler than Wilfred Rhodes or Hedley Verity? For batsmen, you can look at Frank Woolley, Gary Sobers, Graham Pollock, Clem Hill, Martin Donelly, Clive Lloyd; and though it could be argued that Trumper, Hobbs, Grace, Hutton, Compton, Bradman are better bets for the ultimate pinnacles, at least you would still have an argument on your hands.

Much the same applies to tennis. And boxing. Anyone could advance a spirited case that Rod Laver and Jim Driscoll are names that should be placed at the very top.

But look at the history of left-handedness at golf and there is very little for the editor's tribe to be proud of. Yes, Bob Charles, a very good tournament player and a superb putter and winner of *one* major championship. Otherwise, one is quickly looking at Ben Hogan and Johnny Miller, both natural left-handers that were diverted from the true path and played right-handed. Look again at Bob Charles and something more disturbing appears. The man is not really left-handed at all. He's right-handed and right-eyed.

Women come into the outsider category because of the central appeal of golf: to 'get away from it all'. While for most this means going to grass, trees, water, hills, dunes from factory chimney, semi-detached house, articulated lorry and mowing the front lawn, there is also the escape from the people who clutter that environment and, alas, that must include wife and children. Therefore at your local golf club women members are an unwelcome reminder of the world we must go back to after 'just one more drink'.

WOMAN'S PLACE IS IN THE WHAT?   Peter Dobereiner

Four women were playing a friendly game at Effingham Golf Club and as they were putting out a man burst from the bushes beside the green. The uncouth manner of the stranger's approach was as nothing compared to his appearance for, apart from a bowler hat, he was entirely naked.

Although naturally taken aback at the interruption, which at the very least was a breach of golfing etiquette in disturbing players during the act of putting, one sterling spirit among the foursome was neither dumbstruck nor dumbfounded. 'Are you', she asked imperiously in the twinset-and-pearls accent of the Home Counties, 'a member?' Receiving no satisfactory reply, she promptly dispatched the intruder with a well-aimed blow to the bowler with her eight iron.

Reading of this incident I was intrigued by her choice of club. Presumably she laid aside the putter she must have had ready to hand at the time, made a rapid appraisal of the shot that was required and accordingly taken out her eight. Her selection opens up an interesting area of speculation; most authorities with whom I have discussed the problem insist that the wedge is the only club for such occasions.

But even more interesting, surely, is the wording of her question in that moment of crisis. Are you a member? It sounds so utterly irrelevant. But was it? I suspect that it sprang direct from her subconscious, a reflex response to four centuries of brainwashing. If that poor, deranged nude had replied 'Yes, madam, I am in fact the chairman of the greens committee' would the eight iron have been stayed, even momentarily, in its avenging arc? Speculation is idle, but the question at least suggests the possibility.

For the woman golfer in Britain, God's rarest blessing though she may be, is compelled to bow the knee to the lordly male of the species. She is still a second-class citizen, the victim of petty prejudice, masculine condescension and, at times, outright humiliation.

The beheading of Mary, Queen of Scots is the first recorded act of discrimination against a woman golfer. Tongues were set wagging when she was observed knocking a ball about shortly after the murder of her husband. Her political enemies made great play of her heartless behaviour and although there was rather more to her execution than the fact that she played golf, it set a useful precedent. Four hundred years later male opinion is still influenced by that summary tradition. 'What shall we do about the lady members? Oh, chop off their heads,'

Not quite as extreme as that perhaps, since these days we like to think of ourselves as enlightened, but the basic mood persists.

Some clubs ban women entirely although their numbers are steadily dwindling. Oddly enough, this trend is reversed in America where new all-male clubs are being formed. No one would deny that members of a private club are entitled to conduct their affairs to please themselves. If they choose to be stag it is nobody's business but their own. Where the militant feminist has a right, a duty even, to stick an exploratory nose into the affairs of a private club is in the case of those which admit women under rules of membership which would induce apoplexy in the authors of the United Nations charter on human rights.

One club has a bench seat which must not be profaned by the impress of a female bottom; at some places women may play only at prescribed times and have to vanish, like Cinderella, on the stroke of the clock regardless of the state of their matches; other clubs put the public rooms off limits to women or banish them to separate and inferior quarters; a midland club relegates the ladies to a side door and another insists that they may never use a certain flight of steps. No vote, no voice in the club's affairs and even, on occasion, dictation by male committees on how they shall dress. It must be admitted that the destiny which shapes our ends does so in over-liberal degree in the case of some women golfers but the question of whether they should wear trousers is surely one for their own discretion.

I remember an occasion at a swanky English club which allowed women on the course until noon provided that on no account they entered the sacred portals of the clubhouse. In the car park I met two women who had been out playing when one of them was taken unwell. Her partner was saying: 'Perhaps if I knocked on a window one of the men would hand out a glass of water.'

Another incident, at the Royal and Ancient Golf Club of St Andrews, perfectly illustrates the status of women in the golfing scheme of things. A violent rainstorm broke during a tournament and the women spectators, having nowhere else to go, huddled for what protection they could find from the full fury of the squalls under the lee of the granite clubhouse.

After some time the spirits of this bedraggled group were cheered by the sight of a club servant approaching like a lifeboat through the tempest. The women smelled salvation. At last, they thought, they have taken pity on us. Our plight has softened their hearts; they are going to invite us to take shelter, possibly in some snug haven where they house the empty beer crates and the dustbins. 'Ladies, I have a message from the members,' said the functionary with unctuous smile, 'Would you mind putting down your umbrellas as they are obscuring the view of the course from the smoking room windows.'

from The Game with the Hole in it, Faber & Faber (UK)

THE THIN END   Stephen Potter

Not far from the ancient town of Rye there is a sea coast course famous for its mixture of rough beauty and of golf problems—problems so difficult that few men have been able to persuade themselves that women should be allowed even to set foot on it.

Nevertheless women have played this course and round about 1950 Mrs Bassett, a wife well known in gamesmanship circles, was actually made a life member of the Club by her father, a former chairman of committee. She was entitled to play over the course and, though entry to the club house was not allowed, she was permitted, owing to the distinguished record of her parent, to be handed drinks through a small window in a corner of the windward side.

In spite of that, this woman, Mrs Bassett, although there was a *sheltered* outdoor seat for her, used to complain openly, in January and February, and again and again older members asked themselves: how was she elected?

On one occasion she knocked on the window 'because she wanted another', and although I knew I would be criticized, I myself handed her one.

Was I wrong? Twelve years later a woman's room was built. It had a dainty little shelf and a sort of cupboard door which, when opened, led to the back of the bar. But long before that happened I myself took Mrs Bassett to the Woking Club. I was not disappointed. There there was a small women's changing room, complete with wash-basin and a coathanger which (she told me with shining eyes) 'although it had the name Mrs Wilson on it was regarded as being free for use when Mrs Wilson was not present'. But what she did not at first realize was that provided she stuck to a pre-arranged route, clearly recognized and agreed upon, she could walk, partly *through the club premises*, to a dining room *where men and women ate together*. I remember her coming in now, hiding so perfectly her excitement.

from The Complete Golf Gamesmanship, William Heinemann (UK),
MacGraw-Hill Book Co (US)

NEVER PLAY A WOMAN LEVEL   Henry Longhurst

One day in the summer of 1951, when the American women professionals were paying their first visit to England, General Critchley arranged a match for them at Wentworth against a team of London amateurs. These included Leonard Crawley, perhaps the second best player in the country at that time; Gerald Micklem, a Walker Cup player; John Beck, the only man to captain a successful British Walker Cup team, now in his fifties; an English international or two, and, at the very, very bottom your humble servant. However, at the last moment I had to go to France and so, unwittingly, escaped the slaughter. The match was to be played on level terms—an early psychological blunder: one should *never* play a woman level!—and the men, regardless of their doom, assembled with the pleasing prospect of a gallant day's golf in the sunshine, a substantial lunch, and refreshment in congenial company to round off the occasion. They won two of the foursomes and there was a certain amount of chaff at the expense of the other pair who only halved. A few hours later all were laughing on the other side of their faces. In the singles every one of them had been beaten, level, by a woman.

They took it in various ways. One to this day is hardly approachable on the subject. Another was heard to growl that it was 'ridiculous to encourage these people'. Crawley, defeated by Mrs Zaharias, after a good deal of technical stuff about fast-running fairways and not being able to take his driver from the tee, declared that next year, on a course of his own choosing, he would raise a team to give them five strokes a round and beat them . . . .

Anyway, at a convivial pre-Ryder Cup gathering at the home of the Earl and Countess of Carrick, Harlow brought up the topic and I blithely, and as I thought safely, declared that, had I not had to go to France, I should without doubt have defeated my opponent-to-be, Mrs Betty Bush, and thus achieved world celebrity. I ought to have known better. The light of the publicist gleamed suddenly in Harlow's eye. Muttering 'Boy, this is a natural!' he sprang to our host's telephone, located the lady in Chicago, fixed the match as a sort of comedy curtain-raiser to the Ryder Cup, and planted the story in all the New York papers and even, I believe, in London.

This, of course, condemned the reluctant and embarrassed correspondent, playing at that time excruciatingly badly, to long sessions on the practice ground, a tiddler among the big fish, with spectators who had assembled to watch Snead, Mangrum, Faulkner, Rees and the rest asking themselves, had the British really descended to *this*? I borrowed a fine flashy set of clubs—the very worst American club player habitually has four magnificent wooden clubs with leather 'hats', ten gleaming irons, and a cabin-trunk bag for someone else to carry them in. I also acquired a huge bag of practice balls belonging to the president of the Metropolitan Golf Association, Earl Ross, to say nothing of a faintly condescending negro assistant at a pound an hour.

Jack Hargreaves, of the British team, offered sympathetic advice about nonexistent wrist action. Fred Daly, in the course of a kindly half-hour, detected a pronounced hook on the face of the driver and adjusted me till a few flew straight, if not far. 'There you are, sorr!' he said. 'What's the matter with that, sorr?' Even the great Hogan, eyeing from afar, not only offered hints but later on gave the pupil a practical demonstration, not unlike the 'unarmed combat' instruction in the war, of his theory of the straight-right-arm-after-impact. This provided the other occupants of the bar with much innocent amusement and the patient with severe cramp between the third and fourth ribs on the left side.

'Depend upon it, sir,' said Dr Johnson, 'when a man is to be hanged in a fortnight, it sharpens his mind considerably.' To which I echo to any despondent golfer, 'Depend upon it, sir, when you are due to play a diminutive woman professional, level, in circumstances exposing you to extreme ridicule, it sharpens your golf wonderfully'. With two days to go I was hitting as many as three running plumb in the centre of the club.

Seeking to weigh up the opposition, I consulted the Pinehurst assistant professional. Did he know Mrs Bush? Sure he did. And what would she—er—be likely to do on the No. 1 course (par 71)? 'Waal,' he said, leaning his arm on the counter and contemplating for some time, 'I guess she won't do no better than 72.'

At this point there arrived a message from Mrs Bush. As she had said over the telephone, she had recently had an operation. Now her doctor had said she would not be fit to get round the course. She was sorry indeed to let me down like this. Some other time . . .

'Lucky miss', said some.

'Certainly not', said I. 'Lucky Mrs.'

from *Round in 68*, T. Werner Laurie (UK)

DEVIANTS   Michael Murphy

Shivas was left-handed. I did not consider it an important fact until I heard about the recent discoveries concerning the roles of the left and right sides of the brain in mediating various altered states of consciousness. It now appears that mystical states and other inspirations involve a special activation of the right hemisphere, perhaps because the left one is too preoccupied with the functions of speech. The right hemisphere is connected in its motor functions, however, to the left side of the body. So, to take a quick, long leap, all the legends about lefties being just a little daffier than the rest of us may have some basis in this differential action of the brain's two sides: lefties perhaps are more open to the impulses and firings of the mystical half, and inspiration always has an element of surprise and things you would not predict. (What implications for the alignments of politics!) Shivas also had that disconcerting left eye, focused ever so slightly to the center; I remembered when I heard about this recent research that it had not been crossed when he came back from his awesome trance that morning. Was that eye always watching for messages from the inspired side, content to look straight ahead only after it had its fill? Then I remembered that he had originally played the game from the left, changing over to a conventional right-handedness about the time he reached puberty. (In that he was like Ben Hogan, who had also begun from the deviant side.) Did his muscle memory and golfing unconscious carry all that left-handed perspective still? Was his intuition informed by all those thousands of left-handed shots? (I remembered that Hogan had shifted from a tendency to hook to a deliberate fade when he reached the peak of his game: was he still wrestling with the left-hander in his soul?)

from *Gofl in the Kingdom* , The Viking Press (US), Latimer New Dimensions (UK)

A CACK–HANDED STORY WRITTEN BY A LEFTY   Dudley Doust

At this distance in time it perhaps is permissible for an American to recall one particular hardship he suffered during the war. In 1943 there was only one left-handed golf club to be found in the shops of Syracuse, New York. It was a five-iron with a cream-coloured shaft and the glorious name of Bobby Jones stamped on the head.

I bought it. I drove with it, chipped with it and putted with it and, by using it, suffered all the insults that come commonly to left-handed golfers.

We lefties are human, too; if you prick us we bleed. So it was with a feeling of fellowship that I attended a meeting of The Left-Handed Golfers' Society of Great Britain held last week at West Byfleet in Surrey. They were competing for the Quaich Bowl.

The bowl, a beautiful silver replica of a two-handed vessel owned by Charles I and donated by the host club, was first played for 40 years ago this summer and therefore is said to be the oldest golf trophy for left-handers in the world.

Its winners, none of them renowned, are not recorded in the Golfer's Handbook which is a pity, not only because a long line of *one*-armed and Flintshire ladies' champions are published but because the handbook is edited by Percy Huggins, a left-handed golfer himself.

Anyway, 23 lefties were flailing away at West Byfleet and, I must say, they looked a curious lot.

'I don't normally play with left-handers so I'm not a fair judge, but I suppose we do look a wee bit awkward,' said Peter Stuart, a local veterinarian who, with seven victories, has won the bowl more times than any man in history.

'Still,' he said, 'I don't consider myself a freak. I come from the district of Badenoch in the Central Highlands which is sort of a left-handers Brigadoon. About 40 per cent of the golfers up there are lefties. This is because shinty, a form of hockey, is a local game and it is traditionally played left-handed.' With that Stuart shot a gross 77, net 69, and returned to his surgery.

On the course you could spot the lefties a mile away; they wore golf gloves on their right hands. On the left side of the seventh fairway a young competitor chopped about in the woods, looking for his ball.

'Sliced it,' he said, resigned, '99 per cent of all lefties slice the ball but I can't tell you why. Maybe it is because the holes on most courses go anti-clockwise so we slice to stay in bounds.

'Also, bunkers are laid out to catch the right-hander's slice. That is a fact. So, when a left-hander draws a ball, like we ought to do, we get punished. It's not fair.' He resumed his search.

The defending champion, Frank Allen, a burly Henley car dealer, came along. Allen wears white training shoes and plays off 15. We talked about slicing and pretty soon he began hooking the ball, big banana hooks into the trees. He, too, had a grumble.

'Left-handed clubs aren't as good as right-handed clubs,' he said, 'and further-more you can't handle them out first in the shops because there aren't any in the shops. If you order them and then you don't like them you're dead stuck.'

He holed a nice putt on Byfleet's splendid greens and we agreed that lefties were uncommonly gifted around the greens.

'Another thing,' he said, 'the club pros are always saying we ought to learn to play the game right-handed. Johnny Miller. Ben Hogan. Both born lefties. Why is it that nobody ever tells a righty that he would play better golf as a left-hander?'

A whiff of paranoia hangs round left-handed golfers. I think it is deeply rooted in resentment, *Cack-handed*, what a thing to say about a human being. Also, more bothersome, I grew up transposing every key word in golf instructional articles. For 'right' read 'left.' I can remember going through the final chapters of Bobby Jones's classic book, *Down the Fairway*, crossing out every 'right' and pencilling in the word 'left' and vice versa. One missed transposition and you could break an arm or a leg.

Secondly, as Frank Allen said, good clubs are hard to come by. 'That's why we put second-hand clubs up for sale in our news bulletin,' said John Turner, honorary secretary of the Left-Handed Golfers' Society. It's a close freemasonry and, rather like immigrants and homosexuals, the members share the names of shops that cater to their kind. The Croydon Golf Shop, for instance, is the best-stocked shop for left-handed golfers in Britain.

The Society has 180 members, including boxer Henry Cooper and cricketer Peter Parfitt, and schedules 11 annual meetings, including a scratch champion-ship, with a cup donated by Bob Charles, which takes place this October at Hawkstone Park in Shropshire.

In search of members, Turner is a true missionary. Just the other evening he was driving home to Essex when he suddenly saw a lefty practising on Hackney Marshes. Turner stopped his car and chased after the player with membership forms. 'The reason we decided to form the society in 1961,' he said, 'was to defend ourselves.'

By tea time, Frank Allen had retained his Quaich Bowl with a net score of 67 and later he added the better-ball title. At the prize-giving ceremonies he was told, with mock severity, that in future he must play off 13 handicap.

The gathering was adjourned until guest day, June 5, at Ross-on-Wye. As I left, John Turner pressed a gift into my hand. It was the official tie of the

Left-Handed Golfers' Society of Great Britain: several tastefully scribed Ls and Hs on a field, or perhaps a fairway, of green.

from The Sunday Times (UK) 2 June 1974

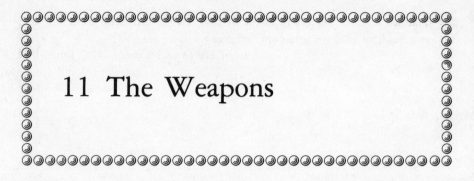

11 The Weapons

IN the days of hickory shafts, hand-forged irons and individually shaped woods a set of clubs was something collected over a lifetime. If a golfer were lucky he would have quite a few favourites but others that he could hardly ever hit a shot with. The advent of steel shafts and matched sets during the 1930s enabled the golfer to choose a set, not a club. This is perhaps a mixed blessing and certainly a highly expensive one.

A man happy with his woods but not the irons, or vice versa, should surely not buy a whole set; to abandon a favourite club is asking for trouble. Perhaps we should not go for sets as automatically as we do, but hunt for key clubs that happen to suit us. Amongst these, I would put the sand and pitching wedges, a long iron, perhaps a fairway wood and above all, the driver. By all means buy another of these to see if it really will make the ball go further and straighter but a least keep the one that has proved its worth to moulder gently in the garage.

We hear of top professionals trying out several sets of clubs before a tournament and, because of contracts, having to use different sets in different countries. But there is another side. Peter Thomson used the same irons for many years, Jack Nicklaus a 3 wood and there is the famous case of Sam Snead's battered driver, so often mended and refaced that it cannot have quite the same characteristics it started out with.

The pieces that follow deal with the history of a few types of clubs and special favourites.

THINGS DO IMPROVE   Horace G. Hutchinson

When it is said that these two malformations are the principal ills which club flesh is heir to, it is not intended to imply that there are not many driving clubs made which are hopeless and impossible in other ways—such as clubs that have spring anywhere, clubs that have spring everywhere, and clubs which have spring nowhere. A plentiful crop of such wretches, whose diseases are too many to enumerate, issues from the club-makers' shops. Likewise, heads that are brittle and shafts that are green; but all these and the like infirmities are too familiar to be worth discussion.

from *Golf*, The Badminton Library (UK) 1893

THE NIBLICK   Sir Walter Simpson

The niblick is too vulgar-looking for description in a polite treatise like this. He is a good fellow, however, ever ready to get you out of a hole . . . .

The mere appearance of a niblick suggests doubts and fear. Other clubs are graceful, smiling, elegant things. The niblick is an angry-looking little cad, coarse, bullet-headed, underbred. Its face looks up as if to say, 'I will raise the ball into the air.' Its smile is treacherous. It does fulfil its promise sometimes; but just as often it smothers its laughter in the sand, leaving you and the ball nonplussed.

from *The Art of Golf*, David Douglas (UK) 1887

THE BULGER   Horace G. Hutchinson

When the first edition of this book was published there was only one man in the kingdom who played with a club whose face was not intended to be a plane—and this was the late Mr Henry Lamb, since, unhappily, deceased. He, and he alone, for he was its inventor, played with a 'bulger.' Now Park also appears to have once made a club with a bulging face, but he does not appear to have played with it. Therefore he failed in seeing the merit of the idea. Mr Lamb did not fail. He went on playing with the new queer thing, in the face of much derision, and with such triumphant success that at least half, and the upper half, of the golfing world plays with bulgers.

Their great merit is that they are easier to drive straight with. Without going into a discussion about the scientific reason, we may note the fact. The scientific reason presents a peculiarly alluring problem, because it is so easy to explain, and also so easy to disprove the explanations. But the effect is this, that a ball hit on the heel of a bulger will not go swerving off to the right, nor a ball hit on the toe to the left, at all in the same degree as they perform these evolutions off the plane-faced club. Speaking in a rough and general way (and no golfer cares the value of a made-up ball for any other way of speaking), we may say that we slice off the heel and that we pull off the toe. It is all the effect of rotation. Now the face of the bulger is convex, with the summit of the convexity at the point of impact with the ball; when, therefore, we strike a ball on the heel of the bulger we strike it on a face which looks towards the left of the proper line of flight of the ball. Conversely, when we strike it on the toe we strike on a face which looks towards the right of that line. And the inclination of the face, in either instance, tends to counteract the rotatory motion which is imparted to the ball owing to the bit of the face with which it was struck. But perhaps that is enough theorising, more especially as the theory is very likely all wrong.

from *Golf*, The Badminton Library (UK), 1893

SNEAD'S IZETT DRIVER   Sam Snead

Just before the firing opened at the Griffith Park course in L.A., Henry Picard walked up and asked, 'How are you hitting, Sam? I hear you are bending them halfway to Santa Monica.'

'I'm so wild I've about decided to quit the tour and go on home.'

Picard watched me whip out some drives and thought my feet might be the problem. He claimed I was spinning around while in the hitting zone onto my right toe, instead of moving more laterally into the ball on the inside of my right foot. Toning down foot action didn't help.

'Let's look at your driver,' said Henry.

'I'll admit it doesn't feel right,' I said, 'but it worked for me in Virginia and in Florida and I don't like to change it.'

'This stick is too whippy for you,' said Henry. 'Do you remember the photographer who tried to catch your swing at Hershey last fall?'

Thinking back, I remembered that Lambert Martin, one of the top cameramen of the New York *World-News*, had set up cameras aimed at catching all points of my swing. Martin 'stopped' the action until we came to the point where my descending clubhead was 2 feet from the ball, and then all he got was a blur—even with the camera set at 1/1,250th of a second. Martin said it was the first time he'd been unable to stop a whole hitting sequence. Later they timed my clubhead speed at almost 150 mph.

'Your hands are too fast for such a light and swingy club,' declared Henry. 'I've got an Izett driver in my car that might be the answer for you.'

The Izett felt like a dream the minute I took ahold of it. The first poke took my breath away. The ball traveled an easy 300 yards down the middle. I waved the caddie back further and further, and even when letting out full shaft, my driving improved about 35 per cent. 'How much will you take for the club, Henry?' I asked.

The Izett was a true-tempered model, stiff-shafted, and a regular telephone pole in weight at more than fourteen-and-a-half ounces; the loft was a normal eight degrees and the length—forty-three inches—likewise. The shaft carried five ounces of the weight, and that was the great difference. George Izett, a top Philadelphia clubmaker, had built it.

'Try it in play, and if you like it, we'll make a deal,' offered Picard.

Lighthorse Harry Cooper smashed par, the tournament record, and all opposition with a 69-70-69-66—274 to win the marbles at Los Angeles, but in my first West Coast showing the Izett enabled me to shoot 71-71-72-69—283, which was good for sixth place and $400 . . . . One week later, with the hook under fair control, I won the Oakland Open, then the Crosby Invitational . . . . Rain washed out all but one round of the Crosby, so that over five rounds in the two competitions my scores read 69-65-69-67-68.

I'd have paid Picard any part of the purses I'd won—$400 at L.A., $1,200 at Oakland, and $762.50 in the Crosby—for that driver. And Henry had every reason to stick me for plenty, having finished a few shots behind me in the latter two events.

'That'll cost you just five-fifty,' said Picard, 'which is what I paid for the club.'

That act of generosity by the Hershey Hurricane could never be repaid, because that No. 1 wood was the single greatest discovery I ever made in golf and put me on the road to happy times. It proved that with the full coil of my body and the strong forward thrust of the right foot which went with my wrist snap at impact with the ball I naturally accelerated the club faster than I could control any ordinary driver. The increased drag of a heavier, stiffer shaft and clubhead compensated for my speed. It harnessed me to just the right degree.

The popular story that I slept with the Picard driver and never let any man swing it is only half true: only the last half of that statement is a fact. It's also a fact that until two years ago [i.e. the late 1950s], twenty-three years later, I was still pulling it from the bag—at least, what was left of it. Most of my major titles have been won with that big blaster: three P.G.A. championships; the British, Argentine, and Brazilian Opens; three Canadian Opens; the All-Americans; the Tam O'Shanter 'World'; the Nassau and Panama Opens; the Tournament of Champions—along with three Masters Tournament titles and a string of Ryder Cup wins.

At the close of 1961, my lifetime record stood at 110 tournaments won and about $400,000 collected, which they say is the world record,* and I'd estimate that I used the Picard driver while accumulating three-fourths of those totals.

Once, in San Francisco, when my back was turned, a local pro drove off the tee with the club. I all but blasted him off the course when I found it out. That's how I felt about that stick.

When it broke, I fixed it and never turned to another wood.

At Sequoiah, California, years ago, the head flew off, sailed down the fairway, and I let out a howl like a hurt wolf and ran all the way after it while the gallery roared. At St Paul the club broke off at the binding close to the head and I didn't hit a satisfactory shot until it was repaired. That five-fifty stick was good for maybe a million drives in every kind of weather, even though as the years went by the club face became eaten out toward the toe and the experts claimed it was finished.

'That'll be the day,' I told them. New inlays were inserted and it behaved as well as ever. This went on until the inserts composed almost a new face. But, no matter what happened, I never thought of the club as changed. Unlike any club I've ever owned, it gave me a feeling of confidence just to pick it up.

The exact Wilson Company duplicate of the original which I use today gives

---

* Not any more. Roberto de Vicenzo has won the most tournaments. Top money winner is, of course...

results, but in the 1959 Greensboro Open, when I was sniping the ball deep right because of getting my hands too flat, or laid over, at the top of the backswing and then rushing the downswing, I brought the Picard out of retirement. And I played seventy holes without missing a fairway.

Hooking has returned to bother me more than once since 1937, but generally the Picard wood saved me the trouble of changing my whole style in order to counteract the hook. It proved one key point in golf to me: find the driving tool that's best suited to your size, reach, and swing; then stay with it.

from *The Education of a Golfer*, Simon & Schuster (US), Cassell & Co (UK)

THE OLD MASTER   Bernard Darwin

Things are always happening to other people in the newspapers which never happen to us in real life. They buy a grubby old picture in a curiosity shop for one shilling and it turns out to be a Rembrandt; they help an old gentleman over a crossing and he leaves them £100,000.

I had long abandoned any such youthful dreams when, by a strange turn of Fortune's wheel, one of these things, in some sort a combination of the two I have cited, happened to me. A gentleman whom I knew only by name wrote to me suddenly out of the blue. He told me that he was going to give me his putter, made by Hugh Philp, that Stradivarius among clubmakers, who first turned a clumsy carpentering craft into a lovely art. I had never met him, still less had I helped him over a crossing; I had never even played with a wooden putter, though perhaps he did not know that . . . .

This wonderful letter reached me when I had only just set out on a holiday, so that I should have to wait some time before actually possessing my treasure. There was a serious temptation to abandon the holiday and take the next train home, but I managed to resist it, and proceeded at once to soothe and inflame my impatience by reading all the literature I could find about putters. There was a photograph of a Philp which sent me into ecstasies, but some of the literature had a sobering effect. First I read Sir Walter Simpson, who was merely flippant. 'A good putter,' he said, 'ought to have the name "Philp" stamped on it by somebody who must not tell you that he did it himself.' Mr Hutchinson, in the *Badminton*, informed me that: 'It is a matter of common knowledge that at least two subsequent clubmakers had a "Hugh Philp" stamp.' It was true that I could afford to disregard this brutal cynicism, because I knew that my putter had a well authenticated pedigree; my benefactor had got it from the younger Bob Kirk, who had inherited it from his father, *the* Bob Kirk. Still, I felt a little depressed, and so turned to Mr John Low, who had written, as I knew, a charming account of the finesse required to get a real putter made leisurely by a true artist. Yet even here was disappointment, for at the end of that classical passage came some words

I had forgotten: 'Even the famous Philp putters were by no means fair of countenance, and were, moreover, in their original shape—that is, before the face was much filed—very hooked in the nose.'

My holiday passed away, not, I am bound to say, wholly leaden-footed. No railway accident intervened. I was home again at last and there was my putter awaiting me, swathed in brown paper, and tied up with the most obstinate string. I hacked my way through and the putter stood revealed, sure enough with the magic H. Philp stamped on the head. And what a beautiful head it is! Not, I admit, of the long, thin type that Mr Low admired. A little stout and even dumpy perhaps, and bearing traces of having had that hooky nose filed away by a knowing hand; but what a fine, deep brown colour it has and with what comfortable solidity it sits down upon the turf! Heavy? Well, yes, perhaps it is a little heavy, but how admirably balanced, and then the grip! so beautifully fat and old-fashioned and filling to the hand and of so rich and oily a blackness. All the dormant collector in me—I hardly knew he existed—seemed to spring into life as I gazed and gloated.

The next step was obvious. I must, in all reverence, try a putt. On my way to the lawn I met the gardener, who is in private life something of a putter, and in the fullness of my heart showed him the club and told him its story. He said it 'looked as if it had been knocking about for a goodish bit of time,' which I took for high praise. Then to the hole, hidden from prying eyes behind a tree. It would be unwise to try too long a putt, since an auspicious start is a great thing. Perhaps it was four feet, or perhaps it was not quite so much. The ball rang on the face, it was truly hit, but heavens! the grass was wet, and I was going to be short. No! by a supreme effort the ball tottered in and the good start was made. It went in again several times and from longer distances, and always it felt sweet and sounded pleasantly.

In my eagerness to hole that first putt there was involved something more than a feeling merely romantic or aesthetic. The fact is that I propose to putt with my putter. My kind benefactor has not laid any positive command upon me, but his letter contained what the lawyers would term perhaps a precatory trust. Having himself putted long and successfully with the club, he does not like to think of it, still hale and hearty and in the plenitude of its powers, being hung up on a wall as a museum piece; he wants it to go on holing putts, and O my goodness! mine is the faulty and trembling hand that must direct it. The question whether I shall be able to hole the putts is only one part of my anxiety. There is another and in some ways a graver question. Even if I do hole them, shall I look the part? Will anybody go so far as to say that I wield the putter as it should be wielded? I am bound to say that I have my doubts, because a wooden putter demands a certain air and carriage. If my parents had realised in my boyhood that I had these great expectations, I should have been differently brought up; I should not have been allowed to begin an infant career on the green with a lofting iron held six inches above the head. Early habits are hard to get rid of, and though I now use an aluminium putter, which is at least an imitation of a wooden one, I am painfully conscious of sagging knees and a drooping nose and, in short, a complete absence of the grand old manner. O Mr Philp, Mr Philp, I hope you won't turn in your grave.

from *Out of the Rough*, Chapman & Hall (UK), reprinted by permission of A. P. Watt & Son

PAINFUL ABSTRACTION   Henry Longhurst

I am the victim of an unfortunate occurrence, namely, that some light-fingered golfing enthusiast in the neighbourhood of Appledore, near Westward Ho!, seeing my clubs in the hall of the local vicarage, abstracted a couple, presumably for his own use on the famous Burrows, where many a distinguished golfer, including the great 'J. H.' [John Henry Taylor, who five times won the Open], started his career.

In the old days when a player lost or broke a club it was always his 'favourite mashie', or even his 'favourite driver'. It had found a place in his collection perhaps after years of patient search.

In these standardized days, when clubs are not the 'personalities' they used to be, but merely members of a set of instruments which must to the layman appear as identical as do those of a dentist (and very much the same shape, at that), one can hardly bemoan the fate of one's 'favourite No. 4'.

On the other hand, I could have wished it to be some other club that he had taken—the No. 2 for instance, or the No. 1, which, like anyone else, I only carry because to discard it would be to confess that I cannot use it. He might even by some blessed chance have taken the putter!

As the years go on, the No. 4 becomes indispensable. It is the club with which one hopes to combat the No. 5, 6, or even 7 of younger but less crafty opponents.

The other missing club was the bigger of two spoons, one of a set made by that great craftsman, J. O. Lovelock, when he was at Mildenhall. It was designed by its owner to fit the close lies prevailing on that noble course and to scoop the ball out of plantain roots and such like. What is more, it did.

The golfer may care to speculate as to which, if he had to lose a wooden club and an iron club, he would sacrifice. He will find it a painful decision, and on the whole I suppose I was lucky. It might have been the driver and the sand-iron— thus rendering the game impossible.

The police inform me that it is out of order to offer a reward in such cases. On the other hand, if the miscreant should happen to read this . . .

from *The Sunday Times* (UK)

THE PLEASURES OF AN UNMATCHED SET   Pat Ward-Thomas

This is the season when the holiday golfer comes into his own. On courses all over the land there are people whose clubs have been resurrected from cupboards and corners, where they have lain idle since the previous summer. Often they are a motley collection, acquired over the years from a multitude of sources—family heirlooms, discards, borrowings and so on. Strange-looking and ill assorted they may be; but, although the expert and the dedicated would not deign to be seen on a course with them, they continue nonetheless to give pleasure to the man whose golf is no more than an occasional relaxation.

In this age when the golfer's equipment comes shining from machines, graded and processed with all the precision that science can devise, it might seem heretical to say that there is overmuch concern with the matched set. The majority of golfers insist upon one, and if a club should be broken or go astray they urgently seek its replica so that the set shall remain intact. They believe that to replace a club with one from an alien family might be courting disaster in some crucial Sunday morning fourball. This is not without its absurdity for the mass of golfers. Their clubs may be as balanced and precise in design as a machine can make them, but their attempts to strike the ball are not. Rarely is their timing, rhythm and arc of swing the same for any two shots in succession. And this by no means applies only to beginners and players with high handicaps.

It is different for the experts. Their swings are so grooved and constant that factors like swing weight and stiffness of shaft can have an appreciable effect on their play, but for most of us I do not think it matters greatly. After all, before the influence of mass production, when clubs were made by hand, a golfer often assembled his set one by one: he liked the feel of this, the way another lay; this head might be heavier, that shaft a shade more whippy; and so on. A man's clubs were more of a personal affair than they are nowadays.

Simply by chance, over the last couple of years, I have begun to assemble a somewhat mixed bag. One day I was in Palmer's workshop in Latrobe, admiring the vast collection of clubs reposing on the shelves, and asked if he would give me a putter. I was told to help myself and was then offered a driver. Naturally I expressed a real doubt that the shaft might be too stiff for me, but he chose one that ever since has served me well, and been the envy of my friends. It certainly does not match the other woods, which are of a set; it is a shade stiffer in the shaft and shorter, and the face is deeper, but, if anything my driving has improved.

When the Open was last at Lytham I was looking at the glass-fibre shafted clubs that Gary Player was using then, not without some curiosity, for they have the look and feel rather more of hickory than steel. He generously offered to have one sent from America, and was true to his word. A seven iron arrived, and once having grown used to it I would not part with it for anything. Again, it is dissimilar to its neighbours in the bag, but I find that this makes no difference.

Last winter, when I was in Bermuda, my wife was in splendid form at the Golf Ball, winning all manner of useful things on the tombola. My return, after a sleepless night over the Atlantic, was warmed by the sight of a beautiful little wooden club, something between a four and a five, which now has a permanent place in my bag. I must hasten to add that my wife does not play golf or this would not be so.

Now the driver and four wood of the original set rest easy in an old heavy leather bag, and I doubt that they or it will be recalled for duty very often. In recent years there has been a remarkable swing towards the light bag, to be carried oneself, as more and more people have realised what a waste of money it can be to pay someone, usually moronic in terms of golf, to carry a large one. A trolley, too, has not left the garage in ages, because I, like many another, have come to regard it as more of a nuisance than a help.

Then there is the jigger,* a discard of Sarazen's a long time ago. I had not realised that such clubs were made, but apparently one American company did so, and I have found it useful on occasion.

At a time when one does not want to carry too many clubs, a couple of other irons can be discarded with no great ill effect. And so it seems that, without any deliberate effort on my part, I have returned to first principles: a remarkably varied collection of clubs and a light bag. And why not? Most of my golf is that of the wanderer, taken as it comes on all manner of courses, and so far it has not suffered, nor has its enjoyment been impaired in consequence.

from *The Long, Green Fairway*, Hodder & Stoughton (UK)

PUTTERS

Patrick Campbell

Of all the tools in the golfer's sack none is as personal to him as his putter.

Bobby Jones, when he won the Grand Slam ... did it with the help of a weapon called Calamity Jane, a hickory shafted stick with three narrow bands of whipping which might have made all the difference to Bobby Jones but subsequently did little for anyone else when Calamity Jane was mass-produced.

Max Faulkner has been the owner of—I think he told me—seventy-two putters in his time. The last time I played with him he was using a tool with a shaft made of driftwood and a rusted head on the back of which was stamped the date 1884.

Some people used to have putters with square heads and play it between their legs like a croquet mallet.

Some elderly gentlemen roll them in from all over the place with horrible things with aluminium heads and a style that obviously shouldn't work, but does, every single time.

---

* Iron with a narrow face.

American women have putters made of white marble with a floral motif.

American professionals hardly ever miss from eight feet with centre-shafted putters.

Wall Street financiers play with putters made of gold.

Some people buy a new putter every month and with it continue to knock the ball harmlessly past the left-hand side of the hole, apart from the very first one which goes in, compelling them to buy yet another new putter, to achieve the same effect.

My father played for years with a putter with a brass head four inches long and a crack in the shaft, so that sometimes it produced an audible clonk when he hit the ball. 'When you get the clonk,' he used to say, 'you're all right,' despite persistent evidence to the contrary.

When he gave it to me I couldn't hole one from eighteen inches with it, even when I did get the clonk.

The next putter I owned was a miracle of design with a beautifully smooth ebony head and a steel shaft precision-bent to get the hands right over the ball. It flew to pieces one day when I missed yet again from two feet and in a tempest of rage tried to hit the next one 200 yards.

After that I came upon a putter with a shaft bent backwards like the starting-handle of a car, so that at the address the hands were a couple of inches ahead of the club-face. It might have started a car.

Some years ago, however, I found my own true love, in Henry Cotton's shop at Temple.*

What first attracted me to it was the length of the shaft. It was about the same as a 2-iron, towering above all the other putters in the rack.

I pounced on it and, being nearly 6 ft. 5 in., was for the first time in my life able to strike a putt without being bent double and subject to rushes of blood, lunch and other pressures.

It didn't go in, but the feeling of relaxation promised success in the future.

From Denis Scanlan in the shop I learnt that the putter had been designed by the Master himself, as a possible solution to his problems on the greens, and that it retailed at £3. 10s.

When the Master arrived in the Cadillac the following weekend I lost no time in striking a deal. 'As I'm the only player for miles around that wouldn't get the handle of that putter stuck in his gullet,' I said, 'I'll take it off you for a quid.'

Henry had a swish with it to see if he still liked it. He didn't. 'If you want it,' he said, 'it will cost you five.'

I protested that the putter was unsaleable to anyone else.

'That,' said Henry, 'is why it will cost you five.'

In the end we settled for £3. 10s.

* Mr Cotton has long since resided in Mediterranean climes.

By hard bargaining of this kind the short game expert finds his own true love and, if he has any sense, remains faithful to her for the rest of his life.

from *Patrick Campbell's Golfing Book*, Blond & Briggs (UK)

LOSS OF FAITH   Peter Alliss

I was playing a practice round with Peter Thomson and some of the other boys when he said very casually, 'Why are you still using that driver?' I was quite startled by this and asked him what he meant. He said he thought the driver had held me back for years and that I'd developed a certain type of swing to fit the club instead of making the club suit my own swing, or finding another club that did. All of a sudden, I couldn't drive. The very next drive after he mentioned this I sliced twenty yards off the fairway. I felt that driving was the most difficult thing in the whole world. Thomson and I are old friends, and I really couldn't imagine he was being arch or calculating in saying what he did, but there is not the slightest possible doubt that this planted a seed in my mind. Driving was something I had to begin thinking about, whereas in the past I had scarcely ever needed to waste any thinking on it. Over the years it has probably been the most reliable part of my game. Even when I was younger and more preoccupied with absolute length, I felt I could hit the fairway more often than anyone else who hit a comparable length. Putting probably filled more of my thoughts than any other part of the game before Troon,* but now here I was, suspicious of the club and of my ability to use it. Harry Weetman had sold me this driver in 1952, and I used it solidly and successfully for ten years, save for a break of about nine months when I broke the shaft and experimented with another driver. But I always felt I could hit a particular type of drive with this club and make it work—I could block out the left side of the fairway and fade the shot down there slightly and make it drift back into the centre. All this is not to say I started hitting tee shots all over the golf course, but I was always conscious, always afraid that a big slice was going to hit me. I felt I was fighting a possibility, fighting something before it happened and in a championship of this intensity I felt I would not have enough concentration, enough thinking power, to spare for such an unexpected burden. I drove very badly in that practice round, and when I telephoned my wife that evening she reacted very sensibly to the situation, saying that I had used the thing perfectly well over the years and there was no possible reason to worry about it now, and to forget what Thomson had said. Yet it perturbed me.

from *Alliss Through the Looking Glass*, Cassell & Co (UK)

---

* Where Alliss was to compete in the 1962 Open—won by Arnold Palmer.

WRITERS RATHER THAN GOLFERS

29 Stephen Potter (1943)   30 George Plimpton (1972)
31 Patrick Campbell (1971)   32 Alistair Cooke (1976)

THREE OF THE FEW LEFT-HANDERS OF QUALITY

33   Laddie Lucas   34   Bob Charles

35 Peter Dawson

GOLF IS A SPECTATOR SPORT

36   Peter Alliss with HRH The Duke of Edinburgh at a golf charity match, Blackpool

37   Ex-King Leopold of Belgium with Princess de Rethy, watching Nicklaus at the Canada Cup golf tournament

38   Race for the last green at the 1960 Canada Cup, Portmarnock

39 Gary Player admonishes a spectator (Fulford, 1976)
40 The crowd make an amphitheatre of the 13th at Augusta during the US
Masters

41 Frank Beard at the 1969 Ryder Cup

42   Henry Cotton

43 Twenty-eight years after his retirement from championship golf, Bobby Jones accepts the Freedom of St Andrews in 1958

44 Henry Longhurst at the microphone

BOPPING IN A FOREST   George Plimpton

. . . Bruno missed his putt, and suddenly his calm left him—it just sidled off—and the rage came in and settled. It was not evident at first. He putted out with dispatch, handed the club to his caddy and accepted his driver in return. But on the way to the next tee, striding along, he suddenly swerved off the path into the woods. He disappeared. We could hear him moving through the underbrush. I thought perhaps he had gone in there to take a pee. Then we heard an odd bopping sound.

Someone looked and said, 'My God, he's in there beating his driver against a stump!'

I peered around a tree to look, and it was true. I saw him in there, a tall figure with his golf hat a startling white in the dark shadows of the eucalyptus forest, flailing away, the club swinging in the air like a willow switch. There was an echoing *bop* as it hit, as if he were trying to drive the stump and its network of roots down into the earth.

We stood around on the path uneasily, wearing the cow-like expressions of children when one of their group collapses into tears. The bopping continued. The caddies moved restlessly, the irons clinking in the golf bags. I wondered vaguely if I should wander into the woods and try to fetch him out—sidle up to him as he toiled at the stump, and say something easy, calming, like: 'Anything I can do to *help*, Bob?' I was, after all, his partner.

The clubbing stopped abruptly. After a while we heard Bruno's footsteps again. He came out on the path. He still held the driver, its shaft down near the clubhead bent in a grotesque curve. He saw us staring at him. He seemed aghast. He was purged and controlled again, but he didn't know how to put it right with us. His caddy, who was a florid-faced youngster, very stout, perhaps still in high school, looked petrified. 'Bob . . . er . . . ah,' he mumbled, 'you want me to try to *straighten that club?*'

'I'll have to use the three wood,' Bruno said. He turned the driver in his hand and stared at it miserably. 'This thing's done with. I got another driver in the back of the car, but this is the one I liked.'

We started along for the tee. 'I'm sorry, everybody,' he said. 'My game is just so damn terrible.'

Our compassion for him was immense. On the tee our team had the honor due to my great putt that had given Bruno and me a birdie on the hole, the exhilaration of which still ticked in me despite the drama in the forest.

'We're on our way, Bob,' I called.

Bruno stepped up first. Due to the loft of the three wood, his drive, despite teeing the ball down low,* soared up until the ball almost lost itself against the

* In fact, teeing low tends to produce a high shot because a descending blow is struck. Sanders for instance uses extra long tees so that he hits on the upswing.

sky before beginning its downward flight, which was nearly vertical from the apex and was completely so as it hit the fairway, so that the ball bounced straight up and came to rest, it seemed to us watching from the tee, not more than a foot or so from where it had landed. There was an obvious loss of yardage due to the trajectory of the ball, but one would not have known this from the chorus of approbation that rose from our little group.

'Sweet shot, Bob!'

'Bob, you really popped it!'

'Great poke, Bob!'

Bruno knew better, and he slumped down on the bench by the side of the tee and stared between his feet . . . .

When our foursome moved off the tee, Bruno's caddy took the bent driver and matter-of-factly worked the woolen cover with the red pompon down over the clubhead and the curved shaft and set the club back in the bag. The club was bent at its end in a curve so pronounced that it seemed as if what was under the woolen cover was a shepherd's crook. I was surprised Bruno didn't fling it away somewhere, into the sea, perhaps, on the ocean holes; but it stayed the day with us, palpable evidence to remind us of the melancholy crisis in the woods.

from *The Bogey Man*, Harper & Row (US), André Deutsch (UK)

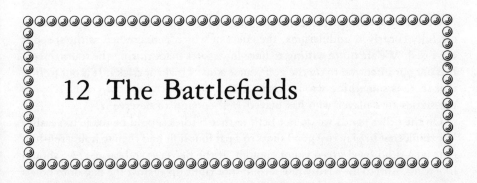

12 The Battlefields

THERE are quite a number of books that attempt to provide a guide to golf courses in Britain and the US. I have not tried to pick out the 'best' courses, but have chosen passages which explain what a great—or unusual—course is like.

BRAINS AS WELL AS BRAWN   H. N. Wethered and Tom Simpson

... a golf course is a field of manoeuvre and action, employing, as it were, the military and engineering side of the game. It opens up a series of tactical and strategical opportunities, the implications of which it would be well for every golfer to grasp ... It is important to emphasise the necessity for the golfer to use his head as much as his hands; or in other words, to make his mental agility match his physical ability.

from *The Architectural Side of Golf*, Longman (UK) 1929

AUGUSTA NATIONAL   R. T. Jones

Our over-all aim at the Augusta National has been to provide a golf course of considerable natural beauty, relatively easy for the average golfer to play, and at the same time testing for the expert player striving to better par figures. We hope to make bogies easy if frankly sought, pars readily obtainable by standard good play, and birdies, except on the par fives, dearly bought. Obviously, with a course as wide-open as needed to accommodate the average golfer, we can only tighten it up by increasing the difficulty of play around the hole. This we attempt to do during the tournament by placing the flags in more difficult and exacting positions and by increasing the speed of the greens. Additionally, we try to maintain our greens of such a firmness that they will only hold a well-played shot, and not a ball that has been hit without the backspin reasonably to be expected, considering the length of the shot.

Generally speaking, the greens at Augusta are quite large, rolling, and with carefully contrived undulations, the effect of which is magnified as the speed is increased. We are quite willing to have low scores made during the tournament. It is not our intention to rig the golf course so as to make it tricky. It is our feeling that there is something wrong with a golf course which will not yield a score in the sixties to a player who has played well enough to deserve it.

On the other hand, we do not believe that birdies should be made too easily. We think that to play two good shots to a par four hole and then to hole a ten-foot putt on a dead-level green is not enough. If the player is to beat par, we should like to ask him to hit a truly fine second shot right up against the flag or to hole a putt of more than a little difficulty. We therefore place the holes on tournament days in such locations on the greens as to require a really fine shot in order to get close. With the greens fast and undulating, the putts from medium distances are difficult and the player who leaves his ball on the outer reaches has a real problem to get down in par figures.

The contours of the greens at Augusta have been very carefully designed. We try to provide on each green at least four areas which we describe as 'pin locations'. This does not mean that the pin is always placed in one very definite spot within these areas, but each area provides an opportunity for cutting the hole in a spot where the contours are very gentle for a radius of four or five feet all around.

The selection of the pin area and the exact location of the hole are decided on the morning of play by a committee appointed for the purpose. The decision will be affected by the condition of the putting surface itself, the state of the weather to be expected, and the holding qualities of the ground. Naturally, the job of placing the holes on tournament days is one which calls for a considerable knowledge of the game and good judgment. I am sure that the players involved would be interested, too, that the committee be composed of individuals of benign and charitable natures. The position of the flags is one of the most controversial matters in any golf tournament, because it can so drastically affect the difficulty of the play.

Even though it is too much to expect that persons deciding on pin locations in the very early morning should be able to foresee what weather conditions will prevail during the actual play, it is nevertheless important that they have in mind what conditions are likely to confront the players. They should also take into account the playing condition of the fairway from which shots to a particular green are to be played.

I think it is also most rewarding for spectators, in watching the play, to be aware of the effect of variables in wind and lie of the ball. If a player is to be asked to play a quickly-stopping shot to a closely guarded green, he has every right to expect that his ball will have a very good chance of finding a clean lie, where it will be accessible to the gripping effect of his club. If the fairway in question, or the fairways in general, are not in good condition, the holes should never be cut too close to guarding bunkers.

Although a following wind tends to rob the ball of back-spin, and so makes more difficult the problem of stopping a pitch in much the same way as a lush lie, I do not believe that it offers the same argument in favour of leniency in the placing of the holes. After all, the wind is a circumstance of play wholly outside the control of those running the tournament and, unlike a bad lie, it is not subject to the vagaries of chance. Since, within reasonable limits, it is the same for all players, the difficulty of the problem to be presented may very properly be decided by the committee.

If one were to set out to make a golf course as difficult as possible, one would place the holes forward, with the wind behind, and at the back of the greens with the wind against. It must be in the light of this basic principle that the committee's decision for each particular hole will be made.

It may not be readily apparent at this point why a far-back location increases the difficulty when playing against the wind. An opposing wind is a great comfort to the player when the flag is located immediately behind a bunker guarding the front of the green. The ball can then be played boldly over the bunker with assurance that it will not finish too far past the hole. But if the pin be moved to the back of the green, and trouble lurks behind, the player must be bold indeed and extraordinarily accurate in his judgment of distance in order to bang his ball right up to the flag. Players of less confidence and skill will be continually leaving themselves far short and with a great deal of putting to do. Several greens at the Augusta National, with shelf-like areas along the back and an abrupt fall-off or bunker in the rear are well suited to emphasize this problem.

It has been said, and I hope it is true, that the Augusta National has exerted influence in the designing or remodelling of several hundred golf courses in the country. I hope this is true, because I sincerely believe that the general concepts which have influenced the construction and later modifications of our course have been quite sound from the stand-point of making the game more enjoyable for the people who support it. I believe our members could be counted upon to testify unanimously to this effect. As for the other side of the coin, I feel quite certain that the contestants in the Masters Tournament would attest very nearly as unanimously that the course provides a real competitive test. It is a fact that hardly ever has any player done exceptionally well in Augusta who has not had a quite respectable record in tournaments played elsewhere.

I believe it is true that with modern equipment and modern players, we cannot make a golf course more difficult or more testing for the expert simply by adding length. The players of today are about as accurate with medium or long irons as with their pitching clubs. The only way to stir them up is by the introduction of subtleties around the greens.

The finishes of the Masters Tournament have almost always been dramatic and exciting. It is my conviction that this has been the case because of the make-or-break quality of the second nine. This nine, with its abundant water hazards, each creating a perilous situation, can provide excruciating torture for the front runner trying to hang on. Yet it can yield a very low score to the player making a closing rush. It has been played in thirty during the tournament and in the medium forties by players still in the running at the time.

from *Golf is My Game*, Doubleday & Co (US), Chatto & Windus (UK)

PINE VALLEY   Pat Ward-Thomas

There is a sense of privilege as well as rare experience in visiting Pine Valley, for it has no parallel anywhere. No course presents more vividly and more severely the basic challenge of golf—the balance between fear and courage. Nowhere is the brave and beautiful shot rewarded so splendidly in comparison to the weak and faltering; nowhere is there such a terrible contrast between reward and punishment, and yet, withal, the examination is just. The fairways are not narrow and the greens, which demand long approach shots are large and welcoming. It is not necessary to be exceptionally long or accurate, but it is essential to be able to hit the ball reasonably well. If the fairways and greens are missed then punishment can be terrible indeed, because the ground about them has been left in its natural state. There is no rough to speak of, for the woods border every hole; but the enormous bunkers are never raked and water comes terrifyingly into play at four holes. Here, surely, is tradition rooted in the first principles of the game, for golfers of olden times were not afraid to play the ball as it lay.

Successful scrambling is quite out of the question. It is impossible to hit the ball badly and score reasonably, and precious few courses, if any, can justly claim likewise. Therefore Pine Valley is not for the meek and frail though thousands come to try their hands, some to curse and some to glory, almost masochistically, in their high scores. Here no one is ashamed of his total. Instead, finishing the course is a matter of pride, for the members well know how easy it is to take an awful number of shots awfully quickly.

When you first play Pine Valley, imagination is tuned to its most destructive pitch. You have heard all the gruesome tales of men taking 27s and the like, of ghastly failures on the brink of success, of the wagers that are laid that the ordinary player will not break 100 for his first round and that receiving five strokes a hole you will not finish eighteen up on bogey. And so the holes look narrower than they are, the carries longer, the trees more menacing, and the water, which must be carried, desperately wide. And yet no hole is beyond the scope of the average golfer, provided he uses and keeps his head. But once let him stray, then 7s and 8s and far worse will crowd thick and fast. The great hazard of Pine Valley is psychological. If one can forget its reputation and overcome the fear of its appearance, then half the battle is won. But therein lies a greater part of the test of golf.

The course is a masterpiece of architecture, imagination, and beauty, and the temptation to describe every hole is great. For of all the courses seen in a lifetime none remains so vividly in the mind. Every hole is different, setting new problems of judgment, control and planning. Many are constructed on the island principle with fairways and greens as oases in a desert of scrub, woods, and sand. Such is the second with its sloping green a pyramid amidst desolation and the seventh, one of the classic long holes of the world. If the drive is good, then an attempt may be made to carry a hundred yards of wilderness; if it is not then it is advisable to play short. The green, too, is surrounded with sand and no one has or ever will reach it in two.

The short holes are magnificent, even if at first they strike terror into the heart of the bravest. The third, a long iron downhill to a lonely, beautiful island green, and the fifth offer no compromise whatsoever. Thinking of the fifth makes one shudder even now. A fair stretch of water lies below the tee and a carry of almost 200 yards to a green tucked high in the woods must be made. All one had to do was hit a driver shot pretty straight into the wind but alas . . . The tenth, a short pitch, is easy if the shot is right; if not the ball may finish in an unprintable part of the devil's anatomy as the bunker beneath the green is locally described. The last short hole is the most famous. Its green lies on a neck of land far below the tee with water on three sides where turtles are wont to play and which once yielded 15,000 balls. Perfectly simple if a medium iron is hit properly. This same water stretches for 150 yards in front of the fifteenth tee. You stand there until you make it and then walk through the woods to one of the longest fairways in existence, which grows narrower after a quarter of a mile.

All, however, is not terrifying. Far from it. Given a straight drive the huge fourth green positively begs hitting; the eighth may bring a birdie if one does not socket a tiny pitch to a tiny green, as may the twelfth where the fairway should be large enough for anyone. The thirteenth is a classic par 4. After a good drive to a plateau the hole swings downhill with all kinds of perdition on the left which cut into the line of the second shot. But like all great holes there is an alternative. Safety and a probable 5 lie to the right. The sixteenth is by no means alarming, once the tee shot is away; neither is the seventeenth, if one ignores what has to be carried with the pitch to the green. It is said that one golfer once took 67 there but he probably lost his temper. One recalls blasting from a cactus plant after just missing this fairway.

From the eighteenth tee the towers of Philadelphia can be seen in the shining distance. The fairway tilts towards the woods far below and sanctuary is near, but first a brave shot must be hit from a sloping lie across a stream. And then Pine Valley has been played and a lifetime's memory made. There remain only post mortems, the like of which are heard nowhere else, in a clubhouse as cool, shadowed, masculine, and peaceful as any Englishman could desire, and infinitely welcoming. A portrait of Crump glows in the darkness and his spirit lives on in men like John Arthur Brown, president these thirty years: men who abhor the modern urge to simplify, who love golf because its challenge is undying, and who are proud of their privilege to preserve it at Pine Valley.

from *The Manchester Guardian*, 1957, reprinted by permission
of Pat Ward-Thomas

BALLYBUNION   Herbert Warren Wind

Ballybunion is a small, gray seaside resort in northern Kerry, forty miles west of Limerick and some twenty-five miles due north of Tralee. It stands on the southern shore of the Shannon estuary, facing the Atlantic, a far less prepossessing village than Lahinch. Though it was thick with holiday people this Sunday, I gathered from Dr O'Sullivan* that it had never been too prosperous. The golf links, he said, had continually suffered down through the years from a lack of funds. In his opinion, the course was potentially the equal of any in Ireland, but the club never had had the wherewithal to maintain it in A-1 condition or to develop it in the manner a rich club might have done. On top of this, the club now had an erosion problem to cope with. Some sections of the high, steep cliffs along the shore were slipping back into the ocean, and not at a geological rate either. There were one or two greens that might be lost in only a matter of years. The principal point he wished to stress, however, was the quality of the course. One Irish Professional Championship, two Irish Amateurs, and two Irish Ladies Amateurs had been held there, and he had yet to meet the golfer who had not been charmed and awed by Ballybunion. 'On the other hand, it's virtually unknown,' he added. 'Very few tourists from Britain or America—or, for that matter, from other parts of Ireland—bother to visit it. They know about Ballybunion, but it's stuck off by itself on the road to nowhere, so in the end they pass it by. They make a tremendous mistake.'

At first glance even the most distinguished linksland courses look utterly ordinary to the man who has never played them before. If he stands, say, before the ante-bellum clubhouse at the Augusta National Golf Club, as he takes in the wide panorama of the lush fairways swinging through the tall pines, he senses instantly that an authentic championship layout awaits him. The same holds true at most of the world's other renowned inland courses. But let him stand on the first tee at St Andrews or Ballybunion, and all that he sees is a treeless sweep of billowing pale-green land, with a few dun-coloured sand hills looming in the distance—a most unpromising vista. A fragment of fairway is visible here and

---

* We have met him before—defeated by the inspired Patrick Campbell in the matchplay chapter.

another fragment there, so what he is looking at is patently a golf course, but it might as easily be pastureland. It is only when the golfer gets out onto a linksland course that he discovers, to his amazement, that it can be filled with great holes, all the more appealing since their strategic features were molded by nature and not by the bulldozer. I should state, before going any farther, that I did not play Ballybunion. In retrospect, I regretted this, but when we arrived that morning a chilly, moisture-laden, twenty-knot wind was busting in off the ocean, and it completely doused what little desire I had to play golf. I could picture myself having one of those sparkling rounds in which I would be standing deep in the alien corn on shot after shot while Dr O'Sullivan patiently studied some adjacent par-3 hole and Slattery ruminated over the decline of the Boston College football teams. Instead we walked the eighteen holes. In the beginning there were just the three of us up from Killarney, but on the second hole, we were joined by Paddy Allen, a dedicated Ballybunion man in his sixties, long one of the club's best players and now a club trustee. (He had been waiting at the small, plain clubhouse to greet us on our arrival, along with his brother Tom, the club steward for upward of fifty years, both of them openly delighted at seeing Dr O'Sullivan. Paddy Allen had then phoned the captain and a few other members about our plans for the day before catching up with us.) By the time we reached the fifth-tee, our walking party had been supplemented by a dozen Ballybunion men, among them the captain, J. D. Mahony; the secretary, Michael Handrahan; and a Dr Walsh, who was forced to leave on the fifteenth hole when a young boy raced out to inform him he was urgently needed to deliver a baby . . .

Despite the ripping wind and some intermittent rain, the two-hour walk was profoundly exciting. Very simply, Ballybunion revealed itself to be nothing less than the finest seaside course I have ever seen. It shows its hand on the very first hole, a par 4 that doglegs to the left and seems a good bit longer than 372 yards, its length on the scorecard. From the tee, the hole appears to be a rather banal par 4, but when, after reaching that point in the fairway where an adequate drive would finish, you study the long, narrow green, a medium-iron away, and the fanciful way the land weaves in the green area, your assessment changes radically. It is, you perceive, a formidable, arresting hole. When I expressed these thoughts to Dr O'Sullivan, he was in full agreement. He went on to observe that he had never seen Ballybunion in such excellent condition. 'Usually it's all kind of shaggy and spotty, but everything's cut so crisp today. Maybe it's because they knew we were coming. Whatever the reason, the course looks grand, doesn't it?'

The second hole certainly did. It is a 413-yard par 4 that runs roughly parallel to the seventy-foot-high cliffs that plunge down to the beach and the water. Actually, the hole is a slight dogleg. The correct line on the tee shot is down the left side of the fairway, for this opens up the entrance to the green, flanked on the left by a massive sand hill and on the right by the cliffs. From the tee, the entire hole is visible and, if this were not an exhilarating enough prospect, farther in the

distance, at the far end of a tight valley between two rows of sand hills, your eye
takes in the minute green of another dazzling cliffside hole, the sixth. I breathed
it all in slowly, wondering first to myself and then aloud who the architect was
who had had the genius to use the duneland in such a thrilling way. Dr O'Sullivan
didn't know, but when I later asked Paddy Allen, he said the credit for both holes
belonged to the late Tom Simpson, a much-admired English architect—they
were two of the holes Simpson had substantially improved when he remodelled
the course in the nineteen-thirties. Allen said this with a dour matter-of-factness
that didn't tally with the pleasure a dedicated Ballybunion man would normally
take in showing these two superior holes to visitors. His voice and countenance
became pronouncedly grimmer a moment later when, after walking us behind the
second green, he pointed out the rude wooden supports that had been rigged
against the face of the cliff. This was one of the places where the erosion was
proceeding at an alarming speed. He shook his head sadly and walked us back to a
sheltered basin on the inland side of the large green-flanking sand hill. 'If we lose
the second green,' he said 'this is where the new green will probably go.'

'It will ruin the hole, Paddy,' Dr O'Sullivan expostulated.

Allen opened his palms in a gesture of resignation. 'Yes, Billy,' he said. 'It will
be just another golf hole.' He then walked silently away to ruminate by himself.

When a tourist drives through Switzerland, he is staggered by its prodigal
beauty: around the corner from the most wondrous view he has ever beheld he
comes upon a view that surpasses it—and on and on, endlessly. Ballybunion is
something like that. I do not mean to suggest that there are other vistas that put
the one from the second tee to shame—there aren't—but there is a corres-
pondence in the way one stirring hole is followed by another and another. The
third, for example, is a 145-yarder that moves through the sand hills to a devilish
little green that tips into an abrupt down-slope on the right and is bunkered on
the left and in front. On the fourth, a 451-yard par 4 on the inland side of the
sandhill belt, the key hazard is a deep bunker carved in the face of a rise in the
middle of the fairway about 20 yards before the plateau green; anything less than a
perfectly struck second shot will end up in it. (A sign wedged into the ground at
the edge of the bunker informs the golfer that it is called the Crow's Nest. There
are similar signs at the five other major hazards on the course—an original touch
and a flavorous one.) The fifth hole, which curves back toward the ocean through
another twisting valley, is a very attractive drive-and-pitch par 4, 340 yards long,
a dogleg to the left this time. The sixth, which I described earlier, is a perfect
beauty, a 450-yard par 4 that tumbles downhill, along the cliffs, to an inviting
green. And that is the way it keeps going at Ballybunion. There is not one prosaic
hole, no one single 'breather,' in the whole eighteen. If the course has a weakness,
I would suppose that it is the comparative plainness of the last two holes—a pair
of par 5s stretching over comparatively featureless interior ground. They are not
trite holes, for they are shrewdly bunkered, but they do lack the eye appeal of the

rest of the course and, as a result, they are somewhat anticlimactic. At the conclusion of our walk, by the way, I found I could remember each of the eighteen holes without much trouble—one of the oldest and soundest rules of thumb for judging the merits of a course that a golfer has just met for the first time. Aside from the first six holes, three others remained especially distinct: the tenth, a 210-yarder over difficult duneland where the prevailing wind, from the west, sweeps across from left to right; the 368-yard thirteenth, where the sand in a fifty-yard-wide bunker called the Sahara is strewn with deer bones, shells, stones, and ashes deposited in the fifteenth century by a tribe that used the cavity as a midden, or dump; and the fourteenth, a 376-yard par 4 that Simpson enlivened by placing in the drive zone a mounded double bunker that the members immediately dubbed Mrs Simpson. Ballybunion is a moderate 6,317 yards in length, par is 71 (34—37), and, as I say, no other links, in my opinion, presents a more satisfying adventure in golf. The course has two unique endowments. First, it is the only links I know of where the bulk of the oceanside holes are perched above spectacular cliffs, à la Pebble Beach (which is not a true links). Second— and this is undoubtedly the secret of its character and charm—it is the only links I know of where the sandhill ridges do not run parallel with the shore but at a decided traverse. This opens all sorts of possibilities—dogleg holes of every description sculptured through the heaving land, and straightaway holes where the sand hills patrol the entrance to the green like the Pillars of Hercules. One more point. Unlike most links, Ballybunion challenges you with target golf. There is none of that bouncing your iron approach short of the green and letting it bobble toward the flag. No, you aim for the flag, and if your shot lands on the green, the green is sufficiently receptive to hold it.

The miracle is that the several golf architects who had a hand in creating Ballybunion recognized how the terrain should be handled. During lunch at the village hotel, Paddy Allen, having pored over the club records at the finish of our walk, supplied some information on these architects. The man who took care of the course when Ballybunion was founded in 1896 was one P. Murphy, who was paid nine shillings a week. When the club was re-formed in 1906, after financial woes had brought down the original organization, Captain Lionel Hewson, for many years the editor of *Irish Golf* magazine, built the nine holes that became the basis of the present layout. In 1926, when the course was extended to eighteen holes, the work was directed by a man named Smyth, a designer on the staff of Carter & Sons, a London firm specializing in the construction of sports grounds. Then, in 1936, Simpson was brought in to remodel the course. He was given carte blanche, but recognizing, as few architects would have managed in their compulsion to edit their predecessors, the unusual worth of the existing layout, he made only four changes: he resited the second, fourth, and eighth greens and introduced the Mrs Simpson double bunker on the fourteenth. Last, the course reflects the devotion of William J. McCarthy, a local solicitor and hotel owner, whose father was one of the club's founders. McCarthy, who is still active in the club, served for more than two decades as Ballybunion's honorary secretary and also performed the duties of a kind of resident architect. In the early nineteen-fifties, he built two first-class new holes to replace the old eleventh and twelfth, but, in truth, there is hardly a hole that McCarthy has not enhanced by some skillful touch, like recontouring a bunker or relocating a tee.

During lunch, Dr O'Sullivan, as the representative of a more thriving and worldly golf club, as well as a regional hero, was kept busy answering a stream of questions by the Ballybunion men as to how they might go about improving their hard-pressed operation. The doctor was very much in favor of the club's acquiring, if it were in a position to do so, the seashore property adjacent to the course. It would be a safeguard against invasion by get-rich-quick realtors. He strongly supported the proposal that a new clubhouse, however modest, be built as soon as was feasible at the edge of the sea, close by either the sixth or the tenth green. (One of the oblique dividends from such a move would be that the order of the holes would necessarily be changed for the better if either the seventh or eleventh became the first hole. Then the present seventeenth and eighteenth would be played in the middle of a round, and the course would roar to a much more stirring finish.) He recommended that the club summon the best professional guidance in dealing with the erosion problem. He was listened to most attentively. There were, in fact, only a few light moments during the lunch. One of them came when Dr Walsh, his delivery completed, rejoined the party. Was it a boy? he was asked. 'No,' he said, 'only a child.'

My overriding memory of the lunch, however, is the unbroken gravity of the Ballybunion men as they discussed with Dr O'Sullivan the steps they should take to make the golf world more conscious of their course. Paddy Allen, I know, was still gripped by that problem when I said goodbye to him. 'We can't expect anything like the number of tourists Portmarnock gets,' he told me, in a small voice that grew emotional despite his efforts to be calm. 'But we need a better bite off the plum, a much better bite. As you saw for yourself, Ballybunion is a fine, fine course. And that champagne air off the ocean . . .' He interrupted himself, then continued. 'The course means everything here. Take away the golf course and you take away Ballybunion.'

from *Herbert Warren Wind's Golf Book*, Simon & Schuster (US)
© *The New Yorker*, 1971

CARNOUSTIE   Peter Thomson

Carnoustie had in fact disappointed. It was dull and uninspiring, due, some said, only to the narrowing of the fairways and the positioning of the cups on the green. But I am inclined to think otherwise. In its own right Carnoustie is a great course in the sense that great things have happened there—at least I am led to believe so. (Indeed one of them I saw—as a youngster of 22 I watched Hogan win his Open which crowned his career.) But under the close scrutiny of the modern more discerning eye it looks old and decrepit. Not all courses on the seaside links land are fine courses even though they be 7,000 yards long and windswept. To earn the highest rating a course must test all the shots and provide at the same time, a chance of scoring low and frighteningly high. It must be possible to score birdies and triple bogies.

Perhaps at Carnoustie it is because after lengthening, so many holes are neither one thing nor the other; neither fours nor fives and, as it was at the 16th neither three nor four.

Even the argument that its length holds no problem for the likes of Nicklaus, holds no water. Courses built for 300-yard tee shot artists are not great courses.

Carnoustie has its old fashioned quota of blind second shots. These no longer serve any purpose in championship golf.

It is difficult to define its other shortcomings. It is like looking at a painting and trying to explain what is missing. Courses like paintings are all different. Some are great and some are bad, and there are more in between.

The fairway bunkering by and large is amateurish and the ones at the 2nd and 6th perfectly ludicrous.

Nor are greenside hazards very inspiring and greens themselves look more accident than design.

This sounds, I know, like sour grapes, but I hope I am looking at it more objectively than that. I am a great lover of seaside links and I have consistently upheld that the greatest of seaside links are the greatest of courses.

Carnoustie could easily satisfy me with a few major renovations. Last July, mistakes were made and from these lessons should be learned. In drawing attention to them I hope they might be avoided in future and that the Open might continue to climb up to its rightful place as the world's foremost golf event. Apart from the general architecture which is so dull, I must speak out against the indiscriminate narrowing of fairways by the ruse of letting the fairway turf grow wild until it is indistinguishable from and merges with, the normal rough. To put it simply, rough should make the hole and not the other way round.

Dog-legging, off-setting of tees and such devices increase the need for judgment and clever thinking. In direct contrast, the plain shrinking of the entire length of the fairway, so that all alternatives are eliminated, robs the game of one of its important aspects—necessity to make a choice.

If golf is a test of threading one's way down narrow, alley-like avenues of untidy growth it is hardly a game. It becomes an examination. It demonstrates neither temperament nor thought. It is boring for players and spectators alike.

Carnoustie can thank providence for the six weeks drought during May and

June, that kept the uncut parts of the fairways sparse. Had they grown lush so that escape was impossible, the championship might had been dubbed absurd!

As it was the rough played little effective part. The winner and most others spent much time in it without more than token penalty.

But there was no need for it.

It had not the slightest bearing on the result and served only nuisance value.

I am convinced that the only answer to the question of how to prepare for a championship, is to hand the matter over to a first class architect who is given a free hand to test his wits against the players.

It is not enough to follow a laid down formula of narrowing and lengthening. By experience we can see that little is gained and sometimes previous features destroyed.

Granted that cutting eighteen greens is a large size job that might take six man hours of work, it is still necessary to cut on the morning of play even if six men and six machines have to do it. At Carnoustie the greens were cut in the evening after play.

By the time the late starters got to them they have about twenty-four hours' growth on them.

This is not good enough. No greens grow absolutely evenly and the longer they grow the more uneven they become.

Championship greens must be absolutely true and the only way to provide this is to cut on the morning of play.

Nor did the cups look to be well cut. Too many had high lips that gave them an appearance something like a moon crater. On a golf course the hole in the green is the only feature fixed in dimension by the rules. It deserves every possible attention.

The positioning of the holes on the greens is the privilege and obligation of the championship committee. It is realised by now that this job is a most important one and one that must not be taken lightly or done by anyone incompetent.

However, good architecture can easily be nullified or destroyed if this job is done badly. In modern construction greens are built with all this in mind and the positioning of flags is almost done by the architect. The Committees do not need to be thoughtful. The positioning of the holes at Carnoustie were certainly not punitive or outrageous, *but several of them were absolutely negative*. At the 4th and 11th and on one particular day at the 8th they just could not be fired at. In fairness to the flag setting committee it should be stated that the wind blew from an entirely unexpected quarter but this only showed up the folly of deciding on all four flag placements on each green the day before the event got under way.

Flag placement must be done with the full consideration of the weather and in particular the wind each day. Only then can the pin placement add to the architecture.

Negative hole settings only serve the purpose of throwing the field together.

Positive flag placings work towards separating, which should be the ultimate idea.

If these criticisms seem harsh on all the largely honorary work done to prepare Carnoustie for the '68 championship, I cannot help it, but as a comfort to the loyal people involved I would like to say that these particular errors are more the rule of championships than the exception. I would not like to nominate any particular championship where the preparations were faultless, and some I can recall were far worse than Carnoustie, but I hope that someone may now give thought to these factors for the improvement of future championships.

The Open at Carnoustie was in many ways the biggest 'production' we have seen in Britain. I believe the attendances broke all records of Opens since the war. My own particular friends who followed me faithfully complained later that they could see very little. This was unfortunate and not really the fault of anyone involved. It was due to the flatness of the Carnoustie course. This has an unfortunate effect in that the spectators are unable to play a more intimate part, not being able to see the details, fine points are missed. Applause or lack of it flows accordingly and the players are unresponsive to any enthusiasm which might lie latent in their hearts. The Old Course has a similar problem. I cannot help feeling that the 'blindness' the crowd must suffer will eventually affect its attendances. These days, television is a far more effective eye-witness and if cricket and lawn tennis were showing I doubt if anyone would in preference go on to the course and stumble around unprepared tracks from which they see very little.

It may be that some courses, even though great ones from the playing point of view, are virtually useless as championship venues. These might have to be struck from the roster. However almost anything in the way of earthmoving and construction can be done in seaside links territory, and it would seem to be an act of wisdom for any town council hoping for a permament place on the championship list to do it. Perhaps when we next come back to Carnoustie it will be a different place . . .

from *This Wonderful World of Golf*, Pelham Books (UK)

MELLAHA—OUTPOST OF THE SAHARA   Michael Hobbs

Golf has spread to all parts of the world where some people have a little time to spare. Golf courses are as various in kind as the countries: anything from a multimillion-dollar construction involving much use of the bulldozer and seed and soil consultants to a few holes laid out near a desert oil rig or an Arctic weather station.

But what happens when a US government signs an agreement with Libya to lease land for an airbase? One result is that several thousand airmen arrive and what they need most is a golf course. It was not too difficult to construct the concrete runways and buildings, but creating a golf course for the men at Wheelus Field demanded ingenuity—and long negotiations with Arab peasants about land and water rights.

The basic material was unpromising: stoney, hardbaked sand and clay land, dotted with palm trees, by the side of the Mediterranean. The palm trees came with rights attached that meant the Arabs must still be able to harvest the date crop. So each and every tree had to remain. The architect could not decide to cut a swathe through *here* for a tee shot, or a few down *there* to set up a subtle line for a dogleg. He had either to avoid them or to make use of those which nature had put in a suitable place.

Bunkers, on the other hand, were no problem at all. Shallow scraped out pits quickly filled up with fine drifting sand. True, when the Sahara *ghibli* blew, they emptied just as quickly.

Golfers kindly referred to what they putted on as 'greens', but they were the colour of damp sand. Constructed as raised platforms of sand soaked in oil waste, there was a top layer of unoiled sand. This had to be kept well watered so that it did not blow away. In the shade of a palm tree reclined an Arab with a large mat. This he dragged over the green to remove the foot and ball marks when the players had gone. The surfaces were true. Grass has a mind of its own but sand is neutral; a well-struck putt held its line exactly.

There were no fairways and no rough. After the rains, if your ball came to rest on one of the patches of grass that then existed for a few days, you would have to seek into your golfing memory to recall how to play a shot from so exotic a surface.

I bought an immense bag from Master-Sergeant Slonski and in it were five woods, eleven irons and an extending rod for retrieving balls from water hazards. The latter implement was essential. Bilharzia was imminent if you took off your shoes and socks and waded in.

Slonski's clubs gave useful clues as to how to play the course. The irons from 1 to 6 were unblemished. So too were the woods, except for the driver, which bore scars on its sole plate as a result of heavy tee shots. The others showed that he had not risked a fairway wood from the baked surface and the stones.

The Mellaha that had emerged was perhaps not the course to test a champion's mettle. Optimism before the shot and a stoic acceptance of fate thereafter were what was needed. You took out the driver, hammered in a tee peg, and the ball took to the air. Once it returned to earth it might skid forwards, ricochet to left or right or come back to you on the rebound from a rock. But eventually it did come to rest. Master-Sergeant Slonski, it seemed, then moved it along with the 7 iron. So, after many ambitious failures, did I. You need a bit of loft for confidence in hitting off concrete and a different hitting action too. Did not the great Hogan change his when he met the hard Scottish links fairway of Carnoustie for the 1953 British Open? He felt his wrists might go if he continued to take his accustomed slab of turf. At Mellaha, that never jolly face would have tautened further, and he would have had to skim the ball off like the rest of us.

After the driver, and the skim with the 7, the green was probably close by. You then had an option: a push towards it with the 7 or perhaps a real target-golf shot at the flag with a lofted club—if you for once braved the risk of injury by taking a divot. If you could hit the green, the oily sand would keep you there.

In due time there came the miracle of a 33 on the back nine that made the splendour of the sunset nothing. What triumphs lay ahead, I wondered? None. The next day the 1967 Arab-Israeli war began. The US airmen withdrew into their Wheelus fortress; I stayed out of harm's way on a country farm.

I never played there again. But at least there are few people around who can claim a 33 on the tough back nine at Mellaha.

EL FASHER

Henry Longhurst

. . . As to the golf course at Fasher, I am conscious of having written about it before but will allow myself the luxury of mentioning it for positively the final time, since out of the four hundred odd courses on which I have played, including some on which no blade of grass has ever grown or ever will, Fasher remains unique. There was no clubhouse and the members, it was said, could be counted on the fingers of two hands, or at any rate on those of the owner of the village adjoining the course, known as Abu Shoke, the 'father of thorns', who had seven on each. There was no clubhouse and no tees, but there were nine greens, each with a hole in, generally with the metal rim sticking up out of the sand, so that a local rule said: 'On the rim counts in.' The course itself was entirely sand, interspersed with a particularly vicious form of camel thorn, the spikes of which were sharp enough not only to penetrate a ball, let alone the seat of your trousers—another local rule said you could 'dethorn' a ball without penalty—but also to be habitually used in place of gramophone needles. Members of the S.D.F.* were riding all over the course, practising for their tattoo, jumping on and off at full gallop, riding two horses at once and so on, and the surface of one green was far from improved by the paw marks of a couple of hyenas. We teed off in the sand at the top of a bluff looking over a magnificent view and played down to the 1st hole, marked by a small boy in a nightshirt holding what turned out to be the club's only flag. No use having permanent flags, they said. If you had wooden ones, the ants would eat them and, if you had metal, the locals would melt them instantly down for spears. So when one had reached within a few yards of the green, the boy doubled off through the camel thorn to hold the flag in the

* Sudan Defence Force—the name of the country's army until independence. It gave the Italians enormous trouble when they attempted invasion from Abyssinia in 1940.

2nd hole, while a hugh coal black caddie advanced in stately fashion to the hole and placed his feet at right angles behind it for the player to putt at. The 7th, I remember, was a short hole with the green surrounded by this ghastly camel thorn, but the Governor described it with a certain amount of local pride as being 'set in a sylvan setting'. The climax came fittingly enough at the 9th, when one of the caddies, distinguished by a blue diamond on the back of his jellaba, became noticeably restive. The blue diamond, it transpired, signified that he had been seconded for duty from the gaol and he feared he was going to be late for lock-up. He was therefore sent back in the Governor's car. One feels somehow that, though he and the Empire of which this was part had long since been dead, Kipling would have approved.

from My Life and Soft Times, Cassell & Co (UK)

16TH AT CYPRESS POINT   George Plimpton

The 16th at Cypress Point is one of the famous golf holes of the world, certainly one of the most difficult and demanding par 3s. In the 1952 Crosby the average score of the entire field on the hole was 5, an average bolstered by Lawson Little getting a 14 and Henry Ransom an 11. Ben Hogan got a 7. The golfer stands on a small elevated tee facing the Pacific Ocean that boils in below on the rocks, its swells laced with long strands of kelp. Occasionally, a sea lion can be seen lolling about, turning lazily, a flipper up, like a log in a slow current. It would be a clear shot to the horizon if it weren't for a promontory that hooks around from the golfer's left. On the end of the promontory, circled by ice plant, is the green, a 210-yard carry across the water.

The green is shallow, with some traps behind, and then the ice plant, and beyond that, ready to receive a shot hit a touch too powerfully, the Pacific Ocean. There is a relatively safe approach to the 16th, which is to aim to the left of the green and carry a shot 125 yards or so across the water onto the wide saddle of the promontory. A lonely storm-bent tree stands in the fairway, and it is in its vicinity that one drops one's first shot. From there the golfer must chip to the green and sink his putt to make his par.

Many players are critical of the 16th at Cypress. Gardner Dickinson told me that he thought it was no sort of golf hole at all. His point was that risking a direct carry to the green, particularly if any sort of wind was blowing in the golfer's face, was ill-advised and 'cotton-pickin' stupid,' and the sensible golfer was penalized for the shot he *should* make—that is to say, to the fairway on the saddle of the promontory, from where he must get down in two for his par. The chances of birdieing the hole playing it that way are, of course, almost nil. Dickinson himself would not try the long shot. (One's whole daily score could be affected; Jerry Barber got a 10 on the hole the year that he was PGA champion.) He always chose the safer route, cutting across as much ocean as he dared with an iron, aiming for the promontory saddle, all the while mumbling and carrying on and pinching up his face in disgust as if the kelp surging back and forth below him in the sea were exuding a strong odor.

The spectators loved the hole, though. They gathered on the wooded bluff above the tee, some perched on the wide cypress branches, squat-shaped, like night herons. When a player motioned—somewhat theatrically, one always felt—to his caddy for a wood, and the caddy, warming to the drama, removed the woolen cover with a flourish, there would be a stirring in the trees, like a rookery at dawn, and a stretching forward, since the spectators up there knew the golfer was going to 'go for it.'

And it was a wonderful thing to hear the click of the club and see the ball soar off over the ocean—as senseless an act, at first glance, as watching someone drive a ball off the stern of a transatlantic liner—the ball rising up against the wind currents and high above the line of the horizon beyond. Then, with its descent, one realized the distant green had become available, until it was a question of *distance*—whether the ball would flash briefly against the cliffs that fronted the green and plummet into the ocean, or whether the green itself would suddenly be pocked by the whiteness of the ball, the feat done, accented by a roar and clatter rising out of the trees behind the tee.

Here was the distinction of this ocean hole at Cypress: it epitomized the feat of golf—excessively, Dickinson would say—namely, the hitting of a distant target with accuracy, a shot so demanding that it was either successful or, with the ocean circling the hole on three sides, emphatically a disaster.

from *The Bogey Man*, Harper & Row (US), André Deutsch (UK)

DON'T COMPLAIN ABOUT THE COURSE—IT COULD BE EXPENSIVE
George Plimpton

Charles B. Macdonald, a financial titan and autocrat of the boom period, . . . was the founder of the National Golf Links of Southampton, Long Island, which has a succession of some of the truly great golf holes of the world. A number of the holes are patterned after those Macdonald had played abroad and admired—the Redan from North Berwick, and then the famous Road Hole of St Andrews, with the deep potholes,* and along the right fairway a line of trees to substitute for the railroad tracks.† Macdonald loved his course so much that his private home was not placed to take advantage of the best possible views but was faced, instead, to look down on his golf links. He ran his club with an iron hand. He was famous for listening to criticisms, rectifying them, and then sending the bill to whoever had

* Potbunkers? Though the road surface was once far rougher than it now is.
† Railway *sheds*?

complained. A member would say, 'Lord, there ought to be a place in the clubhouse where a fellow could play a spot of bridge'—and if MacDonald was within earshot, soon enough a room would be tacked onto the clubhouse, and then charged to the bridge enthusiast. On one occasion a club member had mumbled about the mosquito swarms rising off a pond on the 14th hole. MacDonald had the pond drained and sent the bill to the member. Members either paid up or were dropped from the membership lists. Fortunately, the membership was extremely affluent. But I have always imagined members of the National in MacDonald's time wandering around the course with fixed grins trying to remember not to say anything.

from *The Bogey Man*, Harper & Row (US), André Deutsch (UK)

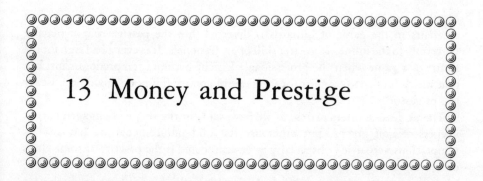

13 Money and Prestige

CADDIES were the first professional golfers. Later a good golfer earned his money as greenkeeper, ball- and club-maker, from small fees for playing a round with a member or giving a lesson, and he might finish the day cleaning clubheads and sandpapering them to remove the rust.

The great British golfers of the 1890s and 1900s made the breakthrough by which names such as Vardon, Ray, Braid, Taylor and Herd became household words. They had prestige but did not become wealthy men. They, and much more so the ordinary club professional, were expected to keep to a lowly station in life.

It took Walter Hagen to change all that, while later the personality of Arnold Palmer and the selling of it by Mark McCormack has done most to make some golfers multimillionaires.

THINGS HAVE CHANGED   Horace G. Hutchinson

It is probable that the rising interest which attaches to the play of amateurs has had an effect in diminishing the interest felt in professional matches and in proportionately diminishing the profits attached to professional play.* There are money prizes in connection with the professional championship, and to other tournaments open to professionals in various parts of the country; but on the whole they are less than they used to be, and the majority live a precarious life, the soldiers of fortune, a capricious goddess who interferes greatly with the golfing sphere.

While the golfing talk of past days was mainly occupied with the achievements of the professional element, it is rather the names and doings of amateurs that are now the subject of discussion. This we may probably regard as a sign of good omen for the future of the game. Where a game falls too much within professional hands, it tends to lose that quality which is implied in the term 'sport.' We see this in the case of baseball in America, more conspicuously perhaps than in any other instance; but we hear a similar complaint with respect to football in the

* This was written just before J. H. Taylor began winning championships. His arrival, of course, was soon followed by Harry Vardon and James Braid.

North of England, and it is certain that much of the active interest on the part of amateurs in the game of billiards is diverted into the passive rôle of playing spectators to the infinitely greater skill of professionals. It is ever a bad sign for the future of a game when the professional element becomes too predominant; but that which is of good promise for the game of golf itself is not of good promise for the professor.

The profession offers prizes, as we have said, in the shape of engagements as keepers of golf greens, but otherwise its solid inducements are few and its temptations very many. Especially to be reprobated is the practice at some clubs of offering a 'drink' to a professional at the close of a round. If you leave him to himself there is no danger of his damaging his health by drinking too little. No golf professional is recorded to have died of thirst. On the other hand, the lives of many have been shortened and degraded by thirst too often satiated. Some of the clubs of the North would be greatly more pleasant places if a fixed price were authoritatively named for the recompense of professional caddies and players. There is a delightful uncertainty upon this point which more than the actual cost deters many from taking out a professional. The 'dour' silence in which he accepts your fee when you give him enough, and the sense of self-contempt for the moral weakness which prompts you to give him too much, are equally annoying with his open dissatisfaction and probable profanity if you give him too little.

Properly treated, however, the professional is almost always a good fellow. He has cheery spirits, a ready wit and humour, which is only denied to the Scotch by those who do not know them, and he will show a zeal and loyalty in defending your performances behind your back—provided you overpay him sufficiently— very much at variance with the opinion which he expresses to your face. He is a little apt to mistake insolence for independence—prone to a criticism which errs on the side of too great candour, but if you can endure a certain measure of this, he is a good companion. Never, however, bet with him; for so will it be best for him and best for you, as he is unlikely to pay you if he loses. This he is apt to do, for he is a bad judge of the merits of a golf match, a point which requires a delicacy of estimate usually beyond his power.

from *Golf*, The Badminton Library (UK) 1893

CREATING THE MARKET   Walter Hagen

I learned early that whatever I got out of life, I'd have to go out and get for myself. And the physical aptitude I possessed gave me the means of beginning. However, I had to create a paying market for that ability to play golf.

Showmanship was needed and happily I possessed a flair for that, too, and I used it. In fact, some fellows sort of believed I invented the kind of showmanship which, in those early days, began to put golf on a big-time money basis.

Apparently, too, it pleased the public to think I lived the easy carefree life, the playboy of golf. Frankly, I was happy to support both those illusions, since I was making money out of the showmanship and I was having a grand time living on the money. I've a lot of clippings which seem to prove that I gave rather effective performances in both lines.

Actually throughout my life, I've assumed nothing without proof. Given the opportunity I checked and double-checked everything from the undulations of a putting green to the figures on a cheque and the curves of a pleasing number. I took nothing for granted, for I could not afford that luxury. I was trying to make a living out of a game which had never in its history supplied more than the bare necessities to its professional players, much less allowed them to live in comparative ease.

from *The Walter Hagen Story*, Simone & Schuster (US),
William Heinemann (UK)

CHANGING IN AN AUSTRO-DAIMLER   Walter Hagen

I invited Jim Barnes to drive down to Deal in my rented limousine so we could look over the course and get acquainted with the setup. I liked the impression the Austro-Daimler, complete with chauffeur and footman, made as we pulled up in front of the club-house. We climbed out of the car and strolled inside. Being early on an off day we couldn't find anyone in the club-house, so we looked for the locker-rooms. We were dressed for golf, except for changing our shoes. While we were making the change the head locker steward—a little man in a white coat—came hurriedly in our direction.

'Are you Mr High-gen?' he inquired brusquely.

'I am,' I said, 'and this is Mr Barnes.'

'Gentlemen,' he said importantly, 'you're in the wrong place.'

'This is Deal?' I asked.

'Oh, yes, indeed,' he assured me. 'But you gentlemen are professionals. You'll be using Mr Hunter's golf shop for dressing.'

'Well, pardon me,' I said and walked out in my golf shoes, giving the other pair to my hired footman to put in the car.

Jim and I went down to the golf shop to pay our respects to Mr Hunter, the pro, and to look over the facilities. One long spike in the wall had several coats hanging on it and in a far corner many pairs of shoes—the toes turned up like skis—were piled disconsolately. I guess the Oakland Hills Golf Club treatment had spoiled me, made me accustomed to being treated as any golfer, pro or amateur, should be. For I took one look at Jim and he followed me out of the place. I knew we weren't going to use that shop for a dressing-room.

'We'll use my car for a dressing-room,' I told Jim. 'We can dress at the tavern in the village, then just change our shoes out here.'

I got my two caddies and we started. I used my footman as a fore-caddie to train him for the Championship. I had told the chauffeur to meet us at the eighteenth green with my polo coat and to leave the car parked directly in front of the club.

When we played around to Deal's eighteenth green the club's Mr Secretary—a small but important little fellow with a waxed moustache—stepped up to greet us. During our walk back to the club-house where my car was parked, he apologised for the incident earlier that morning, but explained again that professionals were not allowed in the club-house.

I told him I was sorry, too, but we did not know the rules and henceforth we'd use my car. 'I'll be living at the near-by pub, so I can easily change my shoes and sweater in the car.'

He didn't like the idea of parking my car in front of the club-house, either, and of having the chauffeur meet me at the eighteenth green.

from *The Walter Hagen Story*, Simon & Schuster (US), William Heinemann (UK)

THE GRAVY   Jack Nicklaus and Herbert Warren Wind

As I remarked earlier, from a commercial standpoint this is the golden age for a professional golfer. No other athletes have the opportunity to do as well as we do, especially when you take into account the subsidiary gravy that comes our way. Since I have gone into the other aspects of the current golf scene in some detail, I think you might find it interesting if I touched briefly on my present business affiliations. First, I play MacGregor clubs and balls. I have been under contract to MacGregor [written in later 1960s] since turning professional.

In foreign tournaments, as I have mentioned, I play Slazenger clubs and balls. Under a deal that Mark McCormack arranged, golf balls bearing my name are merchandized at Firestone outlets—three balls for $1.33. This has been a most successful venture. As regards golf shoes, I endorse a line made by the Plymouth Shoe Company. The ones I wear are kangaroo leather and Corfam, with anodized gold spikes. (If you want to pivot properly, you've got to have anodized gold spikes.)* In the clothes department, my principal affiliation is with Hart, Schaffner, and Marx, who sell Jack Nicklaus slacks and sports jackets. I also have tie-ins with Hathaway-Peerless shirts and sweaters, Robert Lewis rain jackets, Spatz young men's and boys' jackets, Stern, Merritt ties, Host pajamas and robes, Kramer Brothers hosiery, and Hat Corporation headgear. (In Japan a company called Asahi-Kasei put out men's wear that bears my name—something like Nickirasu.) In a different realm of operation, I do a series of golfing tips and occasional articles for *Sports Illustrated*. We began our relationship back in 1962, and it has been an enormously happy and satisfying one for me. The Hall

---

* This is nearly my favourite remark in all of golf literature!

Syndicate handles an illustrated instruction feature I prepare which appears in over a hundred newspapers around the world. I have two fine new contracts with Eastern Airlines and Pontiac. I play some customer golf for the United States Banknote Corporation, I have a promotional arrangement with the Mauna Kea golf resort, I reach for a Coca-Cola when I'm thirsty, and—let me see—I think that's about it. I am not in the laundry business,* but I do endorse lawn mowers through Murray-Ohio.

from *The Greatest Game of All*, Simon & Schuster (US),
William Heinemann (UK)†

A LITTLE SPENDING MONEY   Peter Alliss

One of our travelling companions was Snead. He gave Dai Rees a polythene bag with some of his famous straw hats, and asked Dai to look after them for him. When we met at the airport next day, Snead rushed up to Dai in an agitated way and thanked him for taking care of the bag and pulled all the hats out. Stuck in the hat band of each hat was a $100 bill. Snead said he always liked to have a little spending money with him wherever he went.

Snead ... has made so much money from golf that he probably doesn't know about it, but he certainly takes care of it. His business interests are prodigious. He owns two golf courses, driving ranges, endorses his own clubs, does books, articles, television, real estate in Florida, sponsoring this, that and the other in an endless stream of contracts, contracts, contracts. He keeps himself in remarkable physical condition, never smokes and very rarely drinks. He must be the fittest man in the world at the age of fifty.‡ He can still bend over and pick a golf ball out of the hole without bending his knees, or stand on the first step of a staircase and bend over to touch the floor. Much of this emerges from desire, the desire to succeed. I think people probably succeed in sport or in business for one of two reasons—reward, or a desire for achievement. By reward I mean the urge to amass money, by achievement I mean the urge to do better than anyone else, to win more championships or build bigger empires than anyone else. Snead I imagine would come into the first category, Hogan the second. This is not to say that Hogan does not have a keen appreciation of the value of a dollar. He too has made a vast fortune from golf, but I think he has drawn more pleasure from his achievements, from his status in the history of the game, than from his bank

---

* A reference to Arnold Palmer, who is.
† What Nicklaus has to say of his business endorsements and involvements can equally be said of all golfers and other athletes at the very top. Mark McCormack made the breakthrough when he realized the name of a top golfer can be used to sell and promote just about any product or service, including many with no golf connection.
‡ Sam is now well past 60 and announced his retirement early in 1976. But, like Sinatra's, there have been many 'farewell' performances since then.

balance. But I would imagine that Snead has kept going over the years, as Locke has done, as Cotton has done, because of money and the continuing business opportunities which come from staying at the top.

Cary Middlecoff told me one of the great Snead stories. He arrived at one tournament with lots of gear—clubs, packages, baggage—and with a raincoat over his arm. He decided the easiest way to carry the coat was to wear it. He put it on, put his hands in the pocket and pulled out twenty-five $100 bills. He said, 'My God, I wondered where that $2,500 was—that is my winning take from the pro-amateur at White Sulphur Springs a couple of years ago. I haven't worn the coat since then.'

from *Alliss Through the Looking Glass*, Cassell & Co (UK)

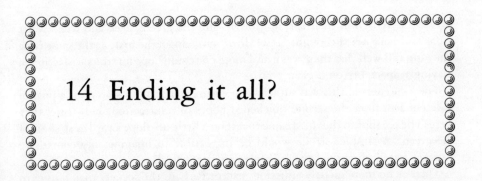

14 Ending it all?

I TOOK up golf as something to do on a wet afternoon when a cricket match was cancelled. Early on, a 36 on the first nine showed me a future of glittering prospects and soon I played golf when the sun shone as well.

In due time I married and gave the game up for a while. I said that it was a gesture to my bride but, looking back, a cancerous slice that had eaten through even to my putting probably had much to do with the decision.

People begin playing for exercise, something to do, because friends have done it, for business contacts, or just out of curiosity. We finally stop through old age or, more often, because we cannot tolerate how bad we have become. Usually no decision is made, however. We just come home with the bag of clubs one day and never go back again.

GIVING UP THE GAME   Pat Ward-Thomas

The other day I came across that rare being—a man who had given up golf for no other reason than that he was weary of its frustrations. He was a cheerful, vigorous person, with all the outward appearances and sounds of assurance, who certainly did not lack the means to play; in fact, he was still a member of the club. That a man, able in every way to play the game, could continue to expose himself to the longings and temptations that the sight of a course always prompt in me, seemed remarkable. In his place I would find them irresistible.

Yet, in a way, I envied a man who, with a single-figure handicap, could cry 'Enough!' This revealed not weakness, an admission that the game had the better of him, but rather strength of mind—the kind it takes to give up smoking—the kind it seems that I do not have!

This was brought home not long after that meeting. We were playing at Sandwich; the morning was still, the haunting mists were beginning to melt, and one of those glorious Sandwich days was starting to unfold. We were alone on the links: the eminent cricket correspondent, a powerful young friend, and myself. There was no haste (although the aforesaid e.c.c. liked to stride along), the fairways were rich in their spring growth, and the greens sleek and true. What more could one ask, I thought, as we drove away down the first, at the same time knowing full well that there was a deal more one could hope for: the satisfaction of playing respectably on a great course.

The awareness of this was sufficient to ensure a tremulous start, but a putt of indecent length at the second quickened hopes of resurrection. How brief they were! The tee shot to the third came to rest on a little up-slope a yard or so short of the green. A simpler stroke would be impossible to imagine; my convulsive attempt barely disturbed the ball from its beautiful lie.

There is no more ghastly affliction, except perhaps the socket, than failure to play a tiny chip or pitch, and always it seems that the easier the stroke the greater the peril. Its very simplicity is the quintessence of the torture, as I was soon to experience again. From just off the fifth green I was miserably short, and a possible four became six; then, such is the irony of the wretched game, from a nasty lie beside the Maiden I chipped stone dead. This was the refinement of misery; soften the victim with a moment of hope so that his downfall will be all the greater. And so it was.

The seventh is ever a substantial hole at St Georges, and it played quite long that morning. The words of a famous and tiresome professional (who is invariably beset with the most appalling misfortune)—'I wouldn't 'ave 'ad it back when I struck it'—applied to my second shot, but, of course, it failed to hold the green and trickled down the bank on the left. There was no problem: a putter was the club; a nice easy stroke over the smooth turf—any novice could have played it. But, as I looked at the ball, an uneasy feeling that I could *not* stole unbidden into my mind. Take your time, head still, smoothly back and through the ball—all the usual enjoinders were useless; the putter blade just touched the top of the ball.

The rest of the round is of no consequence; as it happened, there were no more little chips to fluff. The e.c.c. played with admirable steadiness, the p.y.f. with majestic ease, and I was routed. Then, as we moved towards lunch, I decided positively and calmly to play no more golf for some considerable time. The few matches I had arranged could easily be cancelled. What was the sense in playing if one was defeated by the most elementary shots? What satisfaction was there in hitting two good ones and then taking six? The knowledge that failure was in no sense technical, but entirely from within, was the worst of it. A fault in the method can be understood and remedied, but how do you learn to hit a ball 15 yards or so from a perfect lie, when some fiendish agency jerks your head up—like a marionette on a string—and locks the stroke rigid before the club can make proper contact?

After all, it is possible to enjoy the company of friends, the beauty of a spring morning, the sweetness of the lark songs, the sound of the tide hissing gently on the shingle, and the good pure air without subjecting oneself to the agonies of frustration. Thus my original acquaintance must have argued; and those were my own feelings that noon at Sandwich. There was to be no more of this nonsense. But how feeble resolution can be!

During the afternoon an appointment elsewhere, far removed from golf, was unexpectedly cancelled. The eminent cricket correspondent had gone home, but the powerful young friend remained. The afternoon was filled with sunshine; we looked at each other wondering what to do, and it was I, who but an hour before had been resolved to abandon the game, who suggested a few more holes. So it was; and so, with most of us, it always will be—the golfer and his eternal optimism.

from *The Long, Green Fairway*, Hodder & Stoughton (UK)

GOLF GIVES ME UP   Henry Longhurst

As my travels, writings and broadcasting increased, to say nothing of my age, my golf fell away and it became less and less fun to do progressively more badly something that one had once done reasonably well. I had had every reason to believe that I should turn out in middle age, and even later, to be an accurate and crafty player, always liable to beat an undergraduate, but it was not to be. My swing disintegrated and I became quite pathetically bad. I kept meaning to take myself in hand and go in for a fortnight's serious practice, which I knew was all that was needed, but somehow, with all the travelling about, I never got down to it. If I played on Sunday mornings, I did not enjoy it, and, if I didn't, I had it on my conscience that somehow I ought to be. What settled the problem for me was what we call the twitch and the Americans the 'yips'. This is so ridiculous a disease that non-sufferers can scarcely credit it. It attacks the victim almost always on short putts, though one great professional* who might otherwise have beaten the world had it on short pitches. It does not come on all short putts, but you always know in advance when it is coming. You then become totally incapable of moving a piece of ironmongery to and fro without giving at the critical moment a convulsive twitch. Some people simply stab the ground and move the ball a few inches. Others catch it on the twitch and send it shooting past the hole. Bobby Jones has recounted how he was playing with an American professional called Wild Bill Melhorn, who suffered from it, and on one green Melhorn, trying to hole a yard putt, actually putted it off the green and into a bunker. I was reminded only the other day of an occasion I had forgotten when a caddie had said to me, 'I think it would be better if you stroked the ball a bit more, sir,' and I had replied, 'Dammit, you don't think I *mean* to do it like that, do you?' I am, however, in good company, Jones himself got it†—he described

---

* David Thomas?
† But only after his retirement I suspect, when he competed only in the Masters which he founded in 1934.

the sensation as of the ball 'apparently vanishing from sight just as the club was about to strike it'. The great Harry Vardon got it. Sam Snead, still at fifty-seven* one of the finest swingers in the game, actually had to take to putting croquet-fashion between the legs. Ben Hogan, the most determined golfer of all time, not excluding Palmer, wanted two par fours for a record fifth U.S. Open and not only missed a yard putt on the 17th but 'yipped' it. 'Once you've had 'em, you've got 'em,' they say, and he was never the same again. The Americans tend rather unkindly to call the affliction 'whiskey fingers', and so it may be with some, but Snead is a lifelong teetotaller and Vardon was a most abstemious man—though I particularly like his reply to the lady who asked him to sign the pledge: 'Moderation is essential in all things, madam, but never in my life have I been beaten by a teetotaller.'

I am afraid that by constantly writing about it I may have served to spread the disease, in which context I am reminded of my friend and neighbour Tubby Ionides, who incidentally won the Grand National Irish Sweep on Sundew. Some people have only to read about that other ridiculous golf shot, the socket, in which the ball shoots off, knee high, almost at right-angles, to start doing it themselves, yet quite unable to do it on purpose. Confessing to be one such, my friend added, 'I am worse. I am a *carrier*.' So perhaps am I with the twitch. After one piece I had written about it an old Austrian doctor wrote to me from London saying that he knew the answer, so I naturally hurried to see him. The answer, he said, lay in the angle of the right elbow, i.e., neither stretched straight nor fully bent, as in putting, and there may be something in this, for if you stretch your right arm out as far and as stiffly as possible, you can make some sort of stroke at a putt even when the curse is upon you. What really shook me, however, was when he added casually, 'Violinists sometimes get it.' Here we may imagine the twitch in all its full horror. The hushed Albert Hall and the master, as his elbow bends to the fatal angle, giving a sudden and convulsive jerk and nearly sawing the instrument in half, never to play in public again. I was thoughtless enough to tell this to Hogan in Mexico City once and I have an awful fear that it hastened his downfall.

In the end I think they will find it akin to vertigo, or the case of the rabbit and the stoat. The rabbit can do twenty-five miles an hour and the stoat, I suppose, about four, but the rabbit stands paralysed like a man with a four-foot putt. Similarly you could guarantee, drunk or sober, to walk down a road without touching either side, but putt the same road, unfenced, over Niagara and you would be on your hands and knees within a few paces. Thus I came one day to the last green in the Medal needing a four for a net 69 and a faint chance of defeating at last one of the most tight-fisted bodies in the world, the handicapping committee of the R. and A. My second got on the green, only to roll back into the

* Born 27 May 1912.

Valley of Sin, in which one stands at about eye level with the flag. I pitched up and the ball ran so straight that I had time to think, 'By God, it's in! 68!' It stopped just short, a few inches perhaps—but when I got up onto the green the eye had been deceived from down below and it was a yard short. I was standing idly thinking of nothing while my partner holed out when suddenly it came over me. *I can't do it*. I looked at this hideous thing—just like the one you may have seen poor Doug Sanders missing to win, or rather not to win, the 1970 Open on the same green. I stood over it and remember with the utmost clarity thinking that I would willingly lay down a five-pound note on the green not to have to make this putt. Suddenly I found that the putter had shot to and fro and the ball was as far away the other side. I scuttled round and a moment later it had shot by again and we were back where we started. I doubled back, jerked at it again and this time by sheer good fortune it hit the back of the hole, jumped in the air and went in—but even as it disappeared I knew that my golfing days were numbered.

I forget where it happened but in the middle of a round, which I was regarding with the usual distaste, a small voice within me said, 'You don't *have* to do this,' and I thought, 'No, by God, I don't.' A great wave of relief came over me and on D-Day, 1968, I put the clubs up in the loft with the water tanks, closed the hatch, removed the steps and walked away. Nor have I for one second regretted it. I had travelled a long and happy road since we had cut the holes with our penknives on the Common at Yelverton, but now it was rather like having sucked a very good orange dry and realizing that you were eating the peel. Why not chuck it away and try an apple instead? Which is what I did.

from *My Life and Soft Times*, Cassell & Co (UK)

PINSPLITTERS IN THE CELLAR   Patrick Campbell

A few holes back I was standing in the cellar of this house in France, moistening the still shining heads of my thirty-seven-year-old Pinsplitters with a nostalgic tear, and was about to stuff them back behind the cupboard when the telephone rang. Tony and Bobby, visitors from England, wondering if I would like to play golf!

We had come to live in France three years ago. Since then the only activity taking place around my golf-bag was that conducted . . . by the jersey-munching moths. Three years. Did I even remember which hand went on top? How far away the ground was liable to be? What would happen when I launched that immensely long driver at the digestive tablet? A clean miss? One that shot straight up into the air, decapitating an elderly Contessa standing by? I said I'd play—tomorrow. Far too busy today. But of course I really wanted the interval in which to think myself back into playing golf again. Even to find out what would happen if I were to agitate a golf-ball with the putter on the rug in the hall.

What would it feel like? Would there be a clank—or a thud—as the club-face met the pellet? It had become entirely unfamiliar. I might as well have been shaping up to play polo with you-know-who, without being able to ride a horse.

But the muscles were beginning to remember, on their own. I could almost feel the slow-motion swing with the wedge, the hands coming through first, the little nip of turf and the clubhead going right through the ball as it floated lazily through the air, whizzing with back-spin, to pitch just beyond the stick and roll back again, uphill.

I took the wedge and half a dozen balls out on to the grass behind the house. Not ideal golfing country. The place was covered with immense olive trees, rather close together. But still room enough to lob a wedge shot or two up to the hedge of cypress trees that guard us from the road.

I laid out the balls in a line, had a waggle with the wedge, felt all right, so I shaped up to the first ball, began the old slow-motion back-swing and suddenly everything went mad. I thought I wasn't going to hit it at all. The club was too short. The ball too small. I took a quick little lurch and caught it with the very edge of the sole. The ball took off as though struck by a full 2-iron, a foot above the ground and going like a bullet. It snored between three olive trees and disappeared through the cypress hedge. A split second later there was a tremendous, metallic crash. I had struck either the front or the rear door of a large white car, which had been passing slowly down the road. Seen indistinctly through the hedge, it looked like a Peugeot 504.

It stopped. Four people—elderly, I thought—got out. Two men and two women. At first their voices were muted, by surprise. I heard the beginning of querulous questions.

'What is it that it is?'

'But what, M'sieu Thierry, has passed itself?'

Then fear—and fury—started to take over.

'One has shot at us!'

'Some imbecile has discharged his fowling-piece.'

'We will carry plaint to the police—to the town hall!'

'One must search for the assassin—'

The assassin stood very still, very thin and upright, squeezing himself into the shape of a ruler behind the sheltering trunk of an olive tree. They went on and on.

'But, see, M'sieu Ferracci, one has almost penetrated your door.'

'It is quite possible that all of us might have lost our lives.'

'Madame Thierry, you have the mien of being very pale.'

'What to do? What to do?'

In the end, after scratching about all round the car, looking for shell cases and irrelevant nonsense like that, they all got in again and the car drove slowly away. Voices floated back. 'To the Préfecture . . . a little wine for Madame Thierry . . . disgusting . . . formidable . . .'

I let them get around the corner. Then I picked up the remaining five balls and went back into the house, practice being over for the day.

That evening, I recovered sufficient enthusiasm for golf to ring up the club, to book three caddies and a starting time for 9.30 a.m. The reverberations of the bang on the side of the Peugeot were beginning to subside, but forming in their place was a clear, mental picture of myself attacking a new ball on the first tee with, alternately, every club in the bag, and with the ground around it becoming ever more hacked and scarred, the ball remaining entirely untouched, perched there insolently on its little red peg.

When we arrived at the club the following morning the car-park looked like a Rolls-Royce *concourse d'élégance*. There were seven of the brutes there, with the ultimate insult to Rolls of French number plates. Three Cadillacs, one with Florida plates, a Mustang and a Lamborghini.

I left my little Simca in the middle of them. It had suffered rather a lot of buffeting even before I bought it, third-hand, and had undergone a number of further modifications under my leadership. Once, indeed, when I left it outside the Carlton Hotel in Cannes the commissionaire—the sniffy one with the dark glasses—actually turned away and raised a white-gloved hand to his nostrils, as though in the presence of something physically offensive.

It didn't look much better here.

We went into the Secretary's office, to pay our green fees, and came out 28 francs lighter, each. About £2—a mildly discouraging start to the day. We changed our shoes—we were all extremely nervous. So much so that I suggested a little coffee and brandy to get us going. It was 9.10 a.m. The other men thought it would be unwise. We might miss our starting time.

Far from having three beautiful girl caddies, only to be expected in French golf, we were placed in the care of two Algerian youths, one with a cast in his left eye so pronounced that it made my head swim to look at him. It took them a long, long time to strap one bag on to one trolley, and two on to the other. It looked as if neither of them had ever seen a golf-bag or, indeed, a trolley, before. They were entirely silent.

We walked out to the first tee and into the middle of what looked like a fashion show for *la vie sportive*. There must have been twenty or more people there, nearly all elderly, and every single one of them dressed to the nines for the game of golf. There were cartridge belts studded with tees, Robin Hood hats, black and white shoes, cashmere cardigans, one outbreak of plus-fours, two Bermuda shorts and golfing jackets and golfing slacks and red and white gloves and God knows what else. *Tout*, in fact, *pour le golf*.

There was also a man shaping up to drive off. About fifty years of age, wearing a Sam Snead straw hat very square on his head, red turtle-necked jersey, red corduroy trousers, yellow gloves and black and white shoes. He was engaged upon some private exercise which, though he was standing up to a golf-ball, seemed to me to have no connection with the game.

Slowly and fairly rhythmically he raised his shoulders up round his ears, and lowered them. Up—down. Up—down. Perhaps six times. The other players watched him intently, trying to learn something from his technique.

He got tired of the shoulder work or, perhaps, had completed that portion of the stroke, for now he became absolutely motionless, glaring at the ball as though it had savaged him in some way in the past and he was daring it to do it to him again

At the end of another minute he began to move. He lifted the club very, very slowly into the air until it was approximately vertical, paused for another couple of seconds and then brought it down right on top of the ball with a little cry that sounded like, 'Mimp!' The ball, responding to this pressure like an orange pip squeezed between the fingers, sprang forward perhaps twenty feet, but rather to the left.

The man watched it intently until it came to rest. Then he walked over to his trolley and put the driver back into the bag, covering the head of it with a little sack that appeared to be made of sealskin or some other furry substance. Two miniature poodles were tied to the bag with tartan leashes. It took him some time to disentangle them, but in the end he got all his affairs in order. He seized the trolley by the handle and started to walk after his ball, twenty feet away and well to the left, rather slowly, as though lost in some private reverie. Beyond all doubt or cavil he was playing by himself. And none of the other golfeurs and golfeuses thought it in the least out of the ordinary!

Tony, Bobby and I just failed to avoid catching one another's eye. We looked away, deeply embarrassed and more nervous than ever.

'Looks,' Bobby said—the strain was evident in his voice—'as if it's going to be a bit slow today.'

We got off in the end some time after 10.30 a.m., having been standing on the first tee, swishing at bits of grass, for more than an hour, and watching golf the quality of which would not have occurred even in nightmare. The French had obviously taken to the game with enthusiasm, and a profound and ferociously hopeless ignorance of how it should be played.

Neither were the three of us very much better off. It was difficult, in fact, after the contortions, the tribal dancings and the rigid acrobatics we had been watching, to suppose we were on a golf-course at all.

The first hole here is a short one, about 150 yards. A sunken stream runs across the fairway and there is a hedge behind the green. No trouble, really, anywhere, except for a shallow bunker on the right.

I took out my 5-iron, for the first time for three years, and for the first time for three years balanced a new golf-ball on a new peg. I stood up, then, above the ball, and could find no relation of any kind between it and the club in my hand. I simply didn't know what to do with or to either of them.

The thing was to get it over. Rather too quickly back, swing too short, falling forward, slash at it while still time—and off she went, with exactly the same trajectory as the one that had pierced the cypress hedge and caused Madame Thierry to turn so pale. A rasping big iron that whined through the air, passed non-stop six feet above the green and crashed into the hedge with the sound of a giant redwood being felled.

'Good shot,' Tony said in a low voice. 'Just a bit big.' He and Bobby, with extreme care, struck their tee-shots all of fifty yards, straight into the sunken stream.

It turned out to be heavily populated, up to and including the shoulder-heaving man with the two poodles, who had been in there for more than an hour. There was a ladies' fourball in there, a male octogenarian foursome, and a couple of mixed singles, all flicking and scratching away with wedges and sand-blasters, trying to scoop their ammunition out of the water.

Tony and Bobby joined them. I walked on, up over the green and started rooting in the hedge for my own missile. A moment later something crashed into the foliage immediately beside my head. I heard an accented cry of 'Forrh!' and turned to see a thick-set man wearing a tartan cap with a woolly bobble on top standing on the other side of the green. He'd obviously succeeded in scooping his pellet out of the water, and now had just had another go at it.

He strode forward briskly, pulling his trolley straight across the putting surface, and came to a halt beside me. '*Bonjour, M'sieu*,' he said, with the greatest amiability, '*vous êtes aussi débutant?*' A beginner? Me? The lad that flattened Billy O'Sullivan in that roaring, thrill-packed finish at Portmarnock in 1949?* A debutant. A be*ginner*!

'*Mais, non*,' I replied shortly. '*J'étais professionel.*'

'*Ah, bon*,' he said. He put out his hand. '*Enchanté de faire votre connaissance.*' We shook hands, standing partly in the hedge. An absolutely absurd way to begin a round of golf, specially when one hasn't played for three years.

We waited for twenty minutes on the next tee until two terribly old ladies got far enough ahead up the fairway, striking tiny little shots with complete concentration. They were accompanied by a female wrestler of about sixty, doing caddying work on the side. Among her other equipment she carried a long pole with a wire basket on the end of it, a device for defeating the stream.

I took out my immensely long driver and had an utterly disordered flash with it and got that supremely revolting shot that almost strikes the left shoe, off the very back of the stick, and rolls at right-angles into the ditch behind you.

The man in the tartan cap said, judicially, to the two ladies he appeared to be playing with, '*Il était anciennement professionel.*'

Both the ladies, with equal appreciation, said, '*Ah, bon.*'

* As recounted earlier in this book.

And so the long day wore on. The stream, we found, bisected, bitched and bedevilled almost every hole. We were hardly ever out of it. After the ninth hole the cross-eyed Algerian lad took off his shoes and socks and hung them round his neck, to be ready for the next emergency. 'Hulla hulla hulla,' he said, with a fanged grin. It must have been months since he'd had such an amusing day.

We forged our way through the two little bird-like ladies, after borrowing Ghengis Kate's scooper to retrieve our second shots at the eleventh, and for the first time found ourselves with an open course ahead of us.

It all began to come back. A couple of longish clouts off the tee, an iron shot or two that actually drifted rather sweetly from left to right, instead of howling round in the usual semi-circle. The lovely game of golf, all coming back again.

Off the eighteenth tee I got a real, old-fashioned beezer. Nice and late with the hands, a sort of nudge with the right knee and off she whistled, a really big one. Struck the downward slope of the hill and galloped on to hell and gone, up in the region of 300 yards.

When I reached it, right in the middle of the fairway and further than I'd believed possible, the scene was rendered even more pleasant by the sight of two practically edible portions of French crumpet—early twenties, long yellow hair, silk trousers painted on, and animated with it. They were chatting brightly together as they walked across the course towards the club-house. Spectators, by the look of them, and very possibly the soft furnishings of the Lamborghini in the car-park.

I took a 7-iron out of the bag and then looked back to where Tony and Bobby were searching for their rather lesser tee-shots in the bushes on the right. I judged that the girls, if they had any knowledge of the game at all, would be able to see that I'd hit a genuine steamer and was now shaping to crowd a crisp seven up against the flag-stick.

They stopped, a few yards away, and fell silent. I imagined they'd never seen such a giant tee-shot in all their lives, and must now be waiting with keen expectation for this superb athlete's next production.

It was a beauty, fading gently and coming back out of the pitch mark to finish five or six feet from the hole.

I got together rather a good type of modest grin and let them have it. They didn't even look at it. They walked straight past, chatting together again as brightly as before.

One of them said to the other, clasping her lovely hands, '*Mais, Jean-Claude— lui, il est chic chic chic.*'

Her friend agreed. '*Rrrravissant,*' she said, with a tiger-like purr that would have had Jean-Claude, whoever the hell he was, clutching at his collar.

In the end I holed the putt and got this fabulous three in solitude, unapplauded by anyone, as the other two gents had abandoned the hole and walked into the club-house.

I think I'll probably put the clubs back behind the cupboard and leave it at that, going out in this private blaze of glory.

There's an amateur quality about golf in France that rather gets on the wick of us old (nearly) professionals.

from *Patrick Campbell's Golfing Book*, Blond & Briggs (UK)

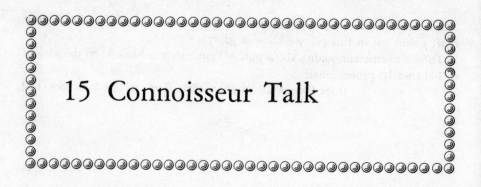

15 Connoisseur Talk

EVERY year a few hundred people are born with the ability to swing a golf clubhead at high velocity and get the sweet spot to meet the centre of a golf ball quite frequently. Alas, you and I are almost certainly not among them. But are we using another talent we may have been born with to counterbalance the fact we swing a club none too well? If you can't do it well, try to talk about it better.

Of course, I'm not referring to the uproar in clubhouses as everyone tells everyone else the details of the magnificent round they have just played, or of the harsh blows of fate that robbed brilliance of its just reward. 'Everyone' is our key word. No good at all allowing your lips even to part in clubhouse or locker room: all are talking and, just as certainly, no one is listening. No, it's out on the course you must seize your audience by the ear.

My space is limited so I'll have to take just a very few of the situations and you, with a wealth of experience untapped and eager to emerge from remote corners of your golfing semiconscious, will be able to take it on from there.

ON BEING, AS USUAL, OUTDRIVEN   Michael Hobbs

This is one of the most emasculating experiences met by the human male. There are few of us who *don't* want to squash a golf ball in the way the ads. show us ought to happen and send it on its way to distant horizons. But unfortunately this takes all the athleticism, rhythm and balance that, alas, we haven't got and are not about to get in this or any other decade. But take heart, the right remark will ease the pain brought on by the sight of our golf ball at rest about 150 yards up the fairway while our opponent's is a faint white speck . . .

The strategic approach
'Of course,' we say, 'I didn't want a long one at this hole. No it's better here to just nudge a little one out to right fairway. Think of the approach to the green. From where I am now, *any* club will knock the ball there. Look at how the shape of the ground is *bound* to gather any kind of shot and steer it along to the green.'

Turn next to your opponent's future problems. 'But your shot has to be just right. A bit fat and you're in the water hazard, a touch too firm and from your angle of approach you'll be way through the back.'

If your opponent's second shot is less than completely successful, you are poised to rub home your psychological advantage at the next par 4. On the tee do not so much as look at a wooden club. Pull out a five iron, pause, look thoughtful, then say: 'No. Stupid. A six is the intelligent club to use here. Need to be left of that hump but *not* past it for the best line home.'

Of course, after hitting that six iron the green will still be a very long way ahead, but those who succeed in talking golf well are prepared to make sacrifices and, quite often, lose not just a hole but the match as well. That is unimportant. If you want to win, learn to play well.

Ill health
Let's suppose your opponent has just achieved a savage and superb blow to the front apron of a 300 yarder, hands a blur as he came into the ball. Shake your head regretfully at memories of times past and say: 'Mmmm ... you got a good hip slide into that one. But you know as long as I got it away straight, I used to be on that green every time when I was your age. Remember I had to take a three wood not to go through the back! But since I got this arthritic hip ... (tendons, discs and the like will do just as well but the golf course is no place for airing more psychological or emotional problems, such as trouble at the office, or the fact your wife has taken yet another new lover. Such ephemera should not disturb the true golfer and would tend to make your opponent feel superior – quite the reverse of what we want.)

A few variations are possible on this theme of the sick and not-so-young you, and the crudely healthy him. For instance, you can try to create an awareness in your opponent that, Hogan-like, you have had to battle against physical problems. But don't make too much fuss about it – gasps of anguish are no good at all. By all means let pain show in your eyes, tauten your lips a little and, perhaps, wince in moderation. If your opponent is a man of feeling he may, after eight or nine holes, come to feel guilty at his relative good fortune and, as we well know, guilt impedes even the most free and flowing of swings.

Not interested in length
We have seen, when discussing what can be said under the 'Strategic approach' heading, how it can be suggested that at certain holes length is actually harmful. But why not take this further and say that, for you, length is of little import. Mention the names of a few players on the US tournament circuit who are well known to have the ability to hit a ball far but have achieved nothing else. Say: 'Jack could hit it further than any of them if he wanted to but he prefers the control he gets from the power fade. I must admit I agree with him

on this one.' (With this remark you can hope to have established that you play rather like Nicklaus, do not blindly accept everything he says as the equivalent of something Moses brought down from the mountain top, and that you too have a power fade. Banish, of course, any humble thought that Jack's fade is an immense shot that drifts a few degrees towards the end of flight, whereas what you produce is a snappy, very rapidly curling, *slice*.)

'Control' then is the key word, and your main interest in golf, you should stress repeatedly. Long, long ago, you can allow yourself to confess with a rueful and charming grin, you *did* like to hit a golf ball out of sight. But nowadays you want to be right there in the middle of the fairway, not fishing your ball from water hazards or up to your knees in lush pastures. Mid fairway is your kingdom. From there the real game of golf is just beginning and you can exercise your true talent – precision play into the green. Burning in a low one through blustery winds, fading one in softly to alight and quickly stop, curling one from right to left to bite against an opposite slope – these are the true delights for you, the golfing aficionado.

EQUIPMENT

Ideally, the good golf talker should, if he can force himself to be so rigidly abstemious, play with an assortment of aged and never-much-good-even-in-their-prime clubs. You should certainly have no more than two woods and both should have no varnish or decals remaining. A strand of thread that hisses through the air as you launch into the ball will add character to them. If they also make very much the *wrong* kind of sound as you strike the ball, so much the better. This sound can be achieved simply enough: loosen each sole-plate screw just half a turn.

But why, you may ask, have clubs of contemptible quality? Why my rusty irons and tired woods? You play well with inferior gear. But allow yourself to say: 'Thought of getting a set of the new ZY 457 aerofoil-shafted irons with those heads they say are made of a new alloy flight tested on the Concorde fuselage but . . .' What you should say next depends on whether the image you want is of wealth or distinctly non-wealth. Having reached a decision you can then continue in one of two ways. Either: 'Jean is insisting on having a vacuum cleaner. Says thirty years on her knees with a handbrush is long enough.' Or: 'Jean just insisted on having a bigger yacht.'

You are now all set to politely examine the clubs he's using. Look at the shafts first. Club manufacturers are always making claims that a new formula material or, God help us, the aerodynamic profile, is about to ensure that you, me and them are all about to hit golf balls new and previously unimaginable distances.

'Ah,' you continue, 'I see . . .' Nothing more is needed for the time being. That pause is the heart of the message and should convey your feeling that the shaft has done it for him.

But at this point, he may smile smugly. You have made what may seem momentarily to be the error of complimenting him on his choice. If so, his pleasure must be dealt with quickly. Pick up any one of your clubs and wave it around reflectively: 'Old Willie MacTavish made these in, when was it, 1933?' Follow up quickly by commenting that X or Y told you the other evening over a beer that metal fatigue, carbon fibre decomposition or whatever has become all too well known to owners of the model he has – all golfers have a vestigial statistical memory that reminds us that with aluminum shafts 86.2 per cent left the average golfer standing perplexed with a shaft in his hands and a head flying independently up the fairway after approximately 2.73 years.

The smug smile should by now be gone. It's entirely possible that he'll swing far too carefully on his next shot . . .

The clubhead

Although club manufacturers tell us a good deal about the special properties of the metal used in their latest line of irons and the advantages of the sole configuration, weight distribution and all the rest of it, the good golf talker will probably find more scope for practising his rare talent in talking about wooden clubs.

At this point, I ought to admit that I'm struck almost dumb at the sight of a head made from date plum – persimmon, if you prefer the word. Though 'real wood' is more effective a term than either. But as his gear is unlikely to be as ancient as yours it's unlikely you'll have to face this problem – they're all plywood these days. Not that this is a word much favoured by manufacturers; for them, or rather their copywriters, 'bonded laminates' and the like are terms that roll more easily off the pen.

So if it's one of the almost omnipresent plywood hosts, make some kind of remark along the lines of 'Yes, 1962 was a very good year in the Baltic timber trade. Something to do with slow growth in NordRhein Westphalia, I think.' But quickly press on to the point you've been aiming at all along. Wood is really an outmoded material. You are about to stress the thinking man's preferences for plastics. Say a few words to the general effect that manufacturers make frequent and lengthy claims about all the wealth of technology that has been ploughed into their latest clubs but that here they are in 1976 still using wood for the space-age golfer. Say: 'I keep telling them to get into plastics for their drivers and fairway woods but they all seem to be the slaves of their marketing people. Obviously a total *stable* material is going to be a better job for a golfer than *wood*. After all, we didn't use much of it to get to the Moon did we?'

PUTTING

If you are putting well

You will cause your opponent a good deal of highly satisfactory irritation — particularly if he's having a bad day on the greens — if you say again and again that there really is nothing to it at all. Throw in a few references from time to time to either a 73-year-old aunt of yours who knocks them into a hole on your front lawn from *any* distance, or, just as good, your four-year-old daughter who has an equal talent. 'Any fool can putt' should thereafter be your theme.

Of course, if this remark is going to be fully effective you will have to putt casually and must give up such common practices as:

1 Pacing with tedious deliberation about a green as you examine the grass in minute detail.
2 Any method of deciding the line such as lying full length on the turf or dangling your putter at arm's length and squinting in a professional-looking sort of way.
3 That tedious habit of removing bits of grass and fluff from your line. Comment that it's a waste of time anyway for they could divert a ball *into* the hole as well as away.
4 The five or so practice strokes you usually allow yourself (I know a man who takes *divots* during this phase).
5 Any nonsenses of putting style such as projecting your left elbow at the hole, shuffling your feet excessively or taking an age of adjustments until you are satisfied your putter head is square to the line.

No, you must stroll up to your ball, a quick glance at the hole, and then, almost before you have stopped moving, give the thing a relaxed-looking tap. If you can manage that, it doesn't actually matter too much whether or not your ball drops for with such simplicity of method you are bound to be better than your opponent for, after he has spent an age over his preparations, he will still jerk it well past, wide or stub the ground.

Yet there is one occasion when it does not do to be devil-may-care, when you may lose prestige in the art of talking golf. If you are faced with a truly impossible putt be grim-faced, talk aloud of the possibilities and alternatives that your keen golfing brain is analysing. But if your ball eventually coasts up hill and down dale and finishes not even respectably near the hole this matters very little; your sudden intense concentration and appearance of acute intellectual effort has been aimed solely at the distant possibility that you *might* sink that absurd putt. If so, you want no one to be able to suggest that there was any luck in your achievement. Say: 'You know I'm quite pleased with the way I thought that one right the way through.' Follow up by outlining your thought processes about the direction of the light breeze (better to say this when there is none at all), what Ben Hogan said to you fifteen years back down at Fort Worth about absolutely anything at all, or perhaps mention that the Putting Maestro Arthur D'Arcy Locke and you both learned your mastery on the nappy greens of South Africa. If you are cultivating a more youthful image, substitute Severiano Ballesteros for Locke.

If you are putting badly

Putting, you can say, is beneath your attention. You enjoy a full swing of the club and a soaring drive or the sharp click and exquisite feel of the perfectly struck iron shot. But these, you may continue, are shots struck through the air and can be judged; putting is a matter of knocking a ball along a bit of turf. The grass grows in all directions, there are little bare patches, worm casts, spike marks and the more serious dents left by aged and heavy gentlemen supporting themselves ponderously on their putters as the time at long last came for them to retrieve their ball from the hole. The whole process is just about impossible.

BUNKERS

Greenside shots

The secret of talking about your last shot from sand always begins with the expression on your face. Nearly always, look disgusted. Above all, never show any emotion or say anything that could be taken as relief at merely having got out of a bunker.

Let's look at a few of the correct reactions. If your shot finishes a couple of feet away, shake your head a little sadly and go through the motions of the shot once more. You expected to hole it, or at least put it within a whisker. If, on the other hand your sand wedge catches the ball about halfway up and your ball flies out low only to strike the flagstick dead centre and then falls, all impetus exhausted, into the hole, nod crisply. Your shot was played precisely as intended. Do not *smile*, do nothing at all to confirm that you may have been *lucky*.

Fairway bunkers

Talking about your shots from these can often follow the same lines as for greenside ones but there is the major difference that the golfer's aim is now distance more than accuracy. The same facial expressions can again be used: however far your ball sails on towards the green, still look disgusted that your stroke has failed to reach your normal standard of perfection. Make remarks such as: 'No, I took just a thimbleful of sand on that one. Cost me a good 50 yards.'

IRON SHOTS

A good deal of what I've said about other departments of the game of golf can be adapted for talking about your shots into the green as well. But there are subtle differences and opportunities are often more favourable for counterattack than beginning the verbal offensive yourself.

For example, you will often come across the man who, triumphant upon the tee of a 170 yarder, turns to you and says: 'Made it with a seven iron!'

Well Henry Cotton was pretty composed about that one. He used to say: 'I am never concerned with the number on a club.'

What Henry meant was that if a crisp little tap with a four iron propelled his ball close to the hole, his composure was not in the least disturbed if a fellow competitors had covered the same distance with a seven. But Henry just thought this – he was not a chatty fellow on a golf course. We, on the other hand, have got to be if we are to talk the game better than we play.

Your repost should be: 'You know I *never* hit full out with an iron. Accuracy is the name of the game. Jack says he's got the same approach – at least until he takes out a one iron.' At this point take out your one iron and execute a practice swing with as much savagery as you can manage.

Having demonstrated how you never hit an iron hard – except the one – return to the assault on your opponent, who by now should be glowing less about the length he got with that seven iron: 'Of course, it's not the number on a club that counts is it? More the way you use it. You seem to hit with a very shut face and hands way out ahead of the ball. Makes a seven into a four, more or less. Remember I used to hit sevens a hell of a way but I couldn't so much as get a three iron off the ground!' (All kinds of benefits may accrue later in the game as a result of this remark. Your opponent may try opening the clubface with potentially disastrous results, get his hands somewhere else, and baby his iron shots.)

By this time your tee shot is a long way overdue and you'd better get on with it. Play your usual more-or-less full out shot with a four iron and, provided your efforts are reasonably satisfactory, say: 'Yes, I thought so. Just a little push but *without breaking the wrists*. That's all this hole needs.'

The man who grasps his wedge at every opportunity offers you a similar opening. As his ball soars magnificently skywards you will be telling him: 'I've never been convinced there's much point in heaving it way up in the air. Think I'll just give it a half six iron and knock it short of the green and let it run up to the hole.'

You should have great success with this for it makes people feel:

1 that they can't play a pitch and run.
2 that they can't play half shots.

3 that so ingrained has 'target golf' become in us all that I am almost *cheating* by trying anything else.

But so far we have not discussed what can be said after a much-less-than-successful iron shot. The key lies in knowing what to praise and what to blame about your shot. If, for instance, your ball soars clear over the green, do not confess to misjudgement of length. Better by far to refer to how superbly you struck the ball: 'You know, I guess I've seldom struck a six iron quite *that* well before.' Or: 'Usually I reckon to hit an iron plumb out of the middle of the club but I was looking at Jack's irons the other day (you'll have to add the magic word 'Nicklaus' if your audience may think you're talking about the club bore, Jack Crabtree) and the impact marks are right up close to the shank. Must have got it in there myself.' (While they ponder the validity. of your technical remarks, you should win the next two holes. Indeed they may shank for weeks to come.)

Readers of this piece will already have said many of the things I've set down. But has it occurred to you to do so in an orderly way, with everything rehearsed and practised beforehand? Or do your *bon mots* just come out on the spur of the moment? This is no good at all except for the rare occasions when happy inspiration strikes you. The good golf talker must be ready at all times, his lines ready and armed for ignition to deal with *every* situation.

These then are a few first thoughts that could set you on your way to becoming a good golf talker. Eventually you may come to agree with me that merely to *play* golf well is too minor an ambition for the likes of us . . .

Index of Golfers

Note: The qualification I have adopted for entry is that a player, if an amateur, should be, or have been, of approximately Walker Cup standard; professionals are past and present tournament players. The form of name used follows common usage: Nicklaus, Jack rather than Nicklaus, J. W. When a golfer is the author of a piece of writing, he is indexed only if the writing in some way refers to his own golf performance.